高等职业教育物流管理专业精品规划教材

物流英语（第3版）

王 艳 张翠玲 主 编
张淑谦 张凤霞 副主编

清华大学出版社
北京

内 容 简 介

随着世界各国之间贸易交往的日益密切,我国物流业已全面挺进国际物流市场,加强我国国际物流从业人员的英语培训已成为目前亟待解决的问题。

本书结合物流英语教学改革的新特点,基于《物流英语(第2版)》进行更新与补充,使其更贴近经济生活,更符合社会发展,更好地为我国物流经济和教学实践服务。全书共10个单元,内容包括物流简介、客户服务、仓储、运输与配送、物流包装、国际物流、物流采购、第三方物流、供应链管理及物流信息管理等。

本书知识系统,案例丰富,注重创新,突出实用性,可以作为高职高专、应用型大学物流管理专业的教材,也可以作为物流企业从业人员的培训教材,对广大社会自学者也是一本非常有益的参考读物。

本书封面贴有清华大学出版社防伪标签,无标签者不得销售。
版权所有,侵权必究。举报: 010-62782989, beiqinquan@tup.tsinghua.edu.cn。

图书在版编目(CIP)数据

物流英语/王艳,张翠玲主编. —3版. —北京: 清华大学出版社,2019(2023.8重印)
(高等职业教育物流管理专业精品规划教材)
ISBN 978-7-302-51725-2

Ⅰ. ①物… Ⅱ. ①王… ②张… Ⅲ. ①物流-英语-高等职业教育-教材 Ⅳ. ①F25

中国版本图书馆CIP数据核字(2018)第266972号

责任编辑: 王剑乔
封面设计: 傅瑞学
责任校对: 赵琳爽
责任印制: 沈 露

出版发行: 清华大学出版社
网　　址: http://www.tup.com.cn, http://www.wqbook.com
地　　址: 北京清华大学学研大厦A座　　邮　编: 100084
社 总 机: 010-83470000　　邮　购: 010-62786544
投稿与读者服务: 010-62776969, c-service@tup.tsinghua.edu.cn
质量反馈: 010-62772015, zhiliang@tup.tsinghua.edu.cn
课件下载: http://www.tup.com.cn,010-83470410

印 装 者: 北京嘉实印刷有限公司
经　　销: 全国新华书店
开　　本: 185mm×260mm　　印　张: 15.5　　字　数: 351千字
版　　次: 2008年4月第1版　　2019年4月第3版　　印　次: 2023年8月第7次印刷
定　　价: 49.00元

产品编号: 080439-01

编 审 委 员 会

主　任：
　　牟惟仲　中国物流技术协会理事长、教授级高级工程师

副主任：
　　翁心刚　北京物资学院副院长、教授
　　冀俊杰　中国物资信息中心原副主任、总工程师
　　张昌连　中国商业信息中心原主任、总工程师
　　吴　明　中国物流技术协会副理事长兼秘书长、高级工程师
　　李大军　中国物流技术协会副秘书长、中国计算机协会市场发展分会秘书长

委　员：
　　林　征　车亚军　张建国　卢亚丽　孙　军　梁　露
　　刘徐方　田振中　张劲珊　李爱华　刘阳威　郑秀恋
　　王　艳　罗佩华　李　青　刘　华　林玲玲　梁　旭
　　王海文　刘丽艳　李耀华　卢亚丽　丁玉书　叶　靖
　　张淑谦　林南南　李秀华　刘文歌　朱凤仙　任　斐
　　崔　娜　李战国　雷　燕　梁红霞　罗松涛　于汶艳

总　编：
　　李大军

副总编：
　　刘徐方　王海文　李爱华　刘　华　田振中

鲁迅全集

序言

preface ▶第3版

物流是国民经济的重要组成部分,也是我国经济发展新的增长点。加快我国现代物流发展,对于调整经济结构、促进产业升级、优化资源配置、改善投资环境、增强综合国力和企业竞争能力、提高经济运行质量与效益、实现可持续发展战略、推进我国经济体制与经济增长方式的根本性转变,具有非常重要而深远的意义。

为推动我国现代物流业的发展,国务院连续下发《物流业调整和振兴规划的通知》(国发〔2009〕8号)、《关于促进物流业健康发展政策措施的意见》国发〔2011〕38号、《关于促进内贸流通健康发展的若干意见》(国办发〔2014〕51号)等多个文件,制定和完善相关配套政策、措施,以有序实施和促进物流企业加大整合、改造、提升、转型的力度,并逐步实现转型发展、集约发展、联动发展、融合发展,通过物流的组织创新、技术创新、服务创新,在保证我国物流总量平稳、较快增长的同时,加快供需结构、地区结构、行业结构、人力资源结构、企业组织结构的调整步伐,创新服务模式,提高服务能力,努力满足经济建设与社会发展的需要。

物流既涉及国际贸易、国际商务活动等外向型经济领域,也涉及交通运输、仓储配送、通关报检等多个业务环节。当前面对世界经济的迅猛发展和国际市场激烈竞争的压力,加强物流科技知识的推广应用,加速物流专业技能型应用人才的培养,已成为我国经济转型发展亟待解决的问题。

需求促进专业建设,市场驱动人才培养,针对我国职业院校沿用多年的物流教材存在知识陈旧和老化而急需更新的问题,为了适应国家经济发展和满足社会就业急需,以及满足物流行业规模发展对技能型人才的需求,在中国物流技术协会的支持下,我们组织北京物资学院、大连工业大学、北京城市学院、吉林工程技术师范学院、北京财贸职业学耽、郑州大学、哈尔滨理工大学、燕山大学、浙江工业大学、河北理工大学、华北水利水电学院、江西财经大学、山东外贸职业学院、吉林财经大学、广东理工大学等多所职业院校及应用型大学物流管理专业的主讲教师和物流企业经理,共同精心编撰了本书,旨在迅速提高职业院校物流管理专业学生和从业者的专业技术素质,更好地服务于我国物流产业和物流经济。

　　本书作为物流管理专业的特色教材,融入了物流运营与管理的最新教学理念,力求严谨,注重与时俱进,根据物流业发展的新形势和新特点,依照物流活动的基本过程和规律,按照物流企业对用人的需求模式,结合解决学生就业、加强实践能力训练,注重校企结合、贴近行业和企业业务实际,强化理论与实践的紧密结合,注重新设施、设备操作技术的掌握,强化实践技能与岗位应用的培养训练,并注重教学内容和教材结构的创新。

　　本书根据高等院校物流管理专业教学大纲和课程设置,对强化物流从业人员教育培训、提高经营管理能力,对帮助学生尽快熟悉物流操作规程与业务管理、毕业后能够顺利走上社会就业具有特殊意义。本书既可作为职业院校物流管理专业教学的首选教材,也可作为物流、商务贸易等企业在职员工的培训教材。

中国物流技术协会理事长　牟惟仲
2018 年 8 月

前言

foreword　第3版

全球经济一体化进程加快,世界各国之间的贸易交往日益密切,中国市场国际化的趋势已逐步形成,面对物流市场国际化的迅速发展与激烈竞争,对从事国际物流运营人员素质的要求越来越高,社会物资流通和物流产业发展急需大量具有物流英语知识与应用技能复合型的专门人才。

英语是工具,是一把打开世界门窗的钥匙,具有加强沟通、扩大交流范围的功能,物流英语已成为我国物流企业进军国际物流市场所必须掌握的关键技能,尽快提高我国涉外物流企业从业人员的英语水平已成为目前亟待解决的问题。

《物流英语》一书的编写正是为培养大量国际物流专门人才,解决物流企业发展对既懂得物流专业知识、又熟练掌握物流英语及实际业务运作技能型人才的急需。本书坚持以科学发展观为统领,严格按照教育部关于"加强职业教育、注重实践教学、强化应用技能培养"等教育教学改革精神和要求,由长期从事物流英语教学的主讲教师及具有丰富经验的企业人士共同编写,本书出版对提高物流从业人员的英语水平,提升物流企业的服务质量,促进我国外向型物流业的健康发展具有十分重要的意义。

本书自2008年出版、2012年再版以来,因写作质量高而深受全国各类职业教育院校广大师生欢迎,2008年被北京市教委评为北京市高等教育精品教材立项项目。本次再版,作者审慎地对原教材进行了知识更新补充,以使其更贴近经济生活,更符合社会发展,更好地为我国物流经济和教学实践服务。

本书作为高等职业教育物流管理专业的特色教材,全书共10个单元,以学习者应用能力培养为主线,根据国际现代物流业的快速发展,围绕物流运作所涉及的领域和业务,结合物流英语教学改革的新特点,系统介绍物流管理、运输、仓储、包装、采购、配送、客户服务及物流信息管理等物流专业英语基本知识,并通过强化实训,培养提高读者的应用能力。

本书融入了物流英语最新的实践教学理念、力求严谨、注重与时俱进，具有知识系统、案例丰富、注重创新、突出实用性、集理论和实践于一体等特点。因此，本书既可以作为高职高专、应用型大学物流管理专业的首选教材，也可以用于物流、外贸与工商企业在职从业者的岗位培训，并为广大社会中小微企业和大学生创业提供有益的学习指导。

本书由李大军筹划并具体组织，王艳和张翠玲任主编，王艳统改稿，张淑谦和张凤霞任副主编，由物流英语专家刘徐方教授审定。作者编写分工：牟惟仲(序言)，张淑谦(第1单元、第5单元)，王艳(第2单元、第10单元、附录)，谭明华(第3单元)，张翠玲(第4单元、第6单元)，梁旭、汤宁(第7单元)，张凤霞(第8单元、第9单元)；李晓新(文字修改、版式调整、制作教学课件)。

在本书再版过程中，我们参考借鉴了国内外有关物流英语的最新书刊和网站资料，并得到编委会和物流协会有关专家的具体指导，在此一并致谢。为配合教学，本书配有电子课件，读者可以从清华大学出版社网站（www.tup.com.cn）免费下载使用。因作者水平有限，书中难免有疏漏和不足，恳请同行和读者批评指正。

编　者

2018年8月

前言
foreword — 第2版

　　全球经济一体化进程加快,世界各国之间的贸易交往日益密切。随着我国加入WTO,我国流通市场已经全面对外开放,中国市场国际化的趋势已在形成,为我国物流企业参与国际物流市场竞争提供了良好的发展契机。英语是一种工具,也是一把打开世界门窗的钥匙,具有加强沟通、扩大交流范围的功能。面对国际物流业的快速发展与激烈竞争,英语已成为我国物流企业进军国际物流市场所必须掌握的技能。尽快提高我国涉外物流企业从业人员的英语水平已成为目前亟待解决的问题。

　　《物流英语》一书的出版,正是为培养大量国际物流专门人才,解决物流企业发展对既懂得物流专业知识、又熟练掌握物流英语及实际业务运作的技能型人才的急需。本书严格按照教育部关于"加强职业教育、注重实践教学、强化应用技能培养"等教育教学改革精神和要求,由长期从事物流英语教学的主讲教师及具有丰富经验的企业人士共同编写。本书的出版对提高从业人员的英语水平,提升物流企业的服务质量,促进我国外向型物流业的健康发展具有十分重要的意义。

　　本书自出版以来,因写作质量高、注重与时俱进,深受全国各类职业教育院校广大师生欢迎,2008年被北京市教委评为北京市高等教育精品教材立项项目。目前本书已重印4次,此为第2次修订再版。作者审慎地对原教材进行了知识更新与补充,以使其更贴近经济生活,更符合社会发展,更好地为我国物流经济和教学实践服务。

　　全书共10个单元,以培养学习者英语书写和口语应用能力为主线,依照国际与国内物流业务活动的基本过程和规律,结合实际讲解知识内容,力求突出实用性。本书内容包括:物流简介、客户服务、仓储、运输与配送、物流包装、国际物流、物流采购、第三方物流、供应链管理及物流信息管理等主要环节基本专业英语知识,以及办证下单日常工作所需的常用词汇用语。

　　本教材与其他相关教材相比,具有以下特点。

　　第一,注重教学实效。针对高职学生英语基础普遍薄弱且水平参差不齐的现状,为了使学生学有所获、学有所用,强化"说"和"写"两方面训练。课文以单元教学为基础,选材新颖,对重点和难点均进行专门注释,方便学生自学。课后针对每单元的主题设计了小组讨论题目,以鼓励学生运用所学物流英语知识来阐述自己的观点,提高口语表达能力;另外,还提供相应的句型翻译,培养学生的写作技能。

第二,注重岗位应用。对话均以常见物流业务场景为背景,证单填写采用真实单据,教学安排有说有写,内容务实,形式活泼,强调交流互动。课后配有相应的对话分组练习和邮件写作训练,充分搭建学生动手平台,提高英语实际应用的技能。

本书作为职业教育物流管理专业的特色教材,注重基础和知识体系的完整,注重实际应用能力的培养,全书采取新颖、统一的格式化设计。本书既适用于职业院校物流管理、交通运输、市场营销、工商管理、电子商务等相关专业教学,还可作为从事国际物流货运代理及其他物流从业人员的岗位培训教材,对于广大社会自学者也是一本有益的读物。

本教材由李大军进行总体方案策划并具体组织编写,王艳主编并统稿,安锦兰、杨昆、董晓霞为副主编;本书由中国物流技术协会副理事长兼秘书长、高级工程师吴明审定。参加编写的人员有:牟惟仲(序言),王艳(第1单元、第2单元),李峥(第3单元),安锦兰(第4单元),黄强新、李耀华(第5单元),杨昆(第6单元),贾相梅(第7单元),董晓霞(第8单元),丁艺(第9单元),刘丽艳、刘华(第10单元),马瑞奇、李人晴、蔡丽伟(附录);华燕萍负责本书修改和版式调整,李晓新制作教学课件。

在教材修订过程中,我们参阅了国内外有关物流英语教学方面的书刊资料和国家颁布实施的相关法规和管理规定,并得到编审委员会和物流协会及从事物流英语教学实践有关专家教授的具体指导,在此一并致谢。因作者水平有限,书中难免存在不足之处,恳请同行和读者批评指正。

编 者

2012 年 2 月

前言

foreword 第1版

全球经济一体化进程加快,世界各国之间的贸易交往日益密切。随着我国加入WTO,我国流通市场已经全面对外开放,中国市场国际化的趋势正在形成,为我国物流企业参与国际物流市场竞争提供了良好的发展契机。英语是一种工具,也是一把打开世界门窗的钥匙,具有加强沟通、扩大交流范围的功能。面对国际物流业的快速发展与激烈竞争,英语已成为我国物流企业进军国际物流市场所必须掌握的技能。尽快提高我国涉外物流企业从业人员的英语水平已成为目前亟待解决的问题。

《物流英语》一书的出版,正是为培养大量国际物流专门人才,解决物流企业发展对既懂得物流专业知识、又熟练掌握物流英语及实际业务运作的技能型人才的急需。本书严格按照教育部关于"加强职业教育、注重实践教学、强化应用技能培养"等教育教学改革精神和要求,由长期从事物流英语教学的主讲教师及具有丰富经验的企业人士共同编写。本书的出版对提高从业人员的英语水平,提升物流企业的服务质量,促进我国外向型物流业的健康发展具有十分重要的意义。

全书共10个单元,以培养学习者英语书写和口语应用能力为主线,依照国际与国内物流业务活动的基本过程和规律,结合实际讲解知识内容,力求突出实用性。本书内容包括：物流简介、客户服务、仓储、运输与配送、物流包装、国际物流、物流采购、第三方物流、供应链管理及物流信息管理等主要环节基本专业英语知识,以及办证下单日常工作所需的常用词汇用语。

本教材与其他相关教材相比,具有以下特点。

第一,注重教学实效。针对高职学生英语基础普遍薄弱且水平参差不齐的现状,为了使学生学有所获、学有所用,强化"说"和"写"两方面训练。课文以单元教学为基础,选材新颖,对重点和难点均进行专门注释,方便学生自学。课后针对每单元的主题设计了小组讨论题目,以鼓励学生运用所学物流英语知识来阐述自己的观点,提高口语表达能力;另外,还提供相应的句型翻译,培养学生的写作技能。

第二,注重岗位应用。对话均以常见物流业务场景为背景,证单填写采用真实单据,教学安排有说有写,内容务实,形式活泼,强调交流互动。课后配有相应的对话分组练习和邮件写作训练,充分搭建学生动手平台,提高英语实际应用的技能。

　　本书作为职业教育物流管理专业的特色教材,注重基础和知识体系的完整,注重实际应用能力的培养,全书采取新颖、统一的格式化设计。正是由于本书具有定位准确、知识系统、内容翔实、案例丰富、贴近实际、突出实用性、适用范围宽泛、通俗易懂及便于学习和掌握等特点,所以本书既适用于物流管理、交通运输、市场营销、工商管理、电子商务等相关专业各学历层次职业教育教学,还可以作为从事国际物流货运代理及其他物流从业人员的岗位培训教材,对于广大社会自学者也是一本有益的读物。

　　本教材由李大军进行总体方案策划并具体组织编写,王艳主编并统稿,李人晴和黄强新为副主编;本书由中国物流技术协会副理事长兼秘书长、高级工程师吴明审定。参加编写的人员有:王艳(第1单元、第2单元、第3单元),李人晴(第4单元),黄强新(第5单元、第9单元),刘华(第6单元),李耀华(第7单元、第8单元),刘丽艳(第10单元),马瑞奇、李晓新(附录);赵茜和蔡丽伟也协助参加了部分单元的编写。

　　在编写过程中,我们参阅了大量国内外有关物流英语教学方面的书刊资料和企业培训教材,并得到编委会牟惟仲、吴明等有关专家教授的具体指导,在此一并表示感谢。由于作者水平有限,书中难免存在不足之处,恳请同行和读者批评指正。

编　者

2008年3月

教学建议

> 第3版

物流英语是物流管理专业的一门主要专业课程。英语是一种工具，也是一把打开世界门窗的钥匙，具有加强沟通、扩大交流范围的功能。面对国际物流业的快速发展与激烈竞争，英语已成为我国物流企业进军国际物流市场所必须掌握的技能；尽快提高我国涉外物流企业从业人员的英语水平也已成为目前亟待解决的问题。希望通过本书的学习能够使学生掌握常见物流场合的基本词汇、物流业务简单对话和日常工作英文邮件，为从事国际物流业务打下坚实的基础。

根据职业教育的特点与要求，在教学过程中，须结合教学对象和教学目标，加强物流英语对话和书写邮件两项技能的培养，注重实践性教学环节的设计。

建议本教材的教学课时为48学时。为了使教师合理安排有限的教学课时，突出教学重点，对课时分配做出如下安排，供教学时参考。

单元	教学内容	总课时	理论教学课时	实践教学课时
1	物流简介	4	2	2
2	客户服务	6	4	2
3	仓储	4	2	2
4	运输与配送	4	2	2
5	物流包装	4	3	1
6	国际物流	6	4	2
7	物流采购	4	3	1
8	第三方物流	6	4	2
9	供应链管理	3	2	1
10	物流信息管理	3	2	1
	机动课时	4		
	课时总计	48		

contents 目录 第3版

Unit 1　Introduction to Logistics ············· 1

　Ⅰ. What Is Logistics ············· 1
　Dialogue 1　Introduction to Logistics Company ············· 6
　Ⅱ. Activities in Logistics System ············· 10
　Dialogue 2　Visiting a Logistics Company ············· 14

Unit 2　Customer Service ············· 19

　Ⅰ. What Is Customer Service ············· 19
　Dialogue 1　Delay of Delivering ············· 24
　Ⅱ. How to Improve Customer Service Level ············· 27
　Dialogue 2　Make a Complaint ············· 31

Unit 3　Warehousing ············· 37

　Ⅰ. Warehouse Operation ············· 37
　Dialogue 1　Visiting a Warehouse ············· 41
　Ⅱ. Inventory Management ············· 44
　Dialogue 2　How Much Should I Order ············· 48

Unit 4　Transportation and Distribution ············· 57

　Ⅰ. Transportation Mode ············· 57
　Dialogue 1　Negotiating About the Transportation
　　　　　　　Conditions ············· 62
　Ⅱ. Distribution Management ············· 66
　Dialogue 2　Partial Shipment and Transshipment ············· 70

Unit 5　Packaging ············· 76

　Ⅰ. Introduction to Packaging ············· 76

Dialogue 1　Packing of Silk Stockings ……………………………… 80
　　Ⅱ．Functions of Packaging ………………………………………… 84
　　Dialogue 2　The Packaging of Beer ……………………………… 88

Unit 6　International Logistics …………………………………………… 94

　　Ⅰ．Containerization …………………………………………………… 94
　　Dialogue 1　Talking About the Unloading Port ………………… 99
　　Ⅱ．Main Logistics Documents …………………………………… 103
　　Dialogue 2　Change the Port of Destination …………………… 107

Unit 7　Purchasing ……………………………………………………… 112

　　Ⅰ．Purchasing ……………………………………………………… 112
　　Dialogue 1　What Is Purchasing ………………………………… 116
　　Ⅱ．Purchasing Process …………………………………………… 120
　　Dialogue 2　Ordering Equipment ………………………………… 125

Unit 8　The Third Party Logistics ……………………………………… 130

　　Ⅰ．The Nature of the Third Party Logistics ……………………… 130
　　Dialogue 1　Searching the 3PL Companies …………………… 134
　　Ⅱ．3PL in China …………………………………………………… 138
　　Dialogue 2　Evaluating 3PL Companies ………………………… 143

Unit 9　Supply Chain Management …………………………………… 149

　　Ⅰ．Supply Chain Management …………………………………… 149
　　Dialogue 1　Developing a Supply Chain ………………………… 153
　　Ⅱ．Developing Trends in Supply Chain Management ………… 158
　　Dialogue 2　The Possibility of Creating a Supply Chain ……… 162

Unit 10　Logistics Information Management ………………………… 167

　　Ⅰ．The Role of Information Management ……………………… 167
　　Dialogue 1　Difference between Legacy System and Present System ………… 173
　　Ⅱ．Pick-to-Light Basics …………………………………………… 175
　　Dialogue 2　Introduction to Supply Chain Management Information
　　　　　　　　System ……………………………………………… 180

参考文献 ………………………………………………………………… 186

Appendix Ⅰ　Logistics Terms ……………………………………………………… 187

Appendix Ⅱ　Reference Keys ……………………………………………………… 194

Appendix Ⅲ　International Logistics Vocabulary ……………………………… 206

Appendix Ⅳ　Logistics Documents ……………………………………………… 220

Unit 1 Introduction to Logistics

- ◆ Knowledge Learning Objectives 知识学习目标 ◆
  - To understand the definition of logistics
  - To know the importance of logistics
  - To learn the activities of logistics
- ◆ Skill Developing Objectives 技能培养目标 ◆
  - Communication skill in receiving the customer
  - Communication skill in introducing the logistics company
  - Writing skill in introducing the logistics company
  - Communication skill in establishing the business relationship

Ⅰ. What Is Logistics

1. The Definition of Logistics(物流的概念)

There are various definitions of different editions. But in general, there are mainly two types of definition in practice.

In *Chinese Logistics Terms*, logistics means the physical movement of goods from the supplier to the receiver. Based on practical need, logistics is integrated organically with the variety of the basic functional activities including transportation, storage, loading and unloading, handling, package, distribution, information management, etc.

The Council of Logistics Management has adopted the following definition of logistics: Logistics is that part of the supply chain process that plans, implements, and controls the efficient, effective flow and storage of goods, services, and related information from the point of origin to the point of consumption in order to meet customers' requirements.

2. Some Interpretation to Logistics(物流的其他概念)

The logistics function of the system goal is to satisfy customer needs. Therefore, from a customer service point of view, some scholars defined logistics as: To the right cost and the right conditions, the right quality and the right quantity, to ensure the right customer at the right time and right place, for the right product for availability, namely, the concept of logistics 7Rs. The so-called product availability, that is, customers who want to get products may face time and space distance issues. In fact, product availability is a functional assessment of the logistics system, and the primary indicators, is also the main objective of the logistics system optimization.

3. The Importance of Logistics(物流的重要性)

Since the beginning of human civilization, there has been the "move" of the goods. So we should say, "Logistics is anything but a newborn baby." However, when it comes to modern logistics, most professionals in the business consider it one of the most competitive and exciting jobs, invisible as it is. "Logistics is a unique global pipeline that operates 24 hours a day, seven days a week and 52 weeks a year, planning and coordinating the delivery of products and service to customers all over the world."

4. Importance of Logistics Management(物流管理的重要性)

In practice, logistics refers to the systematic management of the various activities required from the point of production to the customers. However, logistics management means different things to different organizations. In today's volatile economic environment, logistics management is becoming more important than ever before. It is critical to get the right amount of goods to the right place at the right time, especially in an age when budgets are tight and customers' demands are unpredictable.

A recent US study found that logistics costs account for almost 10% of the Gross Domestic Product. The process itself covers a diverse number of functional areas. Involved in logistics are transportation and traffic, as well as shipping and receiving. It also covers storage and import/export operations.

5. Development of Logistics Management(物流管理的发展)

Logistics management has evolved over the last three decades from the narrowly defined distribution management to the integrated management and to the global supply chain. The mission of logistics management is to plan and coordinate all activities to achieve desired levels of delivered service and quality at the lowest possible cost. In order to succeed in today's global marketplace, companies must be ever cognizant of these trends and develop a logistics management strategy that capitalizes on the best-of-breed technology solution available today, so that they can meet the demands of their customers today and be well prepared for the future.

Unit 1 Introduction to Logistics

New Words and Phrases

logistics [lə'dʒistiks] n. 后勤学，物流
definition [ˌdefi'niʃən] n. 定义，概念
implement ['impliment] v. 履行，推进
civilization [ˌsivilai'zeiʃən] n. 文明
professional [prə'feʃənəl] n. 专家，专业人员
pipeline ['paiplain] n. 管道
acquisition [ˌækwi'ziʃən] n. 获得
manufacture [ˌmænju'fæktʃə] n./v. 加工，制造
storage ['stɔːridʒ] n. 储存，仓储
distribution [ˌdistri'bjuːʃən] n. 配送
maintenance ['meintinəns] n. 维持

disposition [ˌdispə'ziʃən] n. 配置
construction [kən'strʌkʃən] n. 建设，构成
provision [prə'viʒən] n. 供应，提供
volatile ['vɔlətail] adj. 多变的
critical ['kritikl] adj. 关键性的，决定性的
budget ['bʌdʒit] n. 预算
evolve [i'vɔlv] v. 演变，发展
integrate ['intigreit] v. 整合，综合
cognizant ['kɔgnizənt] adj. 知道的，认识的
capitalize ['kæpitəlaiz] v. 变成资本，作资本用

Notes

1. There are various definitions of different editions. 物流的定义有很多不同版本。

2. In *Chinese Logistics Terms*, logistics means the physical movement of goods from the supplier to the receiver. Based on practical need, logistics is integrated organically with the variety of the basic functional activities including transportation, storage, loading and unloading, handling, package, distribution, information management, etc. 《国家标准物流术语》中，物流定义为物品从供应地向接收地的实体流动过程，根据实际需要，将运输、储存、装卸、包装、配送、信息处理等基本功能实现有机结合。

3. The Council of Logistics Management has adopted the following definition of logistics: Logistics is that part of the supply chain process that plans, implements, and controls the efficient, effective flow and storage of goods, services, and related information from the point of origin to the point of consumption in order to meet customers' requirements. 物流管理协会修订了物流的定义：物流是供应链过程中的一部分，是以满足客户需要为目的的，为提高产品、服务和相关信息从起始点到消费点的流动储存效率和效益而对其进行计划、执行和控制的过程。

4. However, when it comes to modern logistics, most professionals in the business consider it one of the most competitive and exciting jobs, invisible as it is. 说到现代物流，业内专家认为，尽管看不见摸不着，却是最富有挑战性和最激动人心的工作之一。

5. In practice, logistics refers to the systematic management of the various activities required from the point of production to the customers. 实际上，物流是指从生产地点到客户所需各种活动的系统管理。

6. It is critical to get the right amount of goods to the right place at the right time, especially in an age when budgets are tight and customers' demands are unpredictable. 尤其是在资金预算紧张和客户需求无法预测时，在正确的地点和时间得到正确数量的货物

才显得颇为关键。

7. Logistics management has evolved over the last three decades from the narrowly defined distribution management to the integrated management and to the global supply chain. 物流管理在最近 30 年中从狭义的配送管理到一体化管理，最后发展为全球供应链管理。

8. In order to succeed in today's global marketplace, companies must be ever cognizant of these trends and develop a logistics management strategy that capitalizes on the best-of-breed technology solution available today, so that they can meet the demands of their customers today and be well prepared for the future. 为了赢得全球市场，在现有的资金和技术条件下，公司必须清楚地知道自己的发展意向以及相关的物流战略，以便公司能够满足客户需求并为未来的发展做好充足的准备。

Exercises

Ⅰ. Pair work: Discuss the following questions.

1. What is logistics?
2. Why is logistics so important?
3. Is logistics anything new? Why?
4. What is the main function of logistics?
5. How do you understand the development of logistics management?

Ⅱ. Fill in the blanks with the words in the following box. Change the forms if necessary.

route	location	movement	originate	importance
inventory	purchase	flow	storage	logistics

1. The aim of _____ management is to minimize the amount of material in stock.

2. _____ is a hot topic in China and the whole world.

3. If the ship had sailed along the recommended _____, it would have been able to avoid the heavy weather.

4. People generally consider logistics as the _____ of goods, it is partly right, but logistics is much more than that.

5. Logistics involves the _____ of goods, but also of people, as well as housing and feeding them.

6. The foreign company has to _____ 500 TEU of garments from China every year.

7. The meaning of the word "logistics" firstly _____ from the military.

8. The _____ expenses will be for your account if you place an order of 100000 tons of roll steel at a time. My workshop uses ten tons a month.

9. With the development of modern economy, people become more and more aware of the _____ of logistics.

10. Whether facilities are owned or rented, the _____ of warehouses is extremely important.

Ⅲ. Translate the following sentences into Chinese.

1. Modern logistics is one of the most challenging and exciting jobs in the world.

2. Every company that sells products need the service of logistics.

3. Many experts hold the opinion that logistics is an iceberg, only the top of which is seen, what is unseen is much bigger.

4. As logistics manager's roles and value have been grown, the need for well-educated, talented professionals with a diverse array of skills is emerged.

5. Logistics is a unique global "pipeline" that operates 24 hours a day, planning and coordinating the transport of products to customers all over the world.

Ⅳ. Translate the following sentences into English.

1. 物流的整体目标是以最低成本获得预期的顾客服务水平。

2. 在物流专家的协助下,公司利润明显上升。

3. 国际物流公司计划、协调和控制着全球产品的运输和交付。

4. 最近几年,我国在物流结构、组织和运作上取得了很大的进步。

5. 海运一直是国际贸易中最重要的运输方式。

Ⅴ. Read the following passages and answer the questions.

After completing a commercial transaction, logistics will execute the transfer of goods from the supplier (seller) to the customer (buyer) in the most cost-effective manner. This is the definition of logistics. During the transfer process, hardware such as logistics facilities and equipment (logistics carriers) are needed, as well as information control and standardization. In addition, supports from the government and logistics association should be in place.

Three major functions of logistics:

(1) Creating time value: same goods can be valued differently at different times. Goods often stop during the transfer process, which is professionally called the storage of logistics. It creates the time value for goods.

(2) Creating location value: same goods can be valued differently at different locations. The value added during the transfer process is the location value of logistics.

(3) Distribution processing value: sometime logistics create distribution processing value, which changes the length, thickness and packages of the goods. Like popular saying, "cutting into smaller parts" is the most commonly seen distribution processing form. Most processing within logistics create added value for goods.

1. What is the meaning "cost-effective"? (   )
   A. Cost reduced.   B. Economically.
   C. Cost evaluate.   D. To add cost.

2. (   ) creates time value.

   A. Transportation   B. Good flow
   C. Different location D. Storage

3. What is the same meaning of location value? (   )

   A. Different value.
   B. Different value of same goods at the different places.
   C. Different good.
   D. Different value of different goods at the same place.

4. What is the distribution processing value? (   )

   A. Distribution.
   B. Processing.
   C. Sales and processing.
   D. Changing the length, thickness and the package of the goods.

5. The distribution process value is available in all logistics activities. Is it correct or not? (   )

   A. Both.   B. Yes.   C. Not.   D. Not clear.

Dialogue 1 Introduction to Logistics Company

(*Li Jian, the sales representative of Zhongji Shipping Company, is talking with Eric, a potential customer.*)

Li: Welcome to our company, Eric. Nice to meet you.

Eric: Nice to meet you, too.

Li: Eric, my name is Li Jian. Here is my card. I'd like to introduce my company.

Eric: Thank you.

Li: Our business covers import and export container transportation and agency, door to door pickup and delivery, customs clearance, warehousing and consolidation.

Eric: I see.

Li: Zhongji has become one of the market leaders in China's freight forwarding and logistics industry today.

Eric: Uh-huh.

Li: We have helped Ford to substantially reduce logistics costs.

Eric: Can you tell me more?

Li: Of course, that was one of the best achivement in the beginning of the 2000s.

Eric: One of the best results? In what way?

Li: We improved their management by optimizing the plans of demonstration before plunging into action. As a result, the overall utilization raised considerably.

Eric: It's amazing.

Li: If you are concerned about logistics questions, you can ask anyone here. We have a reputation for top service.

Eric: I hope so.

Li: If you have a moment, I hope I can talk to you later.

Eric: Well, you are welcome, I'd like to hear your suggestion.

 New Words and Phrases

container [kən'teinə] n. 集装箱
transportation [,trænspɔː'teiʃən] n. 运输
warehouse ['wɛəhaus] v. 仓储,储存
consolidation [kən,sɔli'deiʃən] n. 集货,配货
freight [freit] n. 运输,运费
forward ['fɔːwəd] v. 发送,递送

optimize ['ɔptimaiz] v. 优化,充分利用
demonstration [,deməns'treiʃən] n. 运营
utilization [,juːtilai'zeiʃən] n. 利用
pickup and delivery 货物交接
customs clearance 通关,清关
plunge ... into action 把……投入

 Notes

1. Our business covers import and export container transportation and agency, door to door pickup and delivery, customs clearance, warehousing and consolidation. 我们公司业务涵盖了集装箱进出口运输和代理,门到门交接货物,仓储和配货。

2. We improved their management by optimizing the plans of demonstration before plunging into action. As a result, the overall utilization raised considerably. 我们通过在运营计划投入前对其进行优化,来提高管理水平,从而使整体利用率得以大幅度提升。

 Exercises

Ⅰ. Oral practice: Practice the above dialogue with your partner until you can learn the lines by heart.

Ⅱ. Team work: Make up a dialogue according to the following situation and practice it with your partner.

Situation:

Gary is a clerk of a logistics company. Now he is introducing the company to Jack, who is paying a visit to the company.

Tips:

1. Excuse ...

2. Nice to meet you.

3. It's very kind of you to …

4. Our business covers …

5. Our company provides logistics services such as …

6. I've come here today to see whether you have interest in our service.

7. If you have any questions, please feel freely to contact me anytime.

8. I'm looking forward to our next meeting.

Ⅲ. Write an E-mail to your customer, telling them about the following information.
Contents:

1. 为有合作意向的客户介绍你的公司及主营业务；

2. 附上公司的详细资料；

3. 洽谈初步的合作意向。

Ⅳ. Fill in the blanks with the words in the following box. Change the forms if necessary.

| manager | deal with | establish | luggage |
| honestly | representative | corporation | a good idea |

(Mr. Zhang, are presentative of Beijing Textiles Products Corporation, is coming to a logistics company. He is talking to Miss Wang, the secretary …)

Wang: Hello!

Zhang: Hello!

Wang: What can I do for you? I am the secretary.

Zhang: Yes. Glad to meet you. I am the _____ of Beijing Textiles Products _____.

Wang: Please have a seat, and what would you like to drink, coffee or tea?

Zhang: Thanks, coffee please, and little sugar.

Wang: OK, just a minute.

Zhang: As a representative of Beijing Textiles Products Corporation, I _____ hope to _____ business relation with you.

Wang: We also hope to _____ you. But our _____ is not in at the moment. He will be back in an hour, and would you please wait for him for a while. I'm very sorry.

Zhang: It doesn't matter.

Wang: But if you don't mind I can take you to our restroom and put your _____.

Zhang: That's _____.

Wang: This way please.

Ⅴ. Read the following introduction, and introduce the company "HIT International Transportation Co., Ltd." in your own words.

HIT International Transportation Co., Ltd.

Founded in 1994, HIT is a state-owned enterprise under the HIT Group. Within the short span of 9 years, HIT has become one of the market leaders in China's freight forwarding and logistics industry today. HIT prides itself as

—Class A license holder with full authorization from the government to conduct space booking, customs brokerage and other related services.

—One of the first companies in China to be awarded the ISO 9001/9002 certificates.

—One of the first companies in Shanghai to launch full line of services including nationwide logistics service, project cargo handling, bonded trucking, bonded warehouse facility, city-pair trucking service, exhibition logistics in addition to the air & ocean freight business.

Annual Figures (2003)

Operating revenue	1.65 billion RMB
No. of jobs	200600 Jobs
FCL	75898 TEUs
LCL	10800 TEUs
Air freight	90678 Tons
Employees	1100 People
Customer/auditor complaint ratio	0.025%
Damage ratio	0.0001%

Our Capability & Facility

Air Freight

—24-hour air freight operation

—the customs bonded warehouse (the biggest in Shanghai)

—two operation facility in both Hongqiao & Pudong airport

—involvement in Cargo Terminal Management

—securing the most export space during the peak season with block-space and pallets

Ocean Freight

—HIT's own station at every terminal of the Shanghai port

—EDI linkage with the Customs

—own trucking fleet and CFS warehouse

—service contracts with major carriers

Logistics Services

—providing customized, state-of-the-art solutions offering complete logistics services

—customizing information system to support logistics needs

—daily pick-up service, stock & store with IT scan in/out, pick and pack, inventory, logistics services and other various warehousing facilities around the country.

Ⅱ. Activities in Logistics System

A logistics system can be made up of many different functional activities, some of which are described briefly below.

1. Customer Service(客户服务)

In a broad sense, customer service is the output of the entire logistics system. It involves making sure that the right person receives the right product with the right quantity at the right place at the right time in the right condition at the right cost. At present, many logistics companies may have a customer service department that handle complaints, special orders, damage claims, returns, billing problems, etc.

2. Demand Forecasting(需求预测)

Demand forecasting estimates the need for precise amount of products and services that customers will require in the future. The logistics system can ensure the right products or services are available to meet those requirements. It involves in forecasting how much should be ordered from its suppliers, and how much of finished products should be transported in each market.

3. Transportation(运输)

Transportation refers to the physical movement of goods from one place to another place. It includes specific activities such as selecting the transport mode, choosing the particular route, selecting the right carrier, and complying with various local transportation regulations. Transportation is usually the most costly logistics activity. It may account for 40%~60% of a company's total logistics cost.

4. Warehousing(仓储)

Warehousing is an integral part of every logistics system. It plays an important role in providing a desired level of customer service at the lowest possible total cost. It refers to places where goods can be stored for a particular period of time. Generally, the greater the time lags between production and consumption, the larger the level of warehousing required.

5. Inventory Management(库存管理)

Inventory management deals with balancing the cost of maintaining additional products on hand against the risk of not having those items when the customer wants them. This task has become more complex as firms have gradually lowered inventory levels.

6. Packaging(包装)

Industrial packaging focuses on protecting the product while it is being transported and stored. It conveys important information to inform the customer and provide protection during storage and transport. In a marketing sense, the package acts as a form of promotion or advertising. Its size, weight, color, and printed information attract customers and convey knowledge about the product.

7. Procurement（采购）

Procurement is the purchase of materials and services from outside to support the firm's operations from production to marketing, sales and logistics. It includes the selection of supply source location, timing of purchases, price determination, quality control and many other facets.

8. Material Handling（物资搬运）

Material handling is a broad sense concerning all short-distance movements of raw materials, work in process, or finished goods within a factory or warehouse. As material handling tends to add costs rather than value to logistics systems, managers tend to minimize the number of handling whenever possible.

9. Information Management（信息管理）

Information links all areas of the logistics system together. Information processing is becoming increasingly automated, complex, and rapid. It is critical to the efficient functioning of system.

10. Other Logistics Activities（其他物流活动）

Other activities such as waste disposal, return goods handling, etc. are also important. Logistics managers have to consider the social costs associated with waste disposal. The handling of returned goods, often referred to as reverse distribution, is an important part of the logistics process.

New Words and Phrases

functional ['fʌŋkʃənl] adj. 功能上的，职责上的
output ['autput] n. 产量，产品
complaint [kəm'pleint] n. 抱怨，投诉
damage ['dæmidʒ] n./v. 损失，损坏
claim [kleim] n./v. 要求，索赔
requirement [ri'kwaiəmənt] n. 需求，要求
transport [træns'pɔ:t] n./v. 运输
transportation [,trænspɔ:'teiʃən] n. 运输
regulation [,regju'leiʃən] n. 管制，规则
integral ['intigrəl] adj. 完整的
warehouse ['wɛəhaus] n./v. 储存，仓库
inventory ['invəntri] n. 库存，存货

maintain [men'tein] v. 维持，保持
convey [kən'vei] v. 传送，传递
promotion [prə'məuʃən] n. 促进，提升，促销
procurement [prə'kjuəmənt] n. 采购，获得
purchase ['pə:tʃəs] n./v. 采购
facet ['fæsit] n. （事情之）一面
reverse [ri'və:s] adj. 相反的，逆向的
raw material 原材料
work in process 半成品，在加工产品
finished goods 成品
waste disposal 废弃物处理

Notes

1. In a broad sense, customer service is the output of the entire logistics system. 总的来说,客户服务是整个物流系统的主要产出。

2. It involves making sure that the right person receives the right product with the right quantity at the right place at the right time in the right condition at the right cost. 客户服务就是要以恰当的成本使恰当的客户在恰当的时间,恰当的地点在恰当的条件下以恰当的价格收到恰当的产品。(这7个right就是物流服务的核心理念。)

3. Demand forecasting estimates the need for precise amount of products and services that customers will require in the future. 需求预测就是估计客户将来对产品和服务的确切需求数量。

4. Transportation refers to the physical movement of goods from one place to another place. It includes specific activities such as selecting the transport mode, choosing the particular route, selecting the right carrier, and complying with various local transportation regulations. 运输是指货物在不同地点之间的物理性移动。它包括选择运输方式、具体路线、恰当的承运人以及遵守各种运输法规等具体活动。

5. It plays an important role in providing a desired level of customer service at the lowest possible total cost. 仓储在以最低的可能成本提供相对满意的客户服务水平方面占据着重要的地位。

6. Generally, the greater the time lags between production and consumption, the larger the level of warehousing required. 一般来讲,生产与消费间隔的时间越长,所需求的库存量越大。

7. Inventory management deals with balancing the cost of maintaining additional products on hand against the risk of not having those items when the customer wants them. 库存管理平衡库存持有成本和销售损失成本。

8. Procurement is the purchase of materials and services from outside to support the firm's operations from production to marketing, sales and logistics. 采购是指从企业外部进行原材料和服务的购买,以保证公司生产、销售、物流的正常运转。

9. Material handling is a broad sense concerning all short-distance movements of raw materials, work in process, or finished goods within a factory or warehouse. As material handling tends to add costs rather than value to logistics systems, managers tend to minimize the number of handling whenever possible. 广泛意义上讲,物资搬运是指在工厂或仓库内的原材料、半成品或成品的短距离移动。其在物流系统中只能增加成本而不能创造价值,所以经理们尽可能将搬运的数量降到最低。

10. The handling of returned goods, often referred to as reverse distribution, is an important part of the logistics process. 对退回货物的物流处理,通常被称作逆向物流,是物流流程的重要组成部分。

Exercises

Ⅰ. **Team work: Discuss the following questions.**
1. What are the activities in the logistics system?
2. Why is customer service so important in the logistics system?
3. Why is transportation the most costly logistics activity in the total logistics cost?
4. What is the main difference between warehousing and inventory management?
5. Information management is of great importance in modern logistics, isn't it? Why?
6. What is reverse logistics?

Ⅱ. **Fill in the blanks with the following words. Change the forms if necessary.**

source	activity	success	cost	procurement
analysis	manager	business	alike	land

1. Transport can be done by sea, air, _____, rail and pipe.
2. Mr. Wang is an inventory _____ in a bonded warehouse(保税仓库) in Capital Airport.
3. Logistics managers pay more attention to inventory at present, because inventory management can effectively reduce logistics _____.
4. Information is a key to the _____ of logistics strategy.
5. Warehousing is not a new _____, but it has gained new functions in modern logistics.
6. In every company customer service is _____ of information for demand forecasting.
7. Every firm, large and small _____, needs logistics strategic planning for its development.
8. Packaging is one of the most important _____ which are included in logistics system.
9. _____ deals with the buying of goods and services that keep the organization functioning.
10. Could you give me a brief _____ of the present situation in relation to logistics in China.

Ⅲ. **Translate the following sentences into Chinese.**
1. In the past decades, important changes have occurred with the role of purchasing in modern logistics system.
2. Package can have both a consumer package and logistics package.
3. To make efficient use of the warehouse space, you should decide how large your orders must be.
4. We should keep in mind that one logistics system does not fit all companies. The

number of activities in a logistics system can vary from company to company.

5. The strategic placement of warehouses near the company's major markets can improve the customers service levels.

Ⅳ. **Translate the following sentences into English.**

1. 我们公司拥有非常完善的客户服务系统。
2. 十年来,京东建立了世界一流的物流网络。
3. 过多的库存会最终导致更高的物流总成本。
4. 运价取决于三个因素,即距离、运输和竞争。
5. 包装是确保以最低的成本把产品安全交付给消费者的一种方式。

Dialogue 2　Visiting a Logistics Company

(Gary is from Dazhong Electric Company. Peter is from Zhongji Logistics Company. Gary is making an appointment with Peter on the phone.)

Gary: Hi! This is Gary, is this Zhongji Logistics Company?

Peter: Good afternoon. Can I help you?

Gary: I'd like to speak to Peter please.

Peter: This is Peter. Who's it?

Gary: This is Gary from Dazhong Electric Company. I have been looking for you. Do you have any appointments today?

Peter: Hi! I'm free today.

Gary: Good. I'd like to meet you as soon as possible and hope you can give me more information about your company.

(Gary goes to Zhongji Logistics Company to meet Peter.)

Peter: I appreciate that you give me this opportunity to introduce my company.

Gary: Thank you.

Peter: Our logistics company provides different means of transportation. And we are especially good at transporting goods via railway, highway and airway.

Gary: I'm very impressed. However, I'd like to know how well is your warehousing business.

Peter: Yes, of course. Let me show you around. I'd like to show you the headquarters and warehouse.

Gary: OK, let's go.

Peter: Take it easy. Here is the headquarters. Let's go downstairs. Since the whole company is quite large, we'll take a car to warehouse.

Gary: After you!

(*arriving at the warehouse*)

Peter: This is our warehouse.

Gary: Wow, what a big space!

Peter: Our company can provide customers with a variety of goods inventory, such as raw material, semi-finished products, finished products, spare parts, etc. We have special concessions on predominant goods and long-term contract.

Gary: I'm interested in that. Perhaps we will have the possibility of cooperation in the future.

Peter: That's a good news for us. We are looking forward to it.

New Words and Phrases

warehouse ['wεəhaus] *n.* 仓库
means [mi:nz] *n.* 方法,手段
railway ['reilwei] *n.* 铁路
highway ['haiwei] *n.* 公路
airway ['εəwei] *n.* 空运
headquarters [,hed'kwɔ:təz] *n.* 总部

concession [kən'seʃən] *n.* 优惠
in charge of 负责,主管
raw material 原材料
semi-finished products 半成品
finished products 成品
predominant goods 大宗货物

Notes

1. Our logistics company provides different means of transportation. And we are especially good at transporting goods via railway, highway and airway. 我们公司提供多种不同的运输方式,尤其擅长铁路,公路和航空运输。

2. Our company can provide customers with a variety of goods inventory, such as raw material, semi-finished products, finished products, spare parts, etc. 我们公司可以为客户提供各种货物的库存,诸如原材料、半成品、成品和零部件等。

3. We have special concessions on predominant goods and long-term contract. 对于大宗货物和租期较长的合同,我们都有特别的优惠。

Exercises

Ⅰ. **Oral practice**: Practice the above dialogue with your partner until you can learn the lines by heart.

Ⅱ. **Team work**: Make up a dialogue according to the following situation and practice it with your partner.

Situation:

Mary is a secretary of a logistics company. Now she is receiving the guest, who is willing to cooperate with her company.

Tips:

1. Do you have an appointment …

2. I have an appointment with …

3. I'd like to see the person in charge of …

4. That's the reason I'm here—to build up the business relationship with you.

5. Do you have samples?

6. We will make every effort to give you full satisfaction.

7. We hope to establish regular business relations with you.

8. Looking forward to further news with interest.

9. With the kindest regards.

Ⅲ. Write an E-mail to your customer, telling them about the following information.
Contents:

1. 邀请你的客户来公司参观。

2. 表示你合作的诚意,可以在价格上做出让步。

3. 希望能与客户建立长期的业务关系。

Ⅳ. Fill in the blanks with the words in the following box. Change the forms if necessary.

appointment	treat	workable	enlarge	satisfy
quality	reliable	keep	concession	expect

(*Peter is sitting in the reception room when John, the manager comes in and talks to him …*)

Manager: Excuse me. Are you Peter?

Peter: Yes, and you are …

Manager: I'm John, the manager. My secretary has told me everything about you.

Peter: How do you do!

Manager: How do you do. I'm so sorry for _____ you waiting for so long but I had an important _____ with my customer.

Peter: It doesn't matter. Shall we begin?

Manager: Yes, of course.

Peter: We learn from the Chamber of Commerce in your city that you deal a great deal of logistics business, and we hope to deal with you and _____ our business relation.

Manager: That's true. We promise you will be _____ with our service.

Peter: Uh-huh.

Manager: We have established _____ cooperation with many famous company such as P&G. We have reduced the logistics costs for them.

Peter: It's amazing.

Manager: Our service are of good _____. But I don't know whether the price is

_____ or not.

Peter: If you are really interested in our services, we will make a _____.

Manager: I'd think about it further. Could I let you know tomorrow?

Peter: No problem. I'll _____ you tomorrow.

Manager: OK, Peter. It's time for supper, and we'll _____ you in the Great Wall Hotel. Peter, please.

Peter: That's very thankful.

Ⅴ. Cloze test

Study the words in the box and fill in the blanks with them. Note there are twelve words in the box, but only ten words are needed.

A. focused	B. and	C. access	D. reasons
E. capability	F. information	G. through	H. sellers
I. minimizing	J. status	K. reducing	L. critical

Information System Functionality

From its very beginning, logistics _____ on product storage and flow _____ the distribution channel. There are four _____ why timely and accurate information has become more _____ for effective logistics systems design and operations. First of all, customers consider information about order _____, product availability, delivery schedule, shipment tracking, and invoices as necessary elements of total customer service. Customer demand _____ to real time information. Second, with the goal of total supply chain assets, managers realize that _____ can be used to reduce inventory and human resource requirements. In particular, requirements planning using the most current information can reduce inventory by _____ demand uncertainty. Third, information increases flexibility with regard to how, when, _____ where resources may be utilized to gain strategic advantage. Fourth, enhanced information transfer and exchange utilizing the Internet is changing relationship between buyers and _____ redefining channel relationships.

 Supplementary Reading

Development of Logistics

Logistics is by no means a new subject area. Historically, the concept of logistics systems from specific facets of military and industrial management. In the military sense, logistics is concerned with the various aspects of maintenance and system/product support, particularly from the point in time when systems are in operational use. In the industrial or commercial sector, logistics has been defined to include such activities as material flow, product distribution, transportation, warehousing, and the like. In both situations, however, logistics has been considered as a "downstream" effort, and the requirements for logistics have not been very well defined or integrated.

In recent years, systems and products have become more complex as technology advances, and logistics requirements have increased in general. Not only have the costs associated with system/product acquisition increased significantly in the past decade, but the costs of logistics support have also been increasing at an alarming rate. At the same time, the current economic dilemma of decreasing budgets combined with upward inflationary trends results in less money available for both the procurement of new systems and for the maintenance and support of those items already in use.

I. Answer the following questions.

1. Historically, what does logistics derive from?
2. In the industrial or commercial sector, how has logistics been defined?
3. In recent years, what have become complex technology advances?
4. What have been increasing at an alarming rate?
5. Why is the situation that there is less money available for both the procurement of new systems and for the maintenance and support of those items still exist?

II. Tell whether the following statements are true or false.

(   )1. Logistics is a new subject.

(   )2. The requirements for logistics have been very well defined or integrated.

(   )3. In the military, logistics is concerned with the various aspects of maintenance and system/product support.

(   )4. In recent years, systems and products have become less complex when technology advances.

(   )5. The costs associated with system/product acquisition decreased significantly in the past decade.

Unit 2

Customer Service

> ◆ Knowledge Learning Objectives 知识学习目标 ◆
> - To understand what is customer service
> - To know the role of customer service
> - To learn how to improve the customer service level
>
> ◆ Skill Developing Objectives 技能培养目标 ◆
> - Communication skill in arranging a delivery
> - Communication skill in making a complaint
> - Communication skill in handling a claim
> - Writing skill in handling the complaints and claims

Ⅰ. What Is Customer Service

1. What Is Customer(什么是客户)

In logistics system, the term customer means the object of delivery, or simply speaking, persons or units that receive the goods. In practice, it can be considered as being composed of two parts—internal and external customers. The internal customers involve persons or departments within a firm. In contrast, external customers, in the supply chain, range widely from wholesalers, retailers, end-users to other down-stream enterprises. Whoever the customers are, their demand for logistics service acts as a driving force that stimulates the development of logistics.

2. The Definition of Customer Service(客户服务的定义)

Customer service is normally defined as the service provided to the customer from the time the order is placed until the order is delivered. In fact, it is much more than this. It contains every aspect of the relationship between the manufacturer, supplier and customer. Under this definition it includes price, product range on offer, after-sales service, and product availability, in other words, the total activity of servicing the customer.

3. Two Elements of Customer Service(客户服务的种类)

Almost no company provides all its customers with the same level of customer service. The service contains the flowing two major elements—basic service and value-added service. Basic service refers to the basic level delivered to all customers, whether less profitable or most profitable, they should receive service not lower than this level.

In addition to basic service, firms sometimes offer extra service such as personal package to certain customers, who are considered as key customers by the firm. Such service exceeding the basic level is called value-added customers. Once the firms decide to provide value-added service for customers, they are immediately involved in the activities of customizing. Of course, firms have to undertake basic service promise before engaging in value-added service.

4. The Role of Customer Service(客户服务的作用)

In the process of logistics integration, customer service plays a significant role. Logistics system, with functions of transportation, warehousing and other associated activities, creates time and place utility for products. It tries to ensure that the customers receive the right product in the right place, at the right time, in the right condition, and at the right price. Besides, a customer cannot be satisfied unless he obtains an on-time and accurate delivery which can only be provided by perfect logistics system. Customer service is thus considered as the output of logistics system.

New Words and Phrases

delivery [di'livəri] n. 交付,递送
internal [in'tə:nl] adj. 内部的
external [eks'tə:nl] adj. 外部的
wholesaler ['həulseilə] n. 批发商
retailer ['riteilə] n. 零售商
stimulate ['stimjuleit] v. 刺激,鼓舞
manufacturer [,mænju'fæktʃərə] n. 生产商,制造商
supplier [sə'plaiə] n. 供应商
availability [ə,veilə'biliti] n. 有效性,可利用性
element ['elimənt] n. 元素,成分

exceed [ik'si:d] v. 超出,超越
undertake [,ʌndə'teik] v. 着手,履行
process ['prəuses] n. 过程,进展
utility [ju'tiliti] n. 效用
output ['autput] n. 产出
supply chain　供应链
end-user　终端用户
down-stream enterprises　下游企业
after-sales service　售后服务
value-added service　增值服务

 Notes

1. In logistics system, the term customer means the object of delivery, or simply

speaking, persons or units that receive the goods. 在物流系统中,"客户"一词是指递送服务的对象,简单来说就是接收货物的个人或单位。

2. In contrast, external customers, in the supply chain, range widely from wholesalers, retailers, end-users to other down-stream enterprises. 相反,外部客户分布于供应链各个环节,从批发商、零售商到最终用户或其他下游企业。

3. Whoever the customers are, their demand for logistics service acts as a driving force that stimulates the development of logistics. 不论客户是谁,他们对物流服务的需求驱动刺激着物流业的发展。

4. Customer service is normally defined as the service provided to the customer from the time the order is placed until the order is delivered. 客户服务通常被定义为从下订单开始到订单履行结束期间为客户提供的服务。

5. Under this definition it includes price, product range on offer, after-sales service, and product availability, in other words, the total activity of servicing the customer. 在这种解释下,客户服务包括价格、产品的变化、售后服务以及产品的可获得性。换言之,就是服务客户的所有活动。

6. Almost no company provides all its customers with the same level of customer service. 几乎没有一家公司能为自己的所有客户提供同一水平的服务。

7. Basic service refers to the basic level delivered to all customers, whether less profitable or most profitable, they should receive service not lower than this level. 基本服务是指提供给所有客户的基本服务水平,无论利润微薄还是丰厚,客户都应得到不低于该水平的服务。

8. In addition to basic service, firms sometimes offer extra service such as personal package to certain customers, who are considered as key customers by the firm. 除了基本服务,对于公司的某些关键客户,公司为他们提供诸如个性化包装等的额外增值服务。

9. Of course, firms have to undertake basic service promise before engaging in value-added service. 当然,公司必须在提供增值服务之前履行基本服务的承诺。

10. Logistics system, with functions of transportation, warehousing and other associated activities, creates time and place utility for products. 物流系统通过运输、仓储及其他相关活动的运作为产品创造了时间和空间效用。

 Exercises

Ⅰ. **Pair work: Discuss the following questions.**

1. What is customer service?
2. What is the difference between internal customer and external customer?
3. What is basic service?
4. Why are firms willing to offer value-added service for certain customers?
5. Customer service is the output of the logistics system, isn't it?

II. Fill in the blanks with the words in the following box. Change the forms if necessary.

| available | personal | output | analysis | external customers |
| retail | demand | place utility | response | convenient |

1. Transportation, by moving goods from one place to another place, creates _____ for products.

2. To satisfy customers with special taste, manufactures have to provide _____ services.

3. In the supply chain, _____ may contain wholesalers, retailers and end-users.

4. There is a great _____ for foreign investment in the western part of China.

5. We should make an _____ of products, depending on who use them and how they are used.

6. We must distribute the products to as many places as possible so that our customers find it _____ to get them.

7. Customer service is considered as the _____ of logistics system.

8. The key point in distribution is whether the product is _____ where the customer wishes to consume it.

9. One of the basic tasks of a logistics analyst is to determine customer _____ to service.

10. Generally speaking, soap can be found in a _____ shop.

III. Translate the following sentences into Chinese.

1. In customer service performance, availability means providing a product or material on a predictable basis.

2. Basic customer service is defined in terms of availability, performance and reliability.

3. Little else is significant if the customer's expectations are not fully met.

4. Logistical performance should be modified over time to accommodate changing marketing requirements.

5. It is very important to fully understand customer service deliverables when establishing logistical strategy.

IV. Translate the following sentences into English.
1. 在物流系统中,客户服务是关键活动之一。
2. 出色的顾客服务能够为供应链中的所有成员增值。
3. 客户服务是衡量物流系统有效性的尺度。
4. 众所周知,物流系统的最终目的是让客户满意。
5. 产品和服务只有在客户的手里才具有价值。

V. Read the following passages and answer the questions.
How do you effectively preserve the relationship during tough times? You can't

without the right foundation. Few strong business relationships are built quickly. Every good marketing strategy must include the long term goal of identifying key customers and prospects and building positive relationships. To start the process during tough times is too late. Here are a few suggestions:

- In the beginning don't talk. Yeah, that's right. At the beginning of the relationship do more listening than talking. One of the greatest reasons to keep a supplier is the words: "They know our business." Knowledge and understanding can be the glue to holding the relationship together during tough times.
- Keep the sales brochures in you briefcase. Only pull them out if they can solve a problem the customer has shared. If they don't and you leave them behind they'll be pitched.
- Pick the right sales person for the customer. I don't mean only personality (tough to figure out and a big variable), but length of service and level of industry and company knowledge that would match the size and importance of the customer or prospect.
- Remind the customer of your value proposition each time you meet. It could be on-time performance, fulfillment fates or how much you understand their business and needs.
- Demonstrate cost savings. If your delivery rates are higher but you deliver one day sooner, discuss the savings with the customer in terms of coat of money saved, customer satisfaction, lower inventories with JIT delivery and the implications of not delivering on time or being late.
- Go paperless. A strong e-commerce toolbox can save a customer time, reduce labor costs, paperwork and inconvenience.
- Build your brand's top-of-mind awareness at every opportunity with the goal of being among the first calls made when an RFP is put together. Use case study white papers, press releases, advertising, merchandising, event marketing, web site messages and email marketing.

We've only touched on a few ideas here, and much more can be said about each. But the main point is this. It can be too late when you hear, "Let's build a strong relationship with them," when no foundation has been laid.

1. By saying "Few strong business relationships are built quickly", the author means that (   ).

  A. strong business relationships can be built quickly

  B. strong business relationships cannot be built quickly

  C. business relationships should be strong

  D. business relationships are very important during tough times

2. Which of the following is NOT the merit(好处) of "e-commerce"? (   )
   A. Saving time.
   B. Decreasing labor costs.
   C. Creating convenience.
   D. Making promise contact with suppliers.
3. At the beginning of the business relationship, the author's suggestion is (   ).
   A. "do more listening than talking"
   B. "keep the sales brochures in your briefcase"
   C. "pick the right sales person for the customer"
   D. "Remind the customer of your value proposition each time you meet"
4. Which of the following is the theme(主题) of this passage? (   )
   A. Building the right customer relationship takes the right foundation.
   B. Right customer relationships take time.
   C. Cost is No.1 element in making good business relationships.
   D. Your brand is in your own interest.
5. The passage is more like a(n) (   ).
   A. piece of news
   B. personal idea
   C. advertisement
   D. letter

Dialogue 1 Delay of Delivering

(*Mr. Wang bought a TV set in Dajin Electric Appliance Company just now. Mary is a clerk of Customer Service Department. Now he is in the Customer Service Department.*)

Wang: Here's a TV set I have just bought here. Will you deliver it for me?

Mary: All right. We render the service of delivering goods to customer's house. Please fill in the delivery form with your address, telephone number and the time when you are in.

Wang: Where shall I sign?

Mary: Right here, above the dotted line, please.

(*Today is the delivery time.*)

Mary: Good afternoon. Customer Service Department. Can I help you?

Wang: Good afternoon. This is Mr. Wang. I ordered a TV set two days ago, June 12. It's already five o'clock and it hasn't arrived yet.

Mary: I'm really sorry, sir. It might have been on the way to your place. I'll check it immediately. Can I have your full name, address and phone number?

Wang: Yes. Wang Xinguo, No. 419 Hongqiao Road. My telephone number is 13656785678.

Mary: Thank you, sir. I'll check it with our delivery department and call you back as soon as possible.

Wang: All right, I'll be waiting for your call.

(*Five minutes later*)

Wang: Good afternoon. This is Wang Xinguo.

Mary: Good afternoon. This is Customer Service Department. I must apologize, sir. Due to the traffic jam, we can't make the delivery of your goods today.

Wang: Really? I find it hard to believe. I have already been waiting for nearly a whole day!

Mary: I'm awfully sorry about it. Please accept our sincere apologies. Is tomorrow morning convenient for you? We'll be glad to make arrangements to send it again.

Wang: OK.

Mary: I assure you it won't happen again.

New Words and Phrases

deliver [di'livə] *v.* 交付,递送	assure [ə'ʃuə] *v.* 保证
render ['rendə] *v.* 给予,提供	fill in 填写
check [tʃek] *v.* 查询,核对	due to 由于,因为
awfully ['ɔːfuli] *adv.* 非常,十分	traffic jam 交通堵塞
arrangement [ə'reindʒmənt] *n.* 安排	make the delivery of 交货

Notes

1. We render the service of delivering goods to customer's house. 我们提供送货到家服务。

2. Due to the traffic jam, we can't make the delivery of your goods today. 由于交通堵塞,我们今天无法送货。

3. We'll be glad to make arrangements to send it again. 我们非常乐意再为您安排送货。

Exercises

Ⅰ. **Oral practice**: Practice the above dialogue with your partner until you can learn the lines by heart.

Ⅱ. **Team work**: Make up a dialogue according to the following situation and practice it with your partner.

Situation:

Peter is a clerk of a customer service department. Now he is making arrangement to send goods for the customers.

Tips:

1. Would you please deliver ... for me?
2. Would you send ... to my house?
3. When can we expect the delivery?
4. All goods bought here can be delivered for free.
5. All our goods can be delivered inside the 4th ring road.
6. 24 hours per day delivery is guaranteed.
7. I'll wrap it up nicely for you and have it sent before 5 o'clock this afternoon.
8. Please write your name, address and phone number on the form.

Ⅲ. Write an E-mail to order the book you need, telling them to deliver for you.

Contents:

1. 在网上订购你所需要的书。
2. 说明送货需求。
3. 说明支付方式。
4. 告知你的时间和地点。

Ⅳ. Fill in the blanks with the words in the following box. Change the forms if necessary.

charge any money	order	in cash
delivery department	in store	gold
convenient	sales assistant	charge

(Mary is making a telephone call to order a ring she has seen on TV.)

Clerk: Hello, this is the _____ speaking.

Mary: Hello, I saw a ring in your commercial on TV yesterday. May I _____ that ring by phone?

Clerk: Sure. Do you know the sales number?

Mary: Yes. It's 4805. A 24K _____ ring.

Clerk: Hold on, please. Let me check it for you. Yes, we have this ring _____. It's 900 yuan. You can place an order now. Please tell me your name and address.

Mary: That's Mary, No. 60 Xinhua Street.

Clerk: Mary, No. 60 Xinhua Street. Mary. You need the ring with the sales number 4805.

Mary: When can I get it? Saturday will be _____.

Clerk: Saturday, I will tell the _____.

Mary: Do you _____ for the delivery?

Clerk: Yes, we will _____ 10 yuan for the delivery.

Mary: How will I pay?

Clerk: You may pay _____ to our delivery man on Saturday.

Mary: Thank you.

Ⅴ. **Put the following into Chinese.**

Inquiries in freight forwarding and logistics business are requested for information on sea/air/land freight rates, shipping space, frequency, transit time, etc. Inquiries can be made by letter, fax, E-mail or even telephone. When making an inquiry, it is advisable to observe the following guidelines.

(1) You may begin with the sentence by introducing yourself/your company. If you and the person/company you send inquiries to know each other very well, you need just to go stating direct the subject of your inquiry.

(2) For each item of information you want, better to use a separate paragraph.

(3) Keep your inquiry brief, specific and the point; say what needs to be said, ask what needs to be asked and no more. Then close with a simple "thank you" or "awaiting your reply", "looking forward to your response" etc.

(4) Avoid using long, big, stale words and those over-polite and very formal phrases.

Ⅱ. How to Improve Customer Service Level

1. Urgency of Improving Customer Service(提高客户服务的紧迫性)

In today's fiercely competitive market, customers face a great array of products and brand choices, prices and suppliers. Many firms find it extremely difficult to retain existing customers and to create new customers. Though not every purchase depends on the formation of relationship between the firms and their customers, many actually do. Higher level of customer service resulting from improved logistics system can greatly benefit the implementation of market strategy. Therefore, the managers are now going all out to improve their logistics system to deliver superior customer service.

2. Contradiction Between the Service Level and Cost(服务和成本之间的矛盾)

Firm's ultimate goal is to gain profits, not sales, so both service level and cost have to be taken into account. Higher level of customer service usually results in increased cost. No logistics system can maximize service and minimize logistics cost simultaneously. Maximum customer service implies large inventory, frequent transportation and multiple warehouses, all of which raise logistics cost. Minimum logistics cost means least-cost transportation, low stock levels and few warehouses.

3. Identifying Customers' Needs(确定客户需求)

The start point is to study what the customers require. It is important to remember that no two customers will ever be exactly the same in terms of their service requirements. However, it will be the fact that the customers will fall into groups which are characterized by similar service needs. A three-stage process is suggested here as follows:

- Identify the key parts of customer service as needed by customers.
- Establish the relation of those service parts to customers.
- Identify "group" of customers according to similarity of service preferences.

4. Defining Customers Service Objective(评价客户服务目标)

The purpose of logistics strategy is to provide customers with the level and quality of service that they require at less cost. In developing a market-driven logistics strategy, the aim is to achieve "perfect service" in a cost-effective way. The firm must research the relative importance of these service output. The firm must also take into account competitor's service standards. It will normally want to offer at least the same service level as competitors' service standards. But the objective is to maximize profits not sales. The firm has to look at the cost of providing higher level of services. Some companies offer less service and charge a lower price. Other companies offer more service and charge a higher price. The firm ultimately establishes right objectives to guide its planning.

5. Reducing the Cost of Logistics System(降低物流系统的成本)

An organization cannot achieve logistics efficiency by reducing the cost of each sector in the logistics system. Logistics costs usually interact and are often negatively related. Therefore, the firm has to improve customer service by reducing the total logistics costs.

According to the service standards, the firm designs a logistics system that minimizes the cost of achieving these standards. Cost of logistics system can be calculated by the following formula:

$$TC = TFC + FWC + VWC + LSC$$

TC = total logistics cost of proposed system

TFC = total freight cost of proposed system

FWC = total fixed warehouse cost of proposed system

VWC = total variable warehouse cost of proposed system

LSC = total cost of lost sales due to average delivery delay under proposed system

New Words and Phrases

urgency ['ə:dʒənsi] n. 紧急,紧迫
fiercely ['fiəsli] adv. 强烈地,极度地
competitive [kəm'petitiv] adj. 竞争的
retain [ri'tein] v. 保留,维持
formation [fɔ:'meiʃən] n. 形成

implementation [,implimen'teiʃən] n. 执行,落实
superior [sju'piəriə] adj. 优秀的
contradiction [,kɔntrə'dikʃən] n. 矛盾
ultimate ['ʌltimit] adj. 最终的
simultaneously [,siməl'teiniəsli] adv. 同时地

imply [im'plai] v. 暗示，包含
frequent ['fri:kwənt] adj. 频繁的
multiple ['multipl] adj. 多样的
identify [ai'dentifai] v. 确认
characterize ['kæriktəraiz] v. 以……为特征
process ['prəuses] n. 过程，工序
similarity [ˌsimi'læriti] n. 相似处，相似点
preference ['prefərəns] n. 偏爱
achieve [ə'tʃi:v] v. 完成，达到，实现
competitor [kəm'petitə] n. 竞争者
sector ['sektə] n. 环节

interact [ˌintər'ækt] v. 互相作用，互相影响
negatively ['negətivli] adv. 否定地
calculate ['kælkjuleit] v. 计算
formula ['fɔ:mjulə] n. 公式
variable ['vɛəriəbl] adj. 可变的
a great array of 大量的
result from 发生，引起
result in 致使，导致
take...into account 对……加以考虑
fall into 分类
market-driven 市场驱动

Notes

1. In today's fiercely competitive market, customers face a great array of products and brand choices, prices and suppliers. 在今天竞争激烈的市场，客户面对大量的产品、品牌、价格和供应商可供选择。

2. Higher level of customer service resulting from improved logistics system can greatly benefit the implementation of market strategy. 完善的物流系统带来的高水平物流服务能够极大地促进市场战略的实施。

3. Therefore, the managers are now going all out to improve their logistics system to deliver superior customer service. 因此，经理们都在尽其所能完善他们的物流系统以提供优质的客户服务。

4. Firm's ultimate goal is to gain profits, not sales, so both service level and cost have to be taken into account. 公司的最终目标是获得利润，而不是销售量，因此服务水平和成本均必须考虑进去。

5. No logistics system can maximize service and minimize logistics cost simultaneously. 没有任何一个物流系统能同时做到服务水平最高和成本最低。

6. Maximum customer service implies large inventory, frequent transportation and multiple warehouses, all of which raise logistics cost. 物流服务最大化意味着大量的库存、频繁多次的运输以及多样化的仓库，所有这一切都会增加物流成本。

7. It is important to remember that no two customers will ever be exactly the same in terms of their service requirements. 重要的是没有两个客户的需求完全一致。

8. However, it will be the fact that the customers will fall into groups which are characterized by similar service needs. 然而，在实践中我们必须按照相似的客户需求将客户分类。

9. In developing a market-driven logistics strategy, the aim is to achieve "perfect service" in a cost-effective way. 在推进市场驱动的物流战略中，目标是以有效的成本获得"完美的服务"。

10. The firm must also take into account competitor's service standards. 公司必须考虑竞争者所能提供的服务标准。

11. An organization cannot achieve logistics efficiency by reducing the cost of each sector in the logistics system. Logistics costs usually interact and are often negatively related. 一个组织仅仅通过降低物流系统中一个环节的成本,是不可能提高物流效率的。物流各个部分的成本通常是相互作用以及此消彼长的。

 Exercises

Ⅰ. Team work: Discuss the following questions.

1. Why is it urgent to improve customer service?
2. Every purchase depends on relationship between the firms and their customers. Doesn't it?
3. What is the contradiction between the service level and cost?
4. How do you understand the three-stage process suggested in the text?
5. Why is it necessary to analyze competitor's service standards for the firm?
6. As a logistics manager, how do you reduce the cost of logistics system?

Ⅱ. Fill in the blanks with the words in the following box. Change the forms if necessary.

profit	response	handle	competitive	proximity
offset	basic service	role	coordinate	determine

1. Once their orders are accepted, all customers should be treated equally by receiving _____.
2. It's my job to _____ customer's response to logistics service.
3. Customer service plays a significant _____ in the development of all firms.
4. A firm may have a customer service department or customer service employees that _____ complaints, special orders, damage claims, etc.
5. The mission of logistics management is to plan and _____ all logistics activities to achieve desired level.
6. In today's _____ market, firms find it extremely difficult to create new customers.
7. You can learn about your customer's _____ by analyzing inventory information.
8. Every company's ultimate goal is to gain _____, not sales.
9. I think if our warehouses are located in the _____ of customers, we can offer better after-sale service.
10. Good logistics plan _____ the cost of warehousing and transportation of products.

Ⅲ. **Translate the following sentences into Chinese.**

1. In the Internet age, companies analyze the needs of customers through big data.

2. By the end of this year, the company's profits must be very substantial with increasing market expansion.

3. Many firms are trying to create their unique brand in order to guide customers' preference.

4. Realization of customer's expectation is a core strategy of successful logistics.

5. We must distribute the products to as many places as possible so that our customers find it convenient to get them.

Ⅳ. **Translate the following sentences into English.**

1. 质量好的商品虽然花费高,但从长远来看是经济的。
2. 公司应该采取相应的措施提高客户服务水平。
3. 你很难解释什么是客户服务,客户服务又做些什么?
4. 很多公司已经建立了以客户为中心的市场战略。
5. 除了基本服务,公司还会为关键客户提供特色服务。

Dialogue 2　Make a Complaint

(*Judy, a clerk in Sun Textile Import and Export Co., Ltd. is complaining about the cargo to Sandy, a logistics company clerk.*)

Judy: Hello, may I speak to Sandy?

Sandy: Yes, speaking please.

Judy: This is Judy from Sun Textile Import and Export Co., Ltd.

Sandy: How are you? I think the cargo has already arrived. Is there anything else I can do for you?

Judy: Yes. We regret to tell you that the goods you sent us are not in conformity with the terms of the contract. On examination, we find a shortage in the delivery.

Sandy: Oh? How?

Judy: As soon as the consignment arrived at our port we had inspected it to our disappointment, we found a shortage of 2 cartons.

Sandy: Two cartons?

Judy: Yes. We ordered 20 cartons of garments, but we only received 18 cartons.

Sandy: Did you contact the exporter about the problem?

Judy: Yes. They showed the onboard bill of lading

to us. We all consider the carrier should be liable for the shortage. Therefore, we have to raise a claim against your company as the liability with you.

Sandy: We'd like to have your present proof.

Judy: Here is our onboard bill of lading to claim a settlement.

Sandy: Sorry, the evidence you provided is inadequate.

Judy: Wait a moment, here's a survey report issued by the Commodity Inspection Bureau.

Sandy: Have you got any other evidence?

Judy: Not yet.

Sandy: Sorry, we regret being unable to accept your claim because the goods were in perfect condition when they were loaded.

Judy: What should we do now?

Sandy: We suggest that you approach the insurance company for settlement as the shortage occurred in transit.

Judy: Which evidence do we provide?

Sandy: The full original set of ocean bills of lading, original policy and the original commercial invoice.

Judy: Thanks a lot, bye.

Sandy: Bye.

New Words and Phrases

cargo [ˈkɑːgəu] n. 货物
shortage [ˈʃɔːtidʒ] n. 短量
consignment [kənˈsainmənt] n. 寄送，委托货物
inspect [inˈspekt] v. 检查，检验
carton [ˈkɑːtən] n. 纸箱
carrier [ˈkæriə] n. 承运人
settlement [ˈsetlmənt] n. 解决
approach [əˈprəutʃ] v. 解决，处理

original [əˈridʒənl] adj. 原来的，正本的
policy [ˈpɔlisi] n. 保险单
in conformity with 与……一致，与……相符
onboard bill of lading 已装船提单
be liable for 对……负责
survey report 检验报告
commercial invoice 商业发票

Notes

1. We regret to tell you that the goods you sent us are not in conformity with the terms of the contract. 我们遗憾地通知你，你交付的货物与合同规定不符。

2. We regret being unable to accept your claim because the goods were in perfect condition when the goods were loaded. 非常遗憾我们不能接受你的索赔，因为装货时货物状态完好。

3. We suggest that you approach the insurance company for settlement as the shortage occurred in transit. 由于货物短量发生在运输途中，我们建议你找保险公司解

决问题。

 Exercises

Ⅰ. **Oral practice**: Practice the above dialogue with your partner until you can learn the lines by heart.

Ⅱ. **Team work**: Make up a dialogue according to the following situation and practice it with your partner.

Situation:

Today is the delivery time. Kitty still has not received the toy she ordered on the website. She is making a call to Customer Service Department.

Tips:

1. I'm afraid I have a complaint to make.
2. I'm afraid I have got a complaint about …
3. The last thing we want to do is postpone the delivery date.
4. I must apologize to you for …
5. We again apologize for causing your inconvenience.
6. I assure you it won't happen again.
7. We'll make a thorough investigation.
8. It's nothing serious, I hope.

Ⅲ. **Write an E-mail to the customer service department, telling them about the following information.**

Contents:

1. 你收到的货物与你订的型号不符。
2. 进行投诉。
3. 提出索赔。

Ⅳ. **Fill in the blanks with the words in the following box. Change the forms if necessary.**

| comment | complain | feedback | hesitate | beyond |
| pleased | satisfy | bother | considerate | arrive |

(*Miss Chen, a staff member in the Delivery Department of Air Logistics Co., Ltd. is making a call to a customer, Mr. Zhang.*)

Zhang: Hello. This is Peter Zhang. Who's speaking, please?

Chen: Hello. Mr. Zhang. It's really nice to hear you. This is Kitty Chen from Air Logistics Co., Ltd. I remember that you _____ to us about our delivery yesterday. Is that right?

Zhang: Yes, you are right.

Chen: Mr. Zhang, I'm calling you today just to see if everything is OK now with your washing-machine. I wish I were not _____ you too much.

Zhang: Oh, no, not at all.

Chen: Mr. Zhang, is your washing-machine working properly now?

Zhang: Yes, it is.

Chen: Are you _____ with its performance now, Mr. Zhang?

Zhang: Yes, I am.

Chen: By the way, I'd like to know how soon our delivery man reached your house after you called us.

Zhang: He _____ half an hour after I made the call, which was actually _____ my expectation.

Chen: Was he polite and careful?

Zhang: Yes. He was very careful and _____. He even helped me to clean the floor after he finished his job.

Chen: Thank you very much for your _____, Mr. Zhang. I hope you will be _____ with our service and we appreciate your _____.

Zhang: Thank you.

Chen: Please don't _____ to call us if there is any question. Goodbye.

Zhang: Goodbye.

Ⅴ．Put the following into English.

(1) 请报贵公司最优惠港到港集装箱海运价格，详情如下。

3个20英尺柜，下月出运

货物：家具

起运港：大连　　目的地：汉堡

客户要求直达

请报至少两个船公司价格，以便我公司比较，同时注明船期、船名

希望尽快收到贵公司回复

(2) 就贵公司所询义乌/浙江到西雅图/美国门到港小箱海运价格，我公司报价如下。

义乌—宁波拖柜费：1900RMB/20英尺柜

报关费：100RMB/票

订舱费：200RMB/20英尺柜

海运费：1600美元/英尺柜(已包括BAF、DDC)

船公司：中远/总统轮船

船期：每周三/六 15天到达

(3) 感谢贵公司询价，就320kg电动工具空运上海到纽约，门到门报价如下。

上海报关费：每票US＄40

卫检费：US＄0.01/箱

货运站处理费：US＄0.01/kg

空运费(上海—纽约)：US＄3.10/kg
目的地提/送货费：US＄100
目的地清关费：US＄130/票
目的地关税：US＄180
航空公司：西北航空/每周三/2天到达

Supplementary Reading

Supplementary Reading

The strategic supply chain processes that management has to decide upon will cover the breadth of the supply chain. These include product development, customers, manufacturing, vendors and logistics.

Product Development

Senior Management has to define a strategic direction when considering the products that the company should manufacture and offer to their customers. As product cycles mature or products sales decline, management has to make strategic decisions to develop and introduce new versions of existing products into the marketplace, rationalize the current product offering or whether develop a new range of products and services. These strategic decisions may include the need to acquire another company or sell existing businesses. However, when making these strategic product development decisions, the overall objectives of the firm should be the determining factor.

Customers

At the strategic level, a company has to identify the customers for its products and services, When company management makes strategic decisions on the products to manufacture, they need to then identify the key customer segments（部分） where company marketing and advertising will be targeted.

Manufacturing

At the strategic level, manufacturing decisions define the manufacturing infrastructure and technology that is required. Based on high level forecasting and sales estimates, the company management has to make strategic decisions on how products will be manufactured. The decisions can require new manufacturing facilities to be built or to increase production at existing facilities. However, if the overall company objectives include moving manufacturing overseas, then the decisions may lean towards using subcontracting and third party logistics. As environmental issues influence corporate policy to a greater extent, this may influence strategic supply chain decisions with regards to manufacturing.

Suppliers

Company management has to decide on the strategic supply chain policies with regards to suppliers. Reducing the purchasing spends for a company can directly relate to an increase in profit and strategically a number of decisions can be made to obtain that result. Leveraging the total company's purchases over many businesses can allow company management to select strategic global suppliers who offer the greatest discount. But these decisions have to correspond with the overall company objectives.

Logistics

As well as strategic decisions on manufacturing locations, the logistics function is key to the success of the supply chain. Order fulfillment is important and company management needs to make strategic decisions on the logistics network. The design and operation of the network has a significant influence on the performance of the supply chain. Strategic decisions are required on warehouses, distribution centers which transportation modes should be used. If the overall company objectives identify the use of more third party subcontracting, the company may strategically decide to use third party logistics companies in the supply chain.

1. What is the best title of this passage? (　　)
   A. Strategic Supply Chain Management.
   B. Tactical Supply Chain Management.
   C. Operational Supply Chain Management.
   D. Green Supply Chain Management.
2. All decisions have to be subject to (服从于) (　　).
   A. customers' interest   B. company's objectives
   C. manufacturing capabilities   D. market shares
3. What is most important to the success of the supply chain? (　　)
   A. Product development.   B. Key customer segments.
   C. Global suppliers.   D. Logistics function.
4. To sell existing businesses belongs to the category of (　　).
   A. product development   B. manufacturing
   C. vendors   D. logistics
5. This passage is to (　　).
   A. argue   B. give examples
   C. define   D. introduce

Unit 3

Warehousing

◆ Knowledge Learning Objectives 知识学习目标 ◆
- To understand the role of warehousing
- To know the warehouse activities
- To learn inventory management

◆ Skill Developing Objectives 技能培养目标 ◆
- Communication skill in introducing the warehouse
- Writing skill in introducing the warehouse
- Communication skill in the inventory situation
- Communication skill in the inventory goal

Ⅰ. Warehouse Operation

1. Role of Warehousing（仓储的角色）

Warehousing plays a key role in integrated logistics strategy and in building and maintaining good relationship between supply chain partners. Warehousing affects customer service level, sales and marketing success. Warehousing can link the production facility and the consumer, or supplier and production facility. Warehousing supports production by consolidating inbound materials and distributing them to the production facility at the appropriate time. Warehousing also helps marketing to serve current customers and expand into new markets.

The warehouse is a point in the logistics system where a firm stores or holds raw materials, semi-finished goods, or finished goods for varying periods of time. Holding goods in a warehouse stops or interrupts the flow of goods, adding cost to the product or products.

2. Main Components of Warehousing（仓储的构成要素）

The three basic components of warehousing are warehouse, equipment, and people. Space allows for the storage of goods when demand and supply are unequal. Space affects not only warehousing decisions but also the design of a logistics system. Warehouse equipment includes materials handling, storage racks and conveyor equipment. The equipment helps in product movement, storage, and tracking. People are the most critical component of warehousing. Space and equipment mean nothing without competent people.

The objective is to efficiently receive inventory, possibly store it until required by the market, assemble it into complete orders, and initiate movement to customers. This emphasis on product flow renders a modern warehouse as a mixing facility. As such, a great deal of managerial attention concerns how to perform storage to facilitate efficient materials handling.

3. Types of Warehouses（仓库的类型）

The warehouse is usually divided into private warehouse, public warehouse and contract warehousing.

The private warehouse is owned by the firm using it. Private warehouses provide more control since the firm has decision-making authority over all activities in the warehouse.

The public warehouse is essentially the space that can be leased to solve short-term distribution needs. Using public warehouses offers more flexibility for the users since it requires no capital investment on the user's part.

For many years, firms had two choices with respect to warehousing — public and private. But more recently, contract warehousing (also referred to as third-party warehousing) has emerged as another warehousing alternative. Contract warehousing is a long term, mutually beneficial arrangement which provides unique and specially warehousing and logistics services for one customer.

4. Warehousing Activities（仓储活动）

Warehousing activity is an important link between the producer and the customer. Warehousing activities involve receiving, transfer, storage, picking and shipping. Receiving may take place in railway station, dock, warehouse and so on. Transfer involves physical movement of the goods into the warehouse for storage, movement to areas for the specialized such as consolidation, and movement to out-bound shipment. Storage is a primary function of warehouse. Goods should be stored in areas with right conditions. Picking is conducted after orders are translated into picking slips in many instances. Shipping is the last step. After properly packed and checked on against delivery note, the products should be transferred to staging area and loaded on carrier equipment for transportation.

5. The Function of Warehousing(仓储的功能)

The warehouse serves several value-adding roles in a logistics system. Companies will sometimes face less-than-truckload (LTL) shipments of raw materials and finished goods. Shipping goods long distances at LTL rates is more costly than shipping at full truckload or carload rates. By moving the LTL amounts relatively short distances to or from a warehouse, warehousing can allow a firm to consolidate smaller shipments into a large shipment (a carload or truckload) with significant transportation savings. For the inbound logistics system, the warehouse would consolidate different suppliers' LTL shipments and ship a volume shipment to the firm's plant. For the outbound logistics system, the warehouse would receive a consolidated volume shipment from various plants and ship LTL shipments to different markets.

New Words and Phrases

integrated ['intigreitid] adj. 整体的,综合的
strategy ['strætidʒi] n. 战略,计划
facility [fə'siliti] n. 设备
consumer [kən'sju:mə] n. 消费者,用户
consolidate [kən'sɔlideit] v. 统一,联合
inbound ['inbaund] adj. 内部的
appropriate [ə'prəupriit] adj. 适合的
component [kəm'pəunənt] n. 组成,成分
equipment [i'kwipmənt] n. 设备
rack [ræk] n. 货架
conveyor [kən'veiə] n. 传送,传输
track [træk] v. 追踪
authority [ɔ:'θɔrəti] n. 权力

lease [li:s] v. 出租,租借
flexibility [ˌfleksə'biliti] n. 灵活性,适应性
emerge [i'mə:dʒ] v. 出现
beneficial [ˌbeni'fiʃəl] adj. 有益的,有利的
consolidation [kənˌsɔli'deiʃən] n. 统一,联合
outbound ['autbaund] adj. 外部的
conduct [kən'dʌkt] v. 执行
supply chain 供应链
materials handling 物资搬运
private warehouse 私有仓库
public warehouse 公共仓库
contract warehousing 合同仓储
staging area 待运区,装货区

Notes

1. Warehousing plays a key role in integrated logistics strategy and in building and maintaining good relationship between supply chain partners. 在物流战略的整合以及建立、维持供应链各成员之间良好关系的过程中,仓储占据着重要的地位。

2. Warehousing supports production by consolidating inbound materials and distributing them to the production facility at the appropriate time. 仓储通过整合内部资源支持生产并在恰当的时间将原材料配送到生产点。

3. Warehouse equipment includes materials handling, storage racks and conveyor equipment. 仓储设备包括搬运设备、储存货架和传送设备。

4. People are the most critical component of warehousing. Space and equipment mean nothing without competent people. 人是仓储中最重要的组成部分。没有胜任的员工,空间和设备就显得毫无意义。

5. Private warehouses provide more control since the firm has decision-making authority over all activities in the warehouse. 由于公司对仓库中的所有活动拥有决定权,因此私有仓库具有更大的控制优势。

6. Using public warehouses offers more flexibility for the users since it requires no capital investment on the user's part. 由于不需要对设备进行投资,因此使用公共仓库有更大的灵活性。

7. Contract warehousing is a long term, mutually beneficial arrangement which provides unique and specially warehousing and logistics services for one customer. 合同仓储是一个长期的双方互惠协定,仓储设施的经营人为其客户提供独特的、专门的仓储和物流服务。

8. Warehousing activities involve receiving, transfer, storage, picking and shipping. 仓储活动包括货物接收、传送、储存、分拣和装运。

Exercises

Ⅰ. Pair work: Discuss the following questions.

1. Why is warehousing necessary?
2. How do you understand the role of the warehouse?
3. What are the basic components of warehousing?
4. What are the main types of warehouse?
5. If you are a manager, do you prefer public warehouse to private warehouse?
6. Are you familiar with the warehousing activities?

Ⅱ. Fill in the blanks with the words in the following box. Change the forms if necessary.

| verify | automated | proximity | order | bridge |
| moderate | temporary | desired | achieve | sufficient |

1. Warehouse provides _____ environment conditions and a wide range of products can be stored in this kind.
2. Usually, warehouses are typically viewed as a _____ place to store goods.
3. The cost of small _____ became expensive to transport.
4. Warehousing plays a vital role in providing a _____ level of customer service.
5. Customer service may be the deciding factor for warehouse site location, _____ to markets can improve its service level.
6. Distribution center is a large and highly _____ warehouse designed to receive

goods from various plants and suppliers.

7. A warehouse can be viewed as a _____ between supply and demand.

8. In order to _____ the efficiency they may have to hold stock, but this is not their main role.

9. Retailers found it difficult to source in _____ quantity from a single supplier.

10. After the goods are unloaded from the transportation carrier, they should be _____ against cargo manifest.

Ⅲ. **Translate the following sentences into Chinese.**

1. The sites of warehouse are determined by customer and manufacturing locations and product requirements.

2. Inventories are frequently found in such places as warehouses, yards, shop floors, transportation equipment, and on retail store shelves.

3. A warehouse manager will have to minimize time spending on responding to demand and errors in dispatches.

4. His request for promotion to the position of a warehouse manager was turned down.

5. A data warehouse should be designed for data analysis.

Ⅳ. **Translate the following sentences into English.**

1. 仓储是生产者与消费者之间的重要纽带。

2. 仓库储存所有产品,配送中心以最低库存满足最大需求。

3. 商品的数量越多,所需仓库的规模也就越大。

4. 近年来,仓库的设备与技术发展很快。

5. 产品必须储存,以便日后使用和消费。

Dialogue 1　Visiting a Warehouse

(*Li: a clerk of a warehouse; Wang: a student in logistics major*)

Li: Welcome to the warehouse. Allow me to introduce myself first: I'm a warehouse keeper and I'm responsible for the management of goods.

Wang: How is the warehouse divided?

Li: According to the storage purpose, the warehouse is divided into deliver-center warehouse, storage-center warehouse and logistics-center warehouse.

Wang: What are the procedures after the goods arrived at the warehouse?

Li: First indoor operation, then warehouse management, finally warehouse operation.

Wang: What is indoor operation?

Li: There are a series of procedures including arranging storehouses, checking the goods, enrolling the goods accurately, loading and depositing them in standard.

Wang: What about the warehouse management?

Li: We need to check the products and facilities regularly, keep the warehouse clean and safe, standardize each operation and gather the information.

Wang: And what is the warehouse operation?

Li: It consists of the following five aspects: the warehouse procedures, the quantity of the goods, loading the goods and depositing them in standard, providing the goods according to the shipment list, saving and filing the bills of document.

Wang: Wow, it's very important to be a warehouse keeper. I got it. Thank you very much!

Li: You are welcome.

New Words and Phrases

divide [di'vaid] v. 区分，分割
procedure [prə'si:dʒə] n. 程序，手续
indoor ['indɔ:] adj. 入库的
arrange [ə'reindʒ] v. 安排
enroll [in'rəul] v. 登记

deposit [di'pɔzit] v. 放置，储存
facility [fə'siliti] n. 设备
regularly ['regjuləli] adv. 经常性地
standardize ['stændədaiz] v. 使标准化
gather ['gæðə] v. 收集

Notes

1. The warehouse is divided into deliver-center warehouse, storage-center warehouse and logistics-center warehouse. 仓库被分为配送中心型仓库、存储中心型仓库和物流中心型仓库。

2. First indoor operation, then warehouse management, finally warehouse operation. 首先要进行入库作业，其次是在库管理，最后是出库操作。

3. There are a series of procedures including arranging storehouses, checking the goods, enrolling the goods accurately, loading and depositing them in standard. 这有一系列程序包括安排仓位、核对物品、准确登记、规范装卸。

4. We need to check the products and facilities regularly, keep the warehouse clean and safe, standardize each operation and gather the information. 定期检查产品、设备，保持仓库清洁、安全，规范操作并进行信息汇总。

5. It consists of the following five aspects: the warehouse procedures, the quantity of the goods, loading the goods and depositing them in standard, providing the goods according to the shipment list, saving and filing the bills of document. 仓库运作包括五方面：出库手续齐全、出库数量准确、装卸规范、按出货单先后发放货物、出库单据保存归档。

Exercises

Ⅰ. **Oral practice**: Practice the above dialogue with your partner until you can learn the lines by heart.

Ⅱ. **Team work**: Make up a dialogue according to the following situation and practice it with your partner.

Situation:

Kitty is a clerk of a warehouse. Now she is introducing the warehouse to her customers.

Tips:

1. I want to know how you handle warehouse storage.

2. What kind of goods do you need to keep?

3. I have to operate according to the instruction on the boxes.

4. I have to operate as what you say.

5. I have to operate regarding the order.

6. Keep away from moisture/fire/water.

7. How long do you need to keep?

8. No. 2-10-5-6 means the sixth case of the fifth layer of the tenth shelf in the second warehouse.

Ⅲ. **Write an E-mail to your customer, inviting him to visit the warehouse and hoping to establish the business relationship with him.**

Contents:

1. 介绍仓库的现状（位置及规模等）。

2. 介绍仓库的优势（与竞争者相比）。

3. 洽谈合作意向。

Ⅳ. **Fill in the blanks with the words in the following box. Change the forms if necessary.**

| acquaint | end | discharging | allocate |
| forward | chassis | export | shelf |

Xiao Wang has just been employed by a _____ company at an airport. His job is to _____ the products to different _____. With the help of the warehouse manager, he is getting himself _____ with the work. At that moment, there is a truck that stops at the gate. Xiao Wang goes to find that a container _____ is at the gate and workers are _____ some electronic components in large cases. These cargos are to be _____ to R. O. Korea and Singapore. They will be leaving this afternoon, so Xiao Wang finds two shelves near the other _____ of warehouse for later easier shipment. He is a smart guy who can quickly learn how to work well.

Ⅱ. Inventory Management

1. What Is Inventory(库存是什么)

Inventory refers to stocks of anything necessary to do business. Inventory can be defined as "stocks used to support production, supporting activities and customer service". Inventory applied to finished goods, raw materials, parts and components, MRO (maintenance/repair/operating) and WIP (work-in-process). It includes new products and existing products. It covers all types of manufacturers, distributors, wholesalers, retailers and others in every industry.

2. The Role of Inventory(库存的作用)

There are many reasons why inventories are present in a supply channel. Just consider why a firm might want inventories at some level in their operations and they would also want to keep them at a minimum. Inventories are frequently found in such places as warehouses, yards, shop floors, transportation equipment and on retail store shelves.

Inventory is the key issue to supply chain management success. Customers demand that their orders be shipped complete, accurate and on-time. That means having the right inventory at the right place at the right time. There are five main purposes for inventory within the firm.

- Inventory as a buffer
- Economics of scale
- Balancing supply and demand
- Specialization
- Protection from uncertainties

3. Inventory Goals(库存目标)

Inventory is a large and costly investment. Better management of firm inventories can improve cash flow and return on investment. Theoretically, a firm could stock every item sold in a warehouse dedicated to serve each customer. However, few firms could afford such a large inventory. The objective is to achieve the desired customer service with the minimum inventory with the lowest total cost.

The primary goal of inventory management is to minimize inventory investment while still meeting the functional requirements.

4. Inventory Decision(库存决策)

Inventory decision involves knowing how much to order and when to order.

How much to order

In deciding how much to order, the company needs to balance order-processing costs against inventory-carrying costs. The order-processing costs include supplier selection, receiving, inspection, order paperwork preparation and so on. The inventory carrying costs consist of:

- storage cost
- physical management costs, including handling, housekeeping, accounting etc.
- insurance and taxes
- the risk of obsolescence due to engineering or style change
- the cost of money invested including interest

When to order

When the stock will be near safety stock level of used up, the material has to be reordered. The span of time is called lead time, which includes order preparation time, queue time, processing time, moving time, and receiving and inspection time. If the rate of sale for a product is 50 units per day, and the lead time is 5 days, to ensure that goods arrive just as the last unit is sold, and order should be placed 5 days ahead of the stock-out day.

New Words and Phrases

inventory ['invəntri] n. 库存	obsolescence [ˌɔbsə'lesəns] n. 过时,作废
define [di'fain] v. 下定义	queue [kju:] n./v. 长队,排队
manufacturer [ˌmænju'fæktʃərə] n. 生产商,制造商	finished goods 成品
distributor [dis'tribjutə] n. 经销商	raw materials 原材料
buffer ['bʌfə] n. 缓冲器	parts and components 零部件
balance ['bæləns] v. 平衡,均衡	economics of scale 规模经济
specialization [ˌspeʃəlai'zeiʃən] n. 专业化	order-processing costs 订单处理成本
uncertainty [ʌn'sə:tnti] n. 不确定性	inventory-carrying costs 库存持有成本
investment [in'vestmənt] n. 投资	safety stock level 安全库存水平
dedicate ['dedikeit] v. 致力于	lead time 前置时间
inspection [in'spekʃən] n. 检查,检验	

Notes

1. Inventory can be defined as "stocks used to support production, supporting activities and customer service". 库存定义为支持生产、经营以及客户服务的存储。

2. It covers all types of manufacturers, distributors, wholesalers, retailers and others in every industry. 各行各业的制造商、经销商、批发商、零售商以及其他企业都需要库存。

3. Customers demand that their orders be shipped complete, accurate and on-time. 客户要求完整、准确及准时地装运订单。

4. Inventory as a buffer 库存起到缓冲作用

5. Economics of scale 规模经济

6. Balancing supply and demand 均衡供给和需求

7. Protection from uncertainties 以防不确定性

8. Better management of firm inventories can improve cash flow and return on investment. 对库存的良好管理能够加快现金流动及资金回笼。

9. The objective is to achieve the desired customer service with the minimum inventory with the lowest total cost. 目标是以最低成本的库存达到满意的客户服务水平。

10. Inventory decision involves knowing how much to order and when to order. 库存决策包括下订单的数量和时间两方面。

11. The order-processing costs include supplier selection, receiving, inspection, order paperwork preparation and so on. 订单处理成本包含选择供应商、接收订单、检验、订单文件处理等方面。

12. The risk of obsolescence due to engineering or style change. 由于技术更新或型号改变而造成的货物废弃风险。

13. The cost of money invested including interest. 包括利息在内的机会成本。

14. The span of time is called lead time, which includes order preparation time, queue time, processing time, moving time, and receiving and inspection time. 这个时间周期包括订单准备、等待、处理、传输以及检验时间,这个时间段称作前置时间。

Exercises

Ⅰ. Team work: Discuss the following questions.

1. How do you understand the inventory?
2. Is inventory necessary to every company?
3. What is the primary goal in inventory?
4. Why is inventory used as a buffer?
5. Why is inventory so important to a firm?
6. How many functions of inventory are there?
7. As an inventory manager, how do you achieve inventory goal?
8. As an inventory manager, how do you make inventory decision?

Ⅱ. Fill in the blanks with the words in the following box. Change the forms if necessary.

| cause | expand | warehouse | reorder | specialize |
| inventory | strategic | stocks | balance | decline |

1. Managers must establish and implement inventory policies on the basis of _____ consideration.

2. When he adopted the new strategy in inventory management, he lowered the cost while _____ the sales.

3. The aim of reducing _____ is to make better use of overall assets.

4. Inventory refers to _____ of anything necessary to do business.

5. To make efficient and effective use of the _____ space, you should decide how large your order must be.

6. When the stock is near safety stock level, materials have to be _____.

7. Raw materials, goods in process and finished goods all _____ various forms of inventory.

8. Buffer stock is adopted to maintain _____ in demand or supply.

9. The order cost is _____ with the increase of quantity.

10. Inventory makes it possible for each firm to _____ in the products that it manufactures.

Ⅲ. **Translate the following sentences into Chinese.**

1. Inventory is spread throughout the supply chain from raw materials to work in process to finished goods that suppliers, manufacturers, distributors and retailers hold.

2. Inventory exists in businesses because of a mismatch between supply and demand.

3. Firms must store additional stocks just in case to meet changing demand.

4. If demand is relatively constant but materials are seasonal, then finished inventory helps meet demand when the materials are no longer available.

5. You should pay for the storage cost whether you store your goods in public warehouse, rented private warehouse, or a warehouse of your own.

Ⅳ. **Translate the following sentences into English.**
1. 在消费需求未增加的情况下，补充存货只能是临时刺激。
2. 有些商店每周清点存货一次。
3. 该商品将首先查找本地库存系统。
4. 库存管理的目的是尽量减少库存的数量。
5. 产品分类是选择库存的必要条件。

Ⅴ. **Read the following passages and answer the questions.**

Inventory can serve two basic functions:

1. To provide a reserve for production and sales.
2. To get the price discount by purchasing a large quantities.

Inventory may be raw materials for the factory or finished products for the wholesaler and retailer. Most of inventory is placed in warehouse. Usually, three warehouses are available:

1. Private warehouse. A private warehouse is owned and operated by a company. It is convenient to the owner who can store and process easily. For most factories and big traders, they often have large or small warehouse, more or less space to store goods.

2. Public warehouse. Public Warehouse is developing for the Third Part Logistics and offers special services, including package and arrangement of delivery. Public warehouse has advantage of better service and lower cost than private one by its specialized equipment and marketing share.

3. Contract warehouse. This kind of warehouse is formed and depended on the relation between the suppliers and customer.

When buyer purchases goods, they don't often ship it at the same time and store at the sellers' warehouse. Warehouse equipment consists of folk lift truck, stacker, good shelf and conveyor, etc.

1. Inventory is the same as warehouse. Is it true or not? (　　)
   A. Sometime yes.　　　　　　B. Not.
   C. No relation between them.　D. Different goods at different place.
2. Generally speaking, there are two kinds of inventory which are (　　).
   A. Goods　　　　　　　　　B. Materials
   C. Materials and products　　D. Raw materials and finished products
3. Public warehouse is most efficient. What is your opinion? (　　)
   A. Depend on the situation.　B. Yes.
   C. Not.　　　　　　　　　　D. Not comparable.
4. Usually, contract warehouse doesn't need to pay. Is it correct or not? (　　)
   A. Yes.　　　　　　　　　　B. Not.
   C. It didn't mention it.　　　D. Sometime yes, sometime not.
5. What is the equipment of warehouse? (　　)
   A. Tools.　　　　　　　　　B. Tools for handling, loading and unloading.
   C. Forklift truck.　　　　　　D. Forklift truck and goods shelf.

Dialogue 2　How Much Should I Order

(Xiao Zhang is now in a consulting office where Peter, an expert in logistics, is helping him to solve a problem as how to order.)

Zhang: Excuse me. My name is Zhang Xin.

Peter: Mr. Zhang, What can I do for you?

Zhang: Just call me Xiao Zhang. I have just bought a fruit shop that supplies the market with fruits. And I really don't know how frequently I should put my orders and how much I should order at a time.

Peter: It must be a very complicated thing to do, I guess, as fruits come in different types.

Zhang: Fortunately, I sell only a kind of peach.

Peter: Things are much easier, then. However, there are still other factors.

Zhang: For example?

Peter: The uncertainty of the market, the tax, and so on.

Zhang: According to the past records, the sales are even. The annual sale volume of fruits is 5000kg and they are sold to retail customers in a steady flow.

Peter: It seems to be a very simple question, then. What is your chief concern now?

Zhang: At present, only two costs concern me. One is order-processing costs and another is warehousing costs.

Peter: The order-processing costs include supplier selection, receiving, order paperwork preparation and so on.

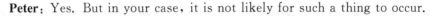

Zhang: Do we need safety stock?

Peter: Since the sales are even, you don't need any safety stock.

Zhang: Do we need safety stock against sudden rise in demand?

Peter: Yes. But in your case, it is not likely for such a thing to occur.

Zhang: Good news.

Peter: Your problem is to find out how many to order with the lowest expenses in warehousing and ordering.

Zhang: Quite right, I would like to know how much I should order at a time with the minimum cost.

Peter: This is, as I see it, a typical question in inventory management. Please provide the clear and accurate information on sales and inventory.

Zhang: OK, I will send them to you tomorrow.

Peter: In that case, I will give you answer tomorrow.

Zhang: How much shall I pay for your service?

Peter: I don't think I will charge you anything for such a trifle thing. But do come if you have any other problems.

Zhang: Sure, I will. See you later.

Peter: See you later.

 New Words and Phrases

consult [kən'sʌlt] *v.* 请教,咨询
frequently ['fri:kwəntli] *adv.* 频繁地
complicated ['kɔmplikeitid] *adj.* 复杂的
factor ['fæktə] *n.* 因素
uncertainty [ʌn'sə:tnti] *n.* 不确定性

annual ['ænjuəl] *adj.* 每年的
retail ['ri:teil] *n.* 零售
trifle ['traifl] *adj.* 微小的,琐碎的
order-processing cost 订单处理成本
safety stock 安全库存

Notes

1. I really don't know how frequently I should put my orders and how much I should order at a time. 我真的不知道我应该多久下一次订单以及每次订多少货物。

2. It must be a very complicated thing to do, I guess, as fruits come in different types. 因为水果有很多种类,这个问题会很复杂。

3. According to the past records, the sales are even. 根据销售记录,销售额是非常有规律的。

4. One is order-processing costs and another is warehousing costs. 一个是订单处理成本,另一个是储存成本。

5. The order-processing costs include supplier selection, receiving, order paperwork preparation and so on. 订单处理成本包括选择供应商、订单接收、订单准备等成本。

6. Do we need safety stock against sudden rise in demand? 我们不需要安全库存以防需求剧增吗?

7. Your problem is to find out how many to order with the lowest expenses in warehousing and ordering. 你的问题就是一次订多少货时储存和订单处理费用能降到最低。

 Exercises

Ⅰ. Oral practice: Practice the above dialogue with your partner until you can learn the lines by heart.

Ⅱ. Team work: Make up a dialogue according to the following situation and practice it with your partner.

Situation:

Tony is consulting Mr. Low, an expert in logistics, about inventory management.

Tips:

1. Excuse me, I'd like to ask you a question.
2. Would you be kind as to tell me how to solve this problem?
3. I wonder if you could tell me how to …
4. I really don't know how to …
5. Could you please give me some advice on how to …
6. Personally, I think …
7. It seems a very hard/simple question.
8. Your problem is how to …
9. In your case, it is very likely/unlikely that …
10. Why don't you …

Ⅲ. Write an E-mail to the expert for advice on inventory management.

Contents:

1. 公司的销售状况。

2. 公司的库存现状。

3. 你希望实现的目标。

Ⅳ. Complete the following sentences with proper forms of the words or phrases given.

1. An overstock of the inventory will result in additional expenses not only in _____ (warehouse), but also in many other aspects.

2. Transportation costs can often be reduced by _____ (ship) large quantities that require less _____ (handle) per unit.

3. _____ (purchase) in quantities greater than immediate needs usually results in a larger inventory.

4. He hasn't much experience in _____ (run firms).

5. Every firm wants to keep inventories _____ (minimum).

Ⅴ. Fill in the blanks with the words in the following box. Change the forms if necessary.

customer service	purchasing	materials	need
goods	warehouse	inventory	period

1. Inventories are stockpiles of raw _____, suppliers, components, work in process and finished _____ that appear at many places such as _____, yards, shop floors, transportation equipment and on retail store shelves.

2. If they are very near to customers, inventories will provide high _____.

3. _____ and transportation costs can often be replaced by buying and shipping in quantities larger than immediate _____.

4. _____ can afford protection at important points throughout the logistics channel and help it operate for a _____ of time.

Ⅵ. Read the following passages and answer the questions.

Inventory is the total amount of goods and/or materials contained in a store or factory at any given time. Store owners need to know the precise number of items on their shelves and storage areas in order to place order or control losses. Factory managers need to know how many units of their products are available for customer orders. Restaurants need to order more food based on their current supplies and menu needs. All of these businesses rely on an inventory count to provide answers.

The word "inventory" can refer to both the total amount of goods and the act of counting them. Many companies take an inventory of their supplies on a regular basis in order to avoid running out of popular items. Others take an inventory to ensure the number of items ordered matches the actual number of items counted physically. Shortages or overages after an inventory can indicate a problem with theft (called "shrinkage" in retail circles) or inaccurate accounting practices.

Restaurants and other retail businesses which take frequent inventories may use a "par" system based on the results. The inventory itself may reveal 10 apples, 12 orange and 8 bananas on the produce shelf, for example. The preferred number of each item is listed on a "par sheet", a master list of all the items in the restaurants. If the par sheet calls for 20 apples, 15 orange and 10 bananas, then the manager knows to place an order for 10 apples, 3 orange and 2 bananas to reach the par number. This same principle holds true for any other retail business with a number of different product lines.

Companies also take an inventory every quarter in order to generate numbers for financial reports and tax records. Ideally, most companies want to have just enough inventories to meet current orders. Having too many products languishing in a warehouse can make a look less appealing to investor and potential customers. Quite often a company will offer significant discounts if the inventory numbers are high and sales are low. This is commonly seen in new car dealerships as the manufacturers release the next year's models before the current vehicles on the lot have been sold. Furniture complies may also offer "inventory reduction sales" in order to clew out their showrooms for newer merchandise.

1. The passage tells us that inventory is important to (　　).
    A. store owners   B. factory managers
    C. restaurants   D. all of those businesses
2. Which of the following statements is TRUE? (　　)
    A. Inventory refers to the total amount of goods only.
    B. Inventory refers to the act of counting goods only.
    C. Too few inventories may cause problems to the company.
    D. Companies generally take an inventory every three months.
3. Which of the following sentences is the main idea of the third paragraph? (　　)
    A. Restaurants and other retail businesses which take frequent inventories may use a "par" system based on the results.
    B. The inventory itself may reveal 10 apples, 12 orange and 8 bananas on the produce shelf, for example.
    C. The preferred number of each item is listed on a "par sheet", a master list of all the items in the restaurants.
    D. If the par sheet calls for 20 apples, 15 orange and 10 bananas, then the manager knows to place an order for 10 apples, 3 orange and 2 bananas to reach the par number.
4. If the inventory numbers within a company are too high, the company may (　　).
    A. offer discounts   B. keep the inventories that way
    C. clean the warehouse   D. use a "par system"

5. In the last paragraph, the word of "appealing" probably means (   ).
   A. surprising   B. attractive   C. had   D. important

Supplementary Reading

Warehouse Operations

Once a warehouse mission is determined, managerial attention focuses on establishing the operation. A typical warehouse contains materials, parts and finished goods on the move. Warehouse operations consist of break-bulk, storage, and assembly procedures. The objective is to efficiently receive inventory, possibly store it until required by the market, assemble it into complete orders, and initiate movement to customers. This emphasis on product flow renders a modern warehouse as a mixing facility. As such, a great deal of managerial attention concerns how to perform storage to facilitate efficient materials handling.

1. Handling

The first consideration focuses on movement continuity and scale economies throughout the warehouse. Movement continuity means that it is better for a material handler with a piece of handling equipment to perform longer moves than to undertake a number of short handling to accomplish the same overall move. Exchanging the product between handlers or moving it from one piece of equipment to another wastes time and increases the potential for product damage. Thus, as a general rule, longer warehouse movements are preferred. Goods, once in motion, should be continuously moved until arrival at their final destination.

Scale economies justify moving the largest quantities or loads possible. Instead of moving individual cases, handling procedures should be designed to move cases grouped on pallets, slip-sheets, or containers. The overall objective of materials handling is to eventually sort inbound shipments into unique customer assortments. The three primary handling activities are receiving, in-storage handling and shipping.

Receiving

Merchandise and material typically arrive at warehouses in large quantity shipments.

The first handling activity is unloading. At most warehouses, unloading is performed mechanically, using a combination of a lift truck and manual processes. When freight is floor stacked on the transport vehicle, the typical procedure is to manually place products on pallets or to use a conveyor. When inbound product has been unitized on pallets or containers, lift trucks can be used to facilitate receiving. A primary benefit of receiving unitized loads is the ability to turn inbound transportation equipment more rapidly. Receiving is usually the unloading of a relatively high volume of similar product.

In-storage Handling

In-storage handling consists of movements within the warehouse. Following receipt and movement to a staging location, product must be moved within the facility for storage or order selection. Finally, when an order is processed it is necessary to select the required products and move them to a shipping area. These two types of in-storage handing are typically referred to as transfer and selection.

There are at least two and sometimes three transfer movements in a typical warehouse. The merchandize is initially moved from the receiving area to a storage location. This movement of typically handled by a lift truck when pallets or slip-sheets are used or by other mechanical means for other types of unit loads. A second internal movement may be required prior to order assembly depending upon warehouse operating procedures. When unit loads have to be broken down for order selection, they are usually transferred from storage to an order selection or picking area. When products are large or bulky, such as appliance, this intermediate movement to a picking area may not be necessary. Such product is often selected from the storage area and moved directly to the shipping staging area. The shipping staging area is the area adjacent to the shipping dock. In order selection warehouses, the assembled customer order is transferred from the selection area to the shipping staging area. Characteristically, in-storage handing involves lower volume movements than receiving but still relatively similar products.

Order selection is one of the major activities within warehouses. The selection process requires that materials, parts, and products be grouped to facilitate order assembly. It is typically for one area of a warehouse to be designated as a selection or picking area to assemble orders. For each order, the combination of products must be selected and packaged to meet specific customer order requirements. The typical selection process is coordinated by a warehouse system.

Shipping

Shipping consists of order verification and transportation equipment loading. Similar to receiving, firms may use conveyors or unit load materials handling equipment such as lift trucks to move products from the staging area into the transportation vehicle. Relative to receiving, warehouse shipping must accommodate relatively low-volume movements of a mixture of product, thus reducing the potential for economies of sale. Shipping unit loads is becoming increasingly popular because considerable time can be saved in vehicle loading. A unit load consists of unitized or palletized product. To facilitate this loading and subsequent unloading upon delivery, many customers are requesting that suppliers provide mixed combinations of product within a unit. The alternative is to floor stack cases in the transportation vehicle. Shipment content verification is typically required when product changes ownership. Verification may be limited to a simple carton count or a piece-by-piece check for proper brand, size, and in some cases serial number to assure shipment accuracy.

2. Storage

The second consideration is that warehouse utilization should position products based upon individual characteristics. The most important product variables to consider in a storage plan are product volume, weight, and storage requirements.

Product volume or velocity is the major factor driving warehouse layout. High volume product should be positioned in the warehouse to minimize movement distance. For example, high-velocity products should be positioned near doors, primary aisles, and at lower levels in storage racks. Such positioning minimizes warehouse handling and reduces the need for frequent lifting. Conversely, products with low volume should be assigned locations more distant from primary aisles or higher up in storage racks.

Similarly, the storage plan should take into consideration product weight and special characteristics. Relatively heavy items should be assigned storage locations low to the ground to minimize lifting. Bulky or low-density product requires cubic space. Floor space along outside walls is ideal for such items. On the other hand, smaller items may require storage shelves, bins, or drawers. The integrated storage plan must consider individual product characteristics.

A typical warehouse is engaged in a combination of active and extended product storage alternatives. Warehouses that directly serve customers typically focus on active short-term storage. In contrast, warehouses use extended storage for speculative, seasonal, or obsolete inventory.

When controlling and measuring warehouse operations, it is important to differentiate the relative requirements and performance capabilities of active storage and extended storage.

Active Storage

Regardless of inventory velocity, most goods must be stored for at least a short time. Storage for basic inventory replenishment is referred to as active storage. Active storage must provide sufficient inventory to meet the periodic demands of the service area. The need for active storage is usually related to the capability to achieve transportation or handling economies of scale. For active storage, materials handling processes and technologies need to focus on quick movement and flexibility with relatively minimal consideration for extended and dense storage.

The active storage concept includes flow-through distribution, which uses warehouses for consolidation and assortment while maintaining minimal or no inventory in storage. The resulting need for reduced inventory favors flow-through and cross-docking techniques that emphasize movement and de-emphasize storage. Flow-through distribution is most appropriate for high-volume, fast-moving products where quantities are reasonably predictable. While flow-through products places minimal demands on storage requirements, it does require that product be quickly unloaded, deunitized, grouped and sequenced into customer assortments, and reloaded into transportation equipment. As a result, the materials handling emphasis is an accurate information-directed quick movement.

Extended Storage

Extended storage, a somewhat misleading term, refers to inventory in excess of that required for normal replenishment of customer stocks. In some special situations, storage may be required for several months prior to customer shipment. Extended storage uses materials handling processes and technologies that focus on maximum space utilization with minimal need for quick access.

A warehouse may be used for extended storage for several other reasons. Some products, such as seasonal items, require storage to await demand or to spread supply across time. Other reasons for extended storage include erratic demand items, product conditioning, speculative purchases, and discount.

Product conditioning sometimes requires extended storage, such as to ripen bananas. Food warehouses typically have ripening rooms to hold products until they reach peak quality. Storage may also be necessary for extended quality checks.

Warehouses may also store goods on an extended basis when goods are purchased on a speculative basis. The magnitude of speculative buying depends upon the specific materials and industries involved, but it is very common in marketing of commodities and seasonal items. For example, if a price increase for an item is expected, it is not uncommon for a firm to buy ahead at the current price and warehouse the product for later use.

The warehouse may also be used to realize special discounts. Early purchase discounts may justify extended storage. The purchasing manager may be able to realize a substantial price reduction during a specific period of the year. Under such conditions the warehouse is expected to hold inventory in excess of active storage. Manufacturers of fertilizer, toys, and lawns furniture often attempt to shift the warehousing burden to customers by offering off-season warehouse storage allowance.

The working principles of WMS system includes six parts, they are inbounding management, shelf operation, storage management, pickout operation, quality inspection and outbounding management, they should all serve for the ERP system, SCM system and CRM system.

Please answer the questions after reading the case.

1. What are the important warehouse activities in the warehouse?
2. How do you explain the order selection?
3. When does the active storage concept include?
4. How do you explain the extended storage?

Unit 4

Transportation and Distribution

◆ Knowledge Learning Objectives 知识学习目标 ◆
- To understand the importance of transportation
- To know the five main modes of transportation
- To learn distribution management

◆ Skill Developing Objectives 技能培养目标 ◆
- Communication skill in talking about the shipment conditions
- Communication skill in advancing the shipment date
- Writing skill in delivering goods
- Communication skill in changing the shipment terms

Ⅰ. Transportation Mode

1. What Is Transportation(什么是运输)

Every firm requires the movement of goods from one place to another place. Transportation refers to the physical movement of goods from the place of origin to the place of consumption. It can involve raw materials being brought into the production process or finished goods being shipped to the customer. Transportation is one of the most significant areas of logistics management. Railway, road, waterway, air and pipeline transportation make up the major modes of transport in modern society. Each mode has its own requirements and features. In the following paragraphs, we will look at some of the different characteristics of each transport mode.

2. Railway Transportation(铁路运输)

Rail offers cost-effective transport of a large number of cargos over long distance. It is especially good for cargos with high volume and low value, such as coal, timber and grain. Over the past years, rail usage has declined as road transport has taken over short haul business and water transport has taken bulk commodities freight. Rail transport is one of the most energy efficient modes of land transport. Environmental and safe consideration also favor rail over road transport. However, the major disadvantages of railway are the inherent inflexibility of operation, fixed time schedules and service from terminal to terminal.

The railroads face some key challenges in this competitive marketplace from other carriers, especially motor carriers. A major factor to rail success is continued productivity. It is interesting in this era of deregulation that the old standard of the railroad industry, the boxcar, is a major concern. Boxcars are decreasing in demand and railroads are facing a real challenge to keep their boxcars in operation. TOFC is the fastest growing area for railroads and probably the most profitable. The railroads must decrease their costs and their prices on boxcar traffic in the future.

3. Road Transportation(公路运输)

Road transport is widely used in inland delivery of goods. This mode tends to be used for higher-value and lower-volume cargo over relatively short distance. It is capable of providing a door to door service. It has not any break in the journey to change from one vehicle to another. So it can be flexible enough to perform "just-in-time" delivery. Any work place in the country can be serviced by road. The advantages of road transport are flexibility of both location and time and speed of delivery. With the development of road transport, new types of problem have emerged, such as a significant growth of fuel consumption, air pollution, traffic congestion and road accidents.

The general commodity truckload part of the motor carrier industry has become fragmented and intensely competitive with resultant turmoil. Leasing companies, truckload specialists, private carriers seeking backhauls, and former household goods movers have all entered this market. Whether the industry's overall financial health will return to previous levels associated with the regulated environment is debatable.

4. Waterway Transportation(水路运输)

Waterway transportation includes maritime and river transportation. As the oldest mode of transport, waterway has developed considerably over the last decades. Waterway is utilized for large loads of low-value-per-unit goods. The carriers are specialized for internal river, canal transport and international deep-sea ships. It is the cheapest method of moving goods world wide. The main advantage of shipping industry lies in moving a large number of cargos in one ship. The main disadvantage is the speed of the ship which is very slow.

Waterway transportation has been hit by escalating fuel costs like other carriers, but they have tried to offset those costs with other economies. New propulsion systems are being investigated, as well as new ship designs. However, intense rate competition has made the situation bleak for deep-water carriers.

5. Air Transportation(航空运输)

Air transport has been increased tremendously and plays a more important role in global logistics than ever before. Air transport accounts for the smallest proportion of cargo transportation. Its growth rate in recent years is the greatest among the modes of transport. It offers rapid and flexible delivery. The major advantage of air freight is the speed of travel. The longer the distance of the flight, the greater the time saving of the customer. Air transport is primarily used for:

- Emergency transport of the critical items

- Speedy transport of high-value, low-weight products
- Speedy transport of perishable items

Labor, fuel, and capital costs have made making a profit difficult for air transportation. Shippers have been sensitive to high rates and this has made air transportation susceptible in spite of promised trade-off savings in inventory costs.

6. Pipeline Transportation(管道运输)

The pipelines will continue to be a major component of the transportation system for the movement of bulk commodities or those commodities that can be made into liquid form by the addition of water in what is then called "slurry". However, the lack of growth in demand for the movement of oil will continue to affect pipelines.

The basic nature of pipeline is unique in comparison to all other modes of transport. Pipelines operate on a twenty-four-hour basis, seven days per week. Pipeline routes are practically unlimited. Pipelines are usually used to transit natural gas, petroleum and coal.

 New Words and Phrases

movement ['muːvmənt] n. 移动,运动
origin ['ɔridʒin] n. 生产地,原产地
consumption [kən'sʌmpʃən] n. 消费

significant [sig'nifikənt] adj. 重大的,有意义的
requirement [ri'kwaiəmənt] n. 需求,需要
feature ['fiːtʃə] n. 特点,特征

characteristic [ˌkærɪktəˈrɪstɪk] n. 特性,特征
coal [kəul] n. 煤
timber [ˈtɪmbə] n. 木材
grain [greɪn] n. 粮食,谷物
haul [hɔːl] n. 拖拉,运输
bulk [bʌlk] adj. 大批的,散装的
environmental [ɪnˌvaɪərənˈmentl] adj. 环境的
inflexibility [ɪnˌfleksəˈbɪlɪti] n. 不变性
schedule [ˈskedʒjuːl] n. 时间表
terminal [ˈtəmɪnl] n. 终点站,终端
vehicle [ˈviːɪkl] n. 车辆,交通工具
pollution [pəˈluːʃən] n. 污染
congestion [kənˈdʒestʃən] n. 堵塞,阻塞
emerge [ɪˈməːdʒ] v. 显现,形成

maritime [ˈmærɪtaɪm] adj. 海运的,海上的
canal [kəˈnæl] n. 运河
tremendously [trɪˈmendəsli] adv. 非常地,惊人地
proportion [prəˈpɔːʃən] n. 部分,比例
emergency [ɪˈməːdʒənsi] n. 紧急情况,紧急事件
perishable [ˈperɪʃəbl] adj. 新鲜的,易腐烂的
petroleum [pɪˈtrəuliəm] n. 石油
raw material   原材料
production process   生产线
finished goods   成品
cost-effective   经济有效的
door to door service   门到门服务
in comparison to   与……比较

Notes

1. Transportation refers to the physical movement of goods from the place of origin to the place of consumption. It can involve raw materials being brought into the production process or finished goods being shipped to the customer. 运输是指从生产地到消费地的物理性移动。具体包括原材料运到生产线以及产成品运到消费者。

2. Over the past years, rail usage has declined as road transport has taken over short haul business and water transport has taken bulk commodities freight. 近些年来,随着公路主要从事短途业务及水路主要从事大批量的散货运输,铁路的业务量逐年呈下降趋势。

3. So it can be flexible enough to perform "just-in-time" delivery. 所以公路运输足够灵活,完成准时制服务。

4. The advantages of road transport are flexibility of both location and time and speed of delivery. 公路运输的优势是位置、时间和交货速度上的灵活性。

5. Waterway is utilized for large loads of low-value-per-unit goods. 水运主要适用于单位价值较低的大批量货物。

6. The longer the distance of the flight, the greater the time saving of the customer. 飞行的距离越长,客户节约的时间就越多。

7. Speedy transport of perishable items   新鲜货物的快速运输

8. The basic nature of pipeline is unique in comparison to all other modes of transport. 与其他运输方式相比,管道运输的特点独特。

Exercises

Ⅰ. Pair work: Discuss the following questions.

1. Why is transportation important to the world?

2. How many kinds of transportation modes do you know? What are they?

3. What are the advantages of road transportation?

4. What are the disadvantages of air transportation?

5. What is the advantage of maritime transportation?

6. What kinds of commodity can be transported by pipeline?

II. Fill in the blanks with the words in the following box. Change the forms if necessary.

| low | important | maritime | feature | door-to-door |
| unique | cheap | advantage | proportion | movement |

1. Waterway transport is the _____ method of moving goods world wide.

2. In recent years air transport has played an _____ role in global logistics.

3. Waterway transport includes _____ and river transportation.

4. Transportation refers to the physical _____ of goods from one place to another place.

5. Each transportation mode has its own requirements and _____.

6. Railway is especially good for cargos with high volume and _____ value.

7. Road transportation can provide _____ delivery service.

8. The nature of pipeline is _____ in comparison to all other modes of transport.

9. Air transport accounts for the smallest _____ of cargo transportation.

10. The major _____ of air freight is the speed of travel.

III. Translate the following sentences into Chinese.

1. Pipelines operate on a twenty-four-hour per day basis, seven days per week, and only are limited by commodity changeover and maintenance.

2. Water carriage is particularly suited for movement of heavy, bulky, low-value-per-unit commodities.

3. The main disadvantages of water transport are the limited range of operation and speed.

4. The two sides finally reached an agreement on the mode of transportation.

5. Freight rates are based on three factors i.e., distance, shipment and competition.

IV. Translate the following sentences into English.

1. 如果铁路运输费用高,我们愿意走海运。

2. 航空运输是最安全的运输方式。

3. 这个公司最近铺了一条地下管道。

4. 这家公司的总物流费用中,运输费用占比最高。

5. 航空运输发展潜力巨大。

V. Put the following mail into Chinese.

From: Martin Gilbert [mail to: martin gilbert@narita.com.cn]

Sent: Tuesday, September 2, 2010, 9:35 A.M.
To: Elie Bismargi [ebismargi@flyingcargo.com]
Cc: Yvonne.wong@narita.com.cn
Subject: RE: Sea Freight Enquiry

Dear Elie,

I believe Yvonne has already forwarded these rates to you earlier. Anyway, resending as per your request…Pls adv. By return your selling rates…Pls mind that those rates are our net cost and on collect basis.

POD: DUBAI

POL/rate in USD

····································

Ningbo:	USD 1350/40'gp/hc
Xingang:	USD 1300/40'gp/hc
Shanghai:	USD 1300/40'gp/hc
Qingdao:	USD 1550/40'gp/hc
Fuzhou:	USD 1550/40'gp/hc
Xiamen:	USD 1450/40'gp/hc

····································

Above rates are valid with immediate effect until September 30, 2010.

As mentioned, offer is inclusive of BAF surcharge, but subject to all local charges where applicable.

Offer is only valid for general, non-hazardous cargo.

Rates for other equipment: formula of 80% out of 40's and 1.125 times 40's will be applied respectively for 20' and HQ containers.

Martin

Narita Shipping Inc.

Dialogue 1 Negotiating About the Transportation Conditions

(*The following is a conversation between Mr. Lin, the clerk in a logistics company and Amy, a customer of the company.*)

Amy: I am glad we have settled the terms of payment, Mr. Lin. When is the earliest shipment you can make?

Lin: It usually takes us two months to deliver, and for a special order, it takes a little longer, three months. You know we should get the goods ready, make out the documents and book shipping space.

Amy: When is the exact shipping date?

Lin: We can make prompt shipment by the end of June.

Amy: I am afraid the date of shipment would be late for us.

Lin: The manufacturers are fully committed. They have no stock on hand.

Amy: But prompt shipment is of great importance for us.

Lin: I see.

Amy: After the arrival of the shipment, the flow of the goods through the marketing channel takes at least two or three weeks before the goods can reach us.

Lin: Well, I see. We will contact the factory and see if they can manage to advance the delivery by a month.

Amy: That will be excellent.

Lin: How about partial shipment? We can ship whatever is ready to meet your urgent need instead of waiting for the whole lot to get ready. I propose that we can make delivery of 50 percent of goods in March and balance in early April.

Amy: Your proposal is workable.

Lin: Another problem is the shipping space. Even we had the goods ready, I do not think we could ship them in March.

Amy: I know there is a great demand on shipping lately.

Lin: I was informed that liner space for Great Wall has been fully booked up to the end of March.

Amy: Maybe tramps are still available.

Lin: Anyhow we will try. We will ask China Shipping Co., Ltd. to meet our needs.

Amy: In case you should fail to effect delivery within the stipulated time, we should have to declare a claim against you for the loss and reserve the right to cancel the contract.

Amy: We know that I assure you the shipment will be effected in time.

Lin: Thank you for your cooperation.

Amy: Not at all.

New Words and Phrases

settle ['setl] v. 安排,解决
document ['dɔkjumənt] n. 文件,单证
prompt [prɔmpt] adj. 迅速的,立即的
commit [kə'mit] v. 委托,从事
balance ['bæləns] n. 余额,剩下的
effect [i'fekt] v. 实现,履行

stipulate ['stipjuleit] v. 指定,规定,约定
tramp [træmp] n. 不定期租船
terms of payment   支付条款
partial shipment   分批装运
shipping space   舱位
declare a claim   索赔

Notes

1. You know we should get the goods ready, make out the documents and book shipping space. 你知道,我们需要时间准备货物,制作单证,预订舱位。

2. We will contact the factory and see if they can manage to advance the delivery by a month. 我们将联系工厂,并看一下他们是否能提前一个月装运。

3. I was informed that liner space for Great Wall has been fully booked up to the end of March. 我接到通知"长城"号的班轮舱位在3月底前已被全部预订完毕。

4. In case you should fail to effect delivery within the stipulated time, we should have to declare a claim against you for the loss and reserve the right to cancel the contract. 如果你们不能在规定的时间内装运,我们将针对损失提出索赔,并保留取消合同的权力。

 Exercises

Ⅰ. **Oral practice**: Practice the above dialogue with your partner until you can learn the lines by heart.

Ⅱ. **Team work**: Make up a dialogue according to the following situation and practice it with your partner.

Situation:

Peter is a clerk of a logistics company. Now he is negotiating with his customer about the transportation conditions.

Tips:

1. What would be your earliest delivery date?
2. I think the earliest shipment we can make is …
3. Prompt shipment is very important to us.
4. We try our best to advance shipment, but we cannot commit ourselves.
5. The last thing we want to do is to postpone the delivery date.
6. It will be better to ship them all at one time so that we couldn't miss the sales season.
7. If you are in urgent need of the goods, we suggest that you allow partial shipment.
8. I assure you the shipment will be effected in time.

Ⅲ. **Write an E-mail to your customer, and tell them about goods transportation.**

Contents:

1. 通知对方货物已准时发出。
2. 已经邮寄给客户运输的相关单证。
3. 请注意查收。
4. 有任何问题请及时联系。

IV. Read the dialogue and translate into Chinese.

Harold: When is the earliest shipment we can expect?

Zhang: I think the earliest shipment we can make is on Nov. 1.

Harold: You may know that the delivery date is very important to us. We are willing to pay an extra fee for immediate delivery.

Zhang: We can't make that kind of delivery. It's our company policy.

Harold: We must have the seafood for the winter sale. Could you advance the shipment by only one month?

Zhang: I'm afraid we can do very little about it.

Harold: But if the goods could not be put on the market in time. Good quality, competitive price, all would mean nothing.

Zhang: Yes, I fully understand. The shipment will be made as early as possible.

V. Read the following passages and answer the questions.

If a shipper has a strict arrival and departure requirements, railroads are at a competitive disadvantage compared to motor carriers. Some of this disadvantage may be overcome through combined transport, which offers the economy of rail movement linked with the flexibility of trucking. Truck trailers are delivered to the rail terminals, where they are loaded on flatbed railcars. At the destination terminal they are off-loaded and delivered to the consignee-the customer who receivers the shipment.

An additional area in which railroads suffer in comparison to motor carriers is equipment availability. Railroad lines use each other's cars, and at times this equipment may not by located where it is most needed. Railcars may be unavailable because they are being loaded, unloaded, moved within railroad sorting yards, or undergoing repair. Other cars may be standing idle or lost within the vast rail network. A number of developments in the rail industry have helped to overcome some of these utilization problems. Advances have included: computer routing and scheduling; the upgrading of equipment, roadbeds, and terminals; improvements in railcar identification systems; and the use of unit trains, cars owned or leased by the shipper; and dedicated through-train service between major metropolitan areas (nonstop shipments of one or a few shippers' products). Railroads own approximately 80 percent of their car fleet. The remaining 20 percent are either leased or owned by shippers.

1. The disadvantages of rail transport compared with motor carrier is (   ).
   A. cost   B. speed
   C. lost and damage ratios   D. transit time and frequency of service
2. The disadvantage above mentioned can be overcome by (   ).
   A. combined transport   B. more frequency
   C. fast train   D. more flexible

3. The advantage of rail transport are (   ).
    A. great amount of shipped
    B. less damage ratio
    C. fast speed、exact schedule、cost saved
    D. direct shipping line
4. Railroads own about (   ) of their car fleet.
    A. half   B. 80%
    C. 20%   D. not mentioned
5. What is the meaning of Metropolitan areas? (   )
    A. Around the city.   B. City itself.
    C. The area near the city.   D. Big city and its neighbor area.

Ⅱ. Distribution Management

1. What Is the Distribution Center(什么是配送中心)

Distribution center is a logistics link. Its main function is to carry on physical distribution. In detail, it is a large and automated center destined to receive goods from various plants and suppliers, take orders, fill them efficiently, and deliver goods to customers on time.

2. The Difference Between Distribution Centers and Warehouses(配送中心和仓库的区别)

Unlike a warehouse, however, the emphasis of a distribution center is on the moving of goods rather than on long-term storage center. It is located close to a major market. It can achieve the rapid processing of orders and shipment of goods to customers. The differences in detail are as follows:

Warehouses(Ws) handle most products in receiving, storing and shipping; while distribution centers (DCs) handle most products in receiving, picking, packaging and shipping.

Ws perform a minimum of value-added activities (receive-store-ship generally in original forms), while DCs perform a great deal of value-added activities, e. g., final assembly.

Ws collect data in batches (generally receive and ship goods in batches), while DCs collect data in real time.

Ws store all products (slow or fast moving), while DCs hold predominantly high demand items.

Ws focus on minimizing the operating costs to meet shipping requirements, while

DCs focus on maximizing the profit impact of fulfilling customer delivery requirement.

3. Operation Flow of Distribution Center(配送中心的运作流程)

There are seven steps of operation flow in the distribution center as follows:
- Goods consolidation: to receive goods from various plants and suppliers.
- Storage: to keep the goods in the warehouses.
- Order picking: to pick up the destined goods according to the orders.
- Purchase: to make orders with the suppliers.
- Order fill: to fill the orders.
- Sorting: to put the goods into separated package according to the order.
- Distribution: to dispatch the goods in the specific transportation mode.

4. Cost of Distribution(配送成本)

Distribution is an important aspect of a company's marketing and production effort and the costs of distribution bear on the final delivered cost of any product.

Transportation costs: The most used mode of transportation is highway motor transport. But the cost of this mode is relatively high. Changing the location and the number of warehouses changes transportation costs in unanticipated and complex ways.

Storage costs: To provide customer service through the company's chosen channels of distribution, some warehousing is required. The keeping of stocks gives rise to costs.

Costs of production: It varies between locations, with the level of investment and with the volume of output. Production decisions must take account of distribution costs.

Communications and data processing costs: It varies with the complexity of the distribution function and operation. This includes the level of customer service provided, order processing, inventory control and transport documentation.

New Words and Phrases

link [liŋk] n. 连接点
destine ['destin] v. 预定,指定
supplier [sə'plaiə] n. 供给者,供应商
efficient [i'fiʃənt] adj. 有效率的,最经济的
emphasis ['emfəsis] n. 强调,重点
collect [kə'lekt] v. 集合,收集
predominantly [pri'dɔminəntli] adv. 压倒性地,主要地
consolidation [kən,sɔli'deiʃən] n. 联合,配货
sort [sɔt] v. 分类,分拣
separate ['sepəreit] v. 分离,隔离

dispatch [dis'pætʃ] v. 派遣,发送
anticipate [æn'tisipeit] v. 预期,预料
complex ['kɔmpleks] adj. 复杂的,合成的
complexity [kəm'pleksiti] n. 复杂性
documentation [,dɔkjumən'teiʃən] n. 文件,单证
value-added 增值
in batches 分批地,成批地
real time 实时
order picking 订单拣选
order fill 订单履行
give rise to 导致,引起

Notes

1. In detail, it is a large and automated center destined to receive goods from various plants and suppliers, take orders, fill them efficiently, and deliver goods to customers on time. 具体地说,配送中心是一个大型的自动化中心,它从工厂和供应者手中接收货物,接收订单,有效执行订单,并将货物准时送给客户。

2. Ws perform a minimum of value-added activities (receive-store-ship generally in original forms), while DCs perform a great deal of value-added activities, e. g., final assembly. 仓库处理极少的增值物流活动,然而配送中心处理大量的增值活动,例如,产品终端装配。

3. DCs collect data in real time 配送中心收集处理实时数据

4. Ws focus on minimizing the operating costs to meet shipping requirements, while DCs focus on maximizing the profit impact of fulfilling customer delivery requirement. 仓库着重最小化运营成本来满足装运需求,而配送中心着重履行客户送货需求时实现利润最大化。

5. To pick up the destined goods according to the orders 根据订单收集指定货物

6. To put the goods into separated package according to the order 根据订单将货物进行不同的包装

7. To dispatch the goods in the specific transportation mode 按指定的运输方式发送

8. Changing the location and the number of warehouses changes transportation costs in unanticipated and complex ways. 改变仓库的位置和数目会以无法预料且极其综合的方式改变运输成本。

Exercises

Ⅰ. **Team work: Discuss the following questions.**

1. What is a distribution center?
2. Why is the distribution center close to the major market?
3. How do you understand the difference between distribution center and warehouse?
4. What basic function do the distribution centers have?
5. How do you understand the cost of distribution?
6. In your opinion, how can the distribution costs be reduced?

Ⅱ. **Fill in the blanks with the words in the following box. Change the forms if necessary.**

automate	focus on	load volume	relationship	advantage
contact	facilitate	fulfill	value-added	transport lane

1. Warehouses _____ minimizing the operating costs to meet shipping requirements.

2. Transportation cost per unit of weight decreases as _____ increases.

3. This short-term storage center is located close to a major market to _____ the rapid processing of orders and shipment of goods to customers.

4. There is a _____ between transport cost and distance.

5. Distribution center is a logistics link to _____ physical distribution as its main function.

6. A _____ refers to movement between origin and destination points.

7. Distribution center performs a great deal of _____ activities, such as packaging, sub-assembly, labeling, etc.

8. The main _____ of the road transportation is door-to-door delivery.

9. As soon as our store comes in new stock, we'll _____ you without delay.

10. Distribution centers are highly _____ places to receive goods from various plants and suppliers.

Ⅲ. **Translate the following sentences into Chinese.**

1. It is not uncommon for transport cost to account for 20% of the total costs of a commodity.

2. Railway provides terminal-to-terminal service instead of door-to-door service.

3. You must deliver the goods before June, or else we won't be able to catch the shopping season.

4. We ask our suppliers to arrange road or rail transport in time to meet the ship.

5. Transport by air is increasing and for certain types of goods, such as fresh food or flowers as well as valuables; air freight is the best choice.

Ⅳ. **Translate the following sentences into English.**

1. 配送是离消费者最近的物流环节。
2. Zara 经常是小批量的用空运从唯一的配送中心西班牙送往别处。
3. 牛奶会从这个配送中心发往北京的各个超市。
4. 这批货物不允许分批装运。
5. 很抱歉,现在我们还无法告诉您确切的装船日期。

Ⅴ. **Put the following mail into Chinese.**

From: Bill Cliton [mail to: bill.cliton@globecargo.com]
To: Lewis@IBR Wuxi
Cc: Lou (Changzhou Overseas Trade)
Date: April 2, 2011 2:40 P.M.
Subject: FW: CIF price for Luko
Importance: High

Dear Bill,

Many thanks for your telephone call. I apologize for any misunderstanding.

Our clients is:

Luko Enterprises LCC

8115 Hunter's Grove Germantown, TN 38158 USA

Phone: +19017082702   E-mail: koreyadam@aol.com

37 boxes with estimated total weight of 115 kilograms. Each box measures 72cm×36cm×30cm. Total estimated value per Changzhou Overseas Trade Company is US $1280.

CIF door to door shipment

Client desires Globe to clear PRC & USA customs.

Client will prepay all import, export, insurance, local fees, and shipping charges.

Please forward us your best estimate of sea or air CIF prices.

As soon as the seal samples are approved, Ms. Lou will inform you with final shipment details and requests a firm price at that time.

Lewis F. Sage

International Business Resources Ltd.

Dialogue 2   Partial Shipment and Transshipment

(*The following is a conversation between Mr. Gong, the clerk in an international logistics company and Mary, a customer of the company.*)

Gong: Speaking of your order, No. 156, Mary, I'm afraid we can't ship the whole lot at one time.

Mary: Why? Is there anything wrong with my order?

Gong: As far as your order is concerned, everything is all right. But it's difficult for us to get so many goods prepared within such a short period.

Mary: What do you propose to do? You are not going to advise me to cancel the order, are you?

Gong: No. I only propose that partial shipment should be allowed.

Mary: But our customers are in urgent need of these goods. So it would be better to ship them all at once.

Gong: Mary, maybe you are not clear about my point yet. It is in your own interests that we put forward such a proposal. If partial shipment is allowed, instead of waiting for the whole lot to get ready, we can ship whatever is ready to meet the urgent need of your end-users.

Mary: Oh, I see. In that case I agree to partial shipment. How do you want the goods divided?

Gong: For those items that are small in size and light in weight, we send them via air freight. It'll be all right to ship other ordinary and large sized items by sea.

Mary: Please by all means guarantee the date of shipment so that we wouldn't miss the sales season.

Gong: We can assure you that the shipment of your order will be effected in June at the latest. There is no need to worry.

Mary: By the way, we do hope you can make a direct shipment.

Gong: We'll do what we can. In case there is no direct shipment, will you consider allowing transshipment?

Mary: I'm afraid not. As you know, Mr. Gong, transshipment takes much more time. And, there are risks of damage to the goods during transshipment. I hope you will try some other ways.

Gong: How about this then? I'll contact the shipping company again and ask them to make delivery half a month in advance. This will ensure the consignment to reach your port in time for your customers' needs.

Mary: That's great! Make delivery half a month in advance, and I'll agree to your suggestion.

New Words and Phrases

urgent ['ə:dʒənt] *adj.* 紧急的,迫切的
divide [di'vaid] *v.* 分割,分类
via ['vaiə] *prep.* 经由,经过
guarantee [ˌgærən'ti:] *v.* 保证,承诺
transshipment [træns'ʃipmənt] *n.* 转运,转船

damage ['dæmidʒ] *n.* 损失,损害
consignment [kən'sainmənt] *n.* 委托,运送之货物
partial shipment 分批装运
end-user 最终用户
in advance 提前

Notes

1. It is in your own interests that we put forward such a proposal. 我们提出这一建议正是为了您的利益。

2. If partial shipment is allowed, instead of waiting for the whole lot to get ready, we can ship whatever is ready to meet the urgent need of your end-users. 如果允许分批装运,我们就可以手头有多少货发多少货,满足贵方用户的急需,而不必等到全部货物备妥才发运。

3. This will ensure the consignment to reach your port in time for your customers' needs. 这将确保货物及时到达贵方港口以应贵方客户需要。

Exercises

Ⅰ. **Oral practice: Practice the above dialogue with your partner until you can learn the lines by heart.**

Ⅱ. **Team work: Make up a dialogue according to the following situation and practice it with your partner.**

Situation:

Gary has received the goods, but the boxes of goods were damaged. So Gary is calling the transport department about the damaged goods.

Tips:

1. On examination, 15 cases were found to be badly damaged.

2. We have to claim on you for …

3. We regret being unable to accept your claim because the case was in perfect condition when the goods were loaded.

4. According to the surveyor's report, the damage is caused by improper …

5. We shall try to make up the loss you sustained.

6. The mistake is on our side. We'll arrange to send you replacement at once and we've also prepared to meet your claim.

7. We've already told you that this is a case of Force Majeure. It's exempt from claim.

8. We hope all disputes can be settled by negotiation.

Ⅲ. **Write an E-mail to your customer, telling them about the following information.**

Contents:

1. 说明货物需要转运。

2. 阐明转运的原因。

3. 说明轮船航班号、日期以及价格。

Ⅳ. **Read the dialogue and translate into Chinese.**

(*Xiao Wang has just been employed by a forwarding company at an airport. It is the first day of his work in the warehouse. His job is to allocate the products to different shelves, waiting for further shipment. At the moment, he is getting himself acquainted with the warehouse facilities with the help of Mr. Chen Weiguo, the assistant of the warehouse manager.*)

Chen: Hi, Xiao Wang! Would you please come over here?

Wang: Yes.

Chen: A truck is at the warehouse gate. Go and find what will be unloaded.

Wang: (*coming back a few minutes later*) Mr. Chen, a container chassis is at the gate and workers are unloading it.

Chen: What is being unloaded?

Wang: Electronic components in large carton cases. Some of them, they said, are hard disks.

Chen: I see. Now you phone the customs officers. Ask them to come. These are cargoes to be exported to Japan and Singapore. The owners need to go through the customs clearance.

Wang: I saw just now some customs officers at the gate.

Chen: In that case, you don't have to make the call. Instead, have a look at the computer and see where we can put the goods.

Wang: When will the goods be leaving?

Chen: I believe they will go on J211 and W403 flights respectively this afternoon.

Wang: Then we'd better find places near the other end of the warehouse. Yes, there are two shelves available, Nos. 41 and 43.

Chen: Good. Now you go and direct the handling.

Wang: Who will be moving the goods?

Chen: Oh, I nearly forgot to tell you. Dial No. 201 and call in a forklift.

Ⅴ. Read the following passages and answer the questions.

The process of logistics integration can be divided into four stages:

Stage 1. Began in the early 1960s in the USA and involved the integration of all activities associated with distribution. Separate distribution departments were to coordinate the management of all processes within physical distribution management (PDM).

Stage 2. PDM was applied to the inbound movement of materials, components, and subassemblies, generally known as "materials management". By the late 1970s, many firms had established " logistics departments" with overall responsibility for the movement, storage, and handling of products upstream and downstream of the production operation.

Stage 3. Logistics plays an important coordinating role, as it interfaces with most other functions. With the emergence of business process re-engineering (BPR) in the early 1990s, the relationship between logistics and related functions was redefined. "Systems integration" occurred. Cross-functional integration should achieve greater results.

Stage 4. Establish Supply Chain Management (SCM) to achieve supply chain optimization and minimize inventory.

1. What is the meaning of integration? (　　)

    A. To link some separate factors as a whole chain.

    B. United.

    C. To put together.

D. Mixture.
2. How many stages in the processing of logistics integration? (   )
   A. One.   B. Two.   C. Three.   D. Four.
3. What is PDM? (   )
   A. Production distribution management.
   B. Physical distribution management.
   C. Processing distribution management.
   D. Pallets distribution management.
4. What is BPR? (   )
   A. Business production relation.   B. Business promotion relation.
   C. Business process re-engineering.   D. Business placement ratio.
5. What is SCM? (   )
   A. Supply Customer Management.   B. Support Customer Management.
   C. Supply Chain Materials.   D. Supply Chain Management.

 Supplementary Reading

Maersk Logistics Company

Maersk Logistics China opened in mid June a large National Distribution Center (NDC) in Jiuting Town in Shanghai, Chinese government officials including Zhou Xuedi, Deputy Magistrate of Songjiang District, Liu Weizhong, Deputy Magistrate of Huangpu District, and officials from Jiuting Town attended the opening ceremony, which was inaugurated by Tom Behrens Sorensen, President of Maersk China Shipping Co., Ltd.

The new Maersk Logistics facility is about 14000m^2 large and is located in the Jiuting Economic Development Zone of Songjiang District, an ideal location for an integrated logistics center in the greater Shanghai area. The NDC is conveniently linked to Shanghai's outer expressway, providing easy access to and from key ports, roads and other distribution channels for importers, local manufacturers and exporters.

"The NDC establishment in Shanghai is an important first step in our fully controlled Pan China Distribution Network" stated Steffen Schiottz Christensen, Managing Director of Maersk Logistics (China) Co., Ltd. "It provides our customers with an unmatched service level efficiently managed by our skilled employees and supported by an advanced IT platform."

The new NDC will offer customers specialized Supply Chain Management services including cross docking, storage, sorting facilities, import, export, and distribution in China. In addition, Maersk Logistics state of the art IT systems MK Logistics will ensure efficient supply chain, inventory and warehouse management.

The distribution center is an important leg in the Pan China Distribution Network of Maersk Logistics China, which is rapidly expanding. Maersk Logistics China has its head office in Shanghai with nine branches and five representative offices across the country.

Maersk Logistics provides customized solutions for integrated supply chain management, warehousing and distribution, and sea or air freight transport in the international logistics market.

Ⅰ. **Answer the following questions.**

1. When and where did Maersk Logistics China open?
2. Does the NDC locate in a suitable place? Why?
3. How will the new NDC offer customers specialized service?
4. What kinds of customized solutions does Maersk Logistics provide?

Ⅱ. **Tell whether the following statements are true or false.**

1. The new Maersk Logistics facility is about 14000m² large and is located in the Jiuting Economic Development Zone of Zhejiang District.   (   )

2. This distribution provides their customers with an unmatched service level efficiently managed by their skilled employees and supported by an advanced IT platform.   (   )

3. It will offer customers non-specialized Supply Chain Management services including cross docking, storage, sorting facilities, import, export and distribution in China.   (   )

4. Maersk Logistics provides customized solutions for integrated supply chain management, warehousing and distribution, and sea or air freight transport only in Chinese logistics market.   (   )

Unit 5 Packaging

- ◆ Knowledge Learning Objectives 知识学习目标 ◆
  - To understand the definition of packaging
  - To know the importance of packaging
  - To learn the types of packaging
- ◆ Skill Developing Objectives 技能培养目标 ◆
  - Communication skill in discussing the consumer package
  - Communication skill in discussing the outer packaging
  - Writing skill in solving the packaging problem

Ⅰ. Introduction to Packaging

1. Package(包装)

A primary package provides means of protection and handling to a product. General term for the total of the means and procedures is applied by the packaging economy to fulfill the task of packaging. Many terms: i. e. acknowledged package, set-up-package, permanent package, one-way package, export package, customary package, consumer package, storage package, multi-way package, multiuse package, standard package, sea-worthy package, deep-cool package, transport package.

2. Packing(包装)

Packing, the selection or construction of the shipping container and the assembling of items or packages therein, includes any necessary blocking, bracing, or cushioning, weatherproofing, exterior strapping, and marking of shipping container for identification of contents.

3. The Role of Packaging(包装的重要性)

Packaging prepares goods for transport, distribution, storage, sale, and use. Thanks to packaging it is possible for products to be available anytime anywhere that gives the consumer a great freedom of choice. One of its basic purposes of packing is to protect the contents. This is important because the items have to withstand a lot of handling between the factory and the consumer. A second purpose is to make item look appealing to the buyer, especially through the use of appealing colors. In recent years, the significance of packing has been increasingly recognized, and today the widespread use of packing is truly a major competitive force in the struggle for markets. Sound packing will help promote the sales, while bad or insufficient packing affects sales. In practice, people are often confused with these words: package, packaging and packing.

4. Packaging(包装方法)

Packaging is the technique of preparing goods for distribution. Creation of a pack or a packaging unit by combination of product with the package, applying methods of packaging using packaging machines or devices by hand. To most people packaging means the carton, bag, jar, can etc., which enable a product to be handled and used.

5. Types of Packaging(包装类型)

There are two basic kinds of packages: the consumer package and the industrial package.

The consumer package is also referred to as the interior, or marketing package, because it is what the customer sees when the product is on the shelf. It is designed to appeal to and inform the final customer.

The industrial package is also known as the exterior package, and is primarily a logistics responsibility. This package is discarded before the products are placed on the shelf, so customer may never see this material.

New Words and Phrases

withstand [wið'stænd] v. 抵抗,经受住
appealing [ə'pi:liŋ] adj. 吸引人的
significance [sig'nifikəns] n. 意义,重要性
widespread ['waidspred] adj. 分布广泛的,普遍的
insufficient [ˌinsə'fiʃənt] adj. 不足的,不够的
confuse [kən'fju:z] v. 搞乱,使糊涂
procedure [prə'si:dʒə] n. 程序,手续
fulfill [ful'fil] v. 履行,实现,完成(计划等)
combination [ˌkɔmbi'neiʃən] n. 结合,联合,合并,化合物
therein [ðɛər'in] adv. 在那里,在其中,在那一点上
weatherproof ['weðəpru:f] adj. 防风雨的,抗风化的
identification [aiˌdentifi'keiʃən] n. 辨认,鉴定,证明,视为同一
interior [in'tiəriə] adj. 内部的,内的
exterior [eks'tiəriə] adj. 外部的,外在的,表面的
discard [dis'ka:d] v. 丢弃,抛弃

Notes

1. General term for the total of the means and procedures is applied by the packaging economy to fulfill the task of packaging. 所有有关包装方法和程序的一般术语都被应用于包装作业中。

2. Packing, the selection or construction of the shipping container and the assembling of items or packages therein, includes any necessary blocking, bracing, or cushioning, weatherproofing, exterior strapping, and marking of shipping container for identification of contents. 包装就是选择或构建货运包装并在其中装上所需运输的货物，包括任何必需的分隔、支撑或缓冲材料以及外部捆绑材料，并在货运包装上标明所运送的货物。

3. Thanks to packaging it is possible for products to be available anytime anywhere that gives the consumer a great freedom of choice. 由于包装的存在，使产品在任何时候和任何地方都可得到，这给消费者极大的自由选择。

4. In recent years, the significance of packing has been increasingly recognized, and today the widespread use of packing is truly a major competitive force in the struggle for markets. 近年来，包装的重要性逐渐被认可，今天，广泛使用的包装已成为产品市场竞争的主要竞争点。

5. Packaging is the technique of preparing goods for distribution. Creation of a pack or a packaging unit by combination of product with the package, applying methods of packaging using packaging machines or devices by hand. 包装是为货物配送准备货物的技术，就是应用手工或机器的包装方法，通过货物包装把货物合并处理成一个包裹或一个包装单位。

Exercises

Ⅰ. Pair work: Discuss the following questions.

1. What are the purposes of packing?
2. What is packaging?
3. What are the differences between packaging and packing?
4. What purpose is the consumer package designed to?
5. What is the difference between the consumer package and the industrial package?
6. Which package do you often see in your daily life?

Ⅱ. Fill in the blanks with the words in the following box. Change the forms if necessary.

| exterior | appealing | discard | widespread | confuse |
| insufficient | withstand | significance | fulfill | containers |

1. I always _____ John with his brother, they are very much alike.
2. We are sure to _____ the task ahead of schedule if everyone bears down.

3. Many plastic _____ are disposed of as waste, although they are reusable.

4. You're supposed to keep your car _____ in good condition by cleaning it.

5. You can schedule a weekend to _____ some things that perhaps you don't actually need.

6. The idea of a holiday abroad is certainly _____.

7. That invention is of great commercial _____.

8. She is strong enough to _____ intellectual challenge.

9. In today's world, trade barriers in international trade are still _____.

10. The case was dismissed because of _____ evidence.

Ⅲ. **Translate the following sentences into Chinese.**

1. Packaging is an important concern for warehousing and materials handling, one that receives increased attention around the world.

2. No matter what environmental conditions are encountered, the package is expected to protect the product, keeping it in the condition intended for use until the product is delivered to the ultimate consumer.

3. New materials and smarter protective packaging systems contribute to reducing the load on our environment.

4. Good packaging allows efficient utilization of storage space as well as transportation cube and weight constraints.

5. This package is discarded before the products are placed on the shelf, so customer may never see this material.

Ⅳ. **Translate the following sentences into English.**

1. 工业包装对物流的成本和效率具有重要的影响。

2. 确认他们已经收到你的包裹。

3. 包装是物流的重要环节之一。

4. 不同的商品需要不同的销售包装。

5. 近几年,物流包装技术突飞猛进。

Ⅴ. **Put the following mail into Chinese.**

From: Michelle Krin (SES Miami)
To: Johnson Smith (SES SHA) Kelly, Xu (SES GUA)
Subject: New a/c secured

Hello Johnson,

Please note that we recently acquired a new customer out of Florida (Kad Furniture) that has awarded us a large portion of their business out of China (approx. 500 FEU). Kad has several vendors within the states that import goods from several different Chinese factories. I have been attempting to make contact with each vendor in order to learn what origin ports they handle for Kad so that I could forward them our office contract information via routing instructions. Also we have asked for factory information to pass onto our overseas offices in order to make instructions.

1. Standard Furniture — US vendor that supplies to Kad.

—factory located in Tianjin (unsue of overseas ctc info.)

2. Riverside Designs — US vendor that supplies to Kad.

—factory located in Dalian

3. Lifestyle — US vendor that supplies to Kad.

—factory located in Guangzhou

There might be additional vendors that import from your territory. I am still in the early stages of introducing and gathering information. However, all have been provided our information and may call you w/o first notifying any of us.

Hope above notification will prevent so many surprises in case you start receiving calls or information in the near future. Let me know if you have any questions.

Michelle

Dialogue 1 Packing of Silk Stockings

(*Mr. Smith, a businessman from America, is talking about the subject of packaging with Mr. Lin, the marketing manager of a company in China.*)

Smith: What are your conditions, Mr. Lin, as far as packaging is concerned?

Lin: Well, as you know, we have unique ways of packing silk stockings for sea shipment. As a rule, we use polythene wrapper for each article, all ready for shelf selling.

Smith: Good. A wrapping that catches the eye will certainly help push sales. With keen competition from similar silk stocking producers, the merchandise must not only be of nice quality, but also look attractive.

Lin: Right. We'll see to it that the silk stockings appeal to the eye as well as to the purse.

Smith: What about the outer packing?

Lin: We will pack them six silk stockings each with a different color in a box, ten boxes in a carton.

Smith: Can you use wooden cases instead?

Lin: Why wooden cases?

Smith: I'm afraid the cardboard boxes are not strong enough for sea transportation.

Lin: Don't worry about that. The cartons are lined with waterproof plastic sheets, and as the cartons are made of cardboard, they shall be handled with care.

Smith: OK, but I am concerned that in case of damage or pilferage, the insurance company will refuse compensation on the ground of improper packing, or packing unsuitable for sea voyage.

Lin: Well, we will use wooden cases if you insist, but the charge for that kind of packing will be considerably higher, and it also slows down delivery.

Smith: Then, I will cable home immediately for instruction on the matter.

Lin: Please do. I will be waiting for your soonest reply.

Smith: I will call you up tomorrow. Good-bye, Mr. Lin.

Lin: Good-bye, Mr. Smith.

New Words and Phrases

polythene ['pɔliˌθiːn] n. 聚乙烯
wrapper ['ræpə] n. 包装材料,包装纸
keen [kiːn] adj. 强烈的,热心的,渴望的
competition [ˌkɔmpi'tiʃən] n. 竞争
attractive [ə'træktiv] adj. 吸引人的,有魅力的
cardboard [ˈkɑːdbɔːd] n. 纸板
waterproof ['wɔːtəpruːf] adj. 防水的

pilferage ['pilfəridʒ] n. 行窃,偷盗
insurance [in'ʃuərəns] n. 保险,保险单,保险业,保险费
compensation [ˌkɔmpen'seiʃən] n. 补偿,赔偿
voyage ['vɔiidʒ] n. 航程,航空
silk stocking 丝袜

Notes

1. With keen competition from similar silk stocking producers, the merchandise must not only be of nice quality, but also look attractive. 丝袜市场的激烈竞争要求商品不仅要有好的质量,而且包装要有吸引力。

2. The cartons are lined with waterproof plastic sheets, and as the cartons are made of cardboard, they shall be handled with care. 纸箱都内衬防水的塑料布,而且一般他们在处理纸箱时,都会相当小心的。

Exercises

Ⅰ. **Oral practice**: Practice the above dialogue with your partner until you can learn the lines by heart.

Ⅱ. **Team work**: Make up a dialogue according to the following situation and practice it with your partner.

Situation:

Mr. Zhang is a manager of China National Native Produce and Animal By-products Import and Export Corporation. Mr. Right is a businessman from Ireland who has ordered a total of $80000 worth of Oolong Tea. He is particular about the way the tea is packed. Now Mr. Zhang is discussing this issue with Mr. Right.

Tips:

1. How are you going to pack our order?

2. For this kind of product we export, each item is individually packed in …

3. … are packed in a paper carton before shipping.

4. I'm afraid the paper cartons are not strong enough for …

5. We've got an excellent record on making deliveries to our customers.

6. All our cartons are lined with shockproof cardboards and are wrapped up with polyethylene sheets.

7. I will cable home immediately for instruction on the matter.

8. I'll be waiting for your reply.

Ⅲ. Write an E-mail to your customer, telling them about the following information.
Contents:

1. 感谢对方对我方的大力支持。

2. 告诉对方我方采用的运输包装材料和包装方法。

3. 征求对方对运输包装的意见。

Ⅳ. Fill in the blanks with the words in the following box. Change the forms if necessary.

| record | safety | take place | rest |
| damp-proof | worry about | consignment | a lot of |

(*Mr. Fred, a businessman from Austria, is talking about the issue of packaging with Mr. Cheng, a salesman of a company in China.*)

F: What kind of packing do you plan to use for this _____ of goods?

C: Cartons. Is that okay?

F: I'm concerned about the possible jolting, squeezing and collision that may _____ when these cases are moved about.

C: Well, what I can tell you is this. We've got an excellent _____ on making deliveries to our customers. Besides, all our cartons are lined with shockproof cardboards and are wrapped up with polyethylene sheets. So they're not only shockproof but also _____.

F: In that case, I guess I can _____ assured.

C: Well, I guess you can say that. The _____ of packing is something we always pay a lot of attention to. Especially for those fragile commodities, we've got to be extra careful. Otherwise, when the things we don't want to see happen have happened, we'll be responsible and that'll cause you _____ inconvenience, too.

F: You're right. But wouldn't it be safer to use wooden cases?

C: We sure if you want us to, but the charge will be much higher.

F: It wouldn't be worth the trouble in that case, would it? Let's still use cartons.

C: Sure, no problem. As I said, cartons are good enough for goods like this. You don't have to _____ it.

V. Read the following passages and answer the questions.

Packaging is the end of production and the start of logistics. But it is more important to the latter than the former because the package is absolutely necessary to transportation and storage. Without it, the logistics can't work. One of the basic functions of packaging is to protect the goods in the process of logistics. It is called industry package. The second function is to make sales easy. For example, a beautiful box of the shoes attracts the customer to buy. This is called commercial package.

Packaging technology can be classified into two categories, one is package materials, the other is packaging methods. The materials consist paper, plastic, wood, metal and glass. Paper is the biggest percentage of the packing materials. It can be used to make outer package, carton (paper box) and corrugated box. Paper is cheap, easy to shape and ventilated. Plastic is new fast developed materials, which is low cost, strong, good resistant to water, acid and so on. Wood has become the less proportion because of environmental protection. It is used to make the wooden box. Metal, exactly aluminum is to make cans for drinks, like Coca-Cola, which is easy to recycle. Glass is mainly used to fill the liquid, like chemical products and liquors. Packaging technique is to adopt several packing methods and containers to protect goods. For example, protection from damage and vibration is the basic packaging method. Protection containers have a lot, such as bag, box, can, bottle and barrel.

1. Which of the following sentence is wrong? (   )
   A. Packaging is the end of production.
   B. Packaging is the start of logistics.
   C. The main function of commercial package is to protect the goods in the process of logistics.
   D. The main function of commercial package is to make sales easy.
2. The main function of packaging is to protect goods. Do you agree? (   )
   A. Yes.　　　B. No.　　　C. Different.　　　D. Same.
3. There are two categories of packaging. Is it a fact? (   )
   A. No, there are two categories.　　B. No, there are only one.
   C. No, there are three categories.　　D. Yes.
4. Packaging material and technique are equal important to packaging technology. Do you agree? (   )
   　　A. No, they are different.　　　B. They have same effect.
   　　C. Yes.　　　　　　　　　　　D. No.
5. Packaging technique is the package shape. Is it a fact? (   )
   　　A. Yes.　　　　　　　　　　　B. No.
   　　C. I don't know.　　　　　　　D. No mention in it.

Ⅱ. Functions of Packaging

When transporting goods from source to customer, packaging is an essential feature of the product and the form this takes is often considered a part of the logistics process. Industrial packaging should perform the following functions to meet integrated logistics requirements. More specifically, packaging performs four functions.

1. Containment(包装商品)

Products must be contained before they can be moved from one place to another. To function successfully, the package must contain the product. If the package breaks open, the item can be damaged or lost, or even cause environmental pollution.

2. Protection(保护商品)

Packaging plays a vital role in protecting products as they go from the manufacturer to the consumer. Packaging is designed to ensure that the product reaches the consumer in good condition. It should protect the goods from damage during handling, storing and transportation. Damages caused by vibration, impact, puncture or compression can happen whenever a package is being transported. Hence, package design and material must combine to achieve the desired level of protection.

3. Improving the Logistics Efficiency(提高物流效率)

Packaging plays a significant role within logistics and its optimal design is important for the efficient functioning of the whole logistics system.

Packaging affects not only marketing and production but also integrated logistics activities. For example, the size, shape and type of packaging material influence the type and amount of material handling equipment. Likewise, package, size and shape affect loading, unloading and the transporting of a product. The easier it is to handle a product, the lower the transportation rate. Therefore, if the package is designed for efficient logistical processing, overall system performance will benefit.

4. Communication(信息传递)

The important logistical packaging function is communication or information transfer. The information contained on the package tells the consumer what the product is and how to use it. The information provided on packaging allows the consumer to decide on the product's purchase and use.

A package must protect what it sells and sell what it protects. Modern methods of consumer marketing would fail were it not for the messages communicated on the package. It is not only the sales package that must communicate. Warehouses and distribution centers would be less efficient if transport packages lacked labels or carried incomplete details. When international trade is involved and different languages are spoken, the use of clear, readily understood symbols on the transport is essential.

To identify package contents of receiving and shipping is the most obvious communication role of packaging. Typical information includes manufacturer, product, container type and count. The communication role of logistics packaging is to provide instruction of how to prevent possible damage.

New Words and Phrases

function ['fʌŋkʃən] n. 功能,职责
source [sɔ:s] n. 来源,出发地
perform [pə'fɔ:m] v. 履行,完成
integrated ['intigreitid] adj. 整体的,综合的,完全的
requirement [ri'kwaiəmənt] n. 需要,需求
specifically [spi'sifikəli] adv. 特别地,具体地,明确地
containment [kən'teinmənt] n. 包含,包括,容纳
manufacturer [,mænju'fæktʃərə] n. 制造商,生产商
consumer [kən'sju:mə] n. 消费者,用户

vibration [vai'breiʃən] n. 振动,动摇
impact ['impækt] n. 冲击,挤压,压紧
puncture ['pʌŋktʃə] n. 刺穿,穿孔
compression [kəm'preʃən] n. 压缩,压制
combine [kəm'bain] v. (使)结合,综合,整合
optimal ['ɔptiməl] adj. 最佳的,理想的
influence ['influəns] v. 影响,改变
lack [læk] v. 缺乏,不足
label ['leibl] n. 标签
identify [ai'dentifai] v. 识别,确认
container [kən'teinə] n. 集装箱,容器
distribution center 配送中心

Notes

1. Industrial packaging should perform the following functions to meet integrated logistics requirements. 工业包装通过履行以下的功能来满足物流整合的需求。

2. If the package breaks open, the item can be damaged or lost, or even cause environmental pollution. 如果包装破裂,商品可能会损坏、丢失,甚至造成环境污染。

3. It should protect the goods from damage during handling, storing and transportation. 在货物搬运、储存和运输过程中,包装可以保护货物不受损坏。

4. Hence, package design and material must combine to achieve the desired level of protection. 因此必须综合利用包装设计和原材料两方面,以实现预期的保护水平。

5. Packaging affects not only marketing and production but also integrated logistics activities. 包装不仅影响市场销售和产品,而且影响物流活动的整合。

6. The easier it is to handle a product, the lower the transportation rate. 货物处理越容易,运输费用就越低。

7. Modern methods of consumer marketing would fail were it not for the messages communicated on the package. 如果包装上没有相关信息,现代的营销手段将不起作用。

8. Warehouses and distribution centers would be less efficient if transport packages lacked labels or carried incomplete details. 如果运输包装上没有标签或标签上的细节信息不完整,仓库和配送中心的工作效率就会受影响。

Exercises

Ⅰ. Team work: Discuss the following questions.

1. What are the main functions of packaging?
2. Are there any other benefits of packaging in addition to what are mentioned in the text? If yes, what are they?
3. Name three products that you consider to be packaged well.
4. Why should we use reusable containers?
5. If packaging cost is reduced, can costs in other aspects of the total logistical operation be cut down? Why?
6. What information can be provided in the package?

Ⅱ. Fill in the blanks with the words in the following box. Change the forms if necessary.

forbid	marketplace	residual	entice	standpoint
instill	oddly	dictate	reinforce	shun

1. We are now in a position to _____ our own demands to our employers.
2. We'll _____ the cease with iron strap.
3. These policies _____ strong feeling of loyalty in P&G employees.
4. The smell of food _____ the hungry children into the hut.
5. I can't figure out why he's been behaving so _____.
6. Consumers may also _____ firms that pollute the environment or engage in unethical practices by not buying their products.
7. What is the reaction to the new car in the _____?
8. It is thus clear that the _____ influences of clannishness must not be underestimated.
9. From the _____ of success, a good work ethic is no less important than an education.
10. More and more public places in the United States _____ smoking.

Ⅲ. Translate the following sentences into Chinese.

1. Over the past two years, the company has increased the investment for its packaging industry in order to meet its customer's need.
2. Good packaging can have a positive impact on layout, design, and overall warehouse productivity.
3. We'll pack them two dozen to one carton, gross weight around 25 kilos a carton.
4. We have especially reinforced our pacing in order to minimize the extent of any possible damage to the goods.
5. The real art of packing is to get the contents into a nice, compact shape that will stay that way during the roughest journey.

Ⅳ. Translate the following sentences into English.
1. 我们的包装是可以回收利用的。
2. 包装材料需要满足绿色物流的需求。
3. 环保包装是未来物流的发展趋势。
4. 冷链物流的运输包装急需改善。
5. 在智慧物流发展大背景下，包装技术需要不断改进。

Ⅴ. Read the following passages and answer the questions.

What is the main difference between the traditional logistics and the modern one? Before 1970, there was no "logistics" as the business word. Transportation and storage represented the flow of goods, like raw materials in and out of factory, and so on. Any truck company or warehouse was an independent unit to handle the goods. Recently, exactly in 1973, the great changes happened in the field. First, containerization transportation has become the most important role in the ocean transport. Container as a loading and unloading unit is very convenient. Before that, 10000 tons ship should be filled in 48 hours. After the container adopter, 35000 tons container ship can be loaded in eight hours. It is a revolution in the transportation! And more, containerization links all functions, making package, loading and unloading, transport, storage and distribution as an integration. In this point, the logistics came as a new part in the commerce. Secondly, computer technology helps the logistics greatly. When the information system was introduced in logistics, we find it is very easy to operate, save us a lot of money and time.

I think you have got the answer already.

1. Traditional logistics is the same as the modern one. Is it true or not? (　　)

    A. No.

    B. Yes.

    C. They can't be compard with each other.

    D. The comparance hasn't practical value.

2. What make traditional logistics upgrading modern one? (　　)

    A. Information technology and modern ship.

    B. Container ships and trucks.

    C. Containerization and information technology.

    D. Container and computer.

3. Containerization is not a revolution but a transportation method. What is your opinion? (　　)

    A. I agree.　　　　　　　　B. It is only a story.

    C. It is only a kind of technology.　　D. It is a real revolution to the logistics.

4. What is the meaning of integration? (　　)

    A. Putting together.

B. Holding one by one.

C. Putting some elements into a whole linkage.

D. Connecting two or more things.

5. What is the usage of information system to the logistics? (   )

A. To provide information.

B. Recording of information.

C. Transmitting information.

D. To manage and control the operation of the logistics.

Dialogue 2 The Packaging of Beer

(Mr. Lin is a marketing manager of Tsingtao Brewery Group in China. Peter is a businessman from the European Union. Now Mr. Lin is discussing the packaging of Beer with Peter.)

Peter: Mr. Lin, I'm very glad we've settled the terms for the transaction of 500 cases of Tsingtao Beer in general, and I would like to know what's your packing for transportation.

Lin: As a rule, when packing these small bottles of beer, we pack them six bottles in one carton, and four cartons in one box. Besides, all these boxes should be lined with shockproof cardboard from inside and reinforced with straps from outside.

Peter: That's OK. But I still want to discuss the matter of packing the beer. Would you hear my comments?

Lin: Certainly. We warmly welcome your comments and suggestions.

Peter: Your present packing is in glass bottles of two sizes, large and small. One large bottle is too much for an ordinary person to consume at one time, while the small size seems just right.

Lin: This comment of yours is very good. We should consider the normal quantity that an ordinary person consumes at one time, when we decide on the size of the beer bottle.

Peter: I don't think glass-bottles are popular nowadays for liquids. The shortcomings are obvious: first, they can easily be broken in transit even though you put 24 bottles in a well-lined box; second, glass-bottles are too heavy and it would increase the cost of freight; third, it is not convenient to drink the beer packed in bottles because you have to use a bottle-opener to open them.

Lin: Yes, all these shortcomings exist as a matter of fact. Do you have any good ideas?

Peter: Liquids are now packed in tins, which have been gaining popularity on the world market. Many leading companies of beverage, such as Coca Cola, they pack their liquids in tins. I think you could use similar packing and incorporate an opener on the top of each tin.

Lin: As far as you know, when we pack our export liquids in tins, it will greatly increase the cost of packing. Now we are making efforts to reduce the production cost of tins.

Peter: I can understand that. But I hope that you will speed up your efforts in that direction. In fact I've already seen some good results.

Lin: Is that so? What's that?

Peter: At the last Guangzhou Fair, I tasted black tea ready-made, and packed in paper cartons. That packaging would greatly reduce the cost of the goods.

Lin: The paper tins can only be used to pack liquids like tea and milk, but not beer perhaps, because there is some gas as well as the pressure from inside of the container when the container is opened. So, I'm afraid paper tins cannot stand the pressure.

Peter: You are right. You see I've forgotten the difference between beer and soft drinks.

Lin: Your opinion is very helpful. I'll transfer your valuable proposals mentioned today to our production department for study so as to improve our packing. Thank you very much.

New Words and Phrases

beer [biə] n. 啤酒
transportation [ˌtrænspɔːˈteiʃən] n. 运输,运送
reinforce [ˌriːinˈfɔːs] v. 加强,增援,加固
strap [stræp] n. 带,皮带
liquid [ˈlikwid] n. 液体,流体
shortcoming [ˈʃɔːtkʌmiŋ] n. 缺点,短处
transit [ˈtrænsit] n. 搬运,运输,运输线

beverage [ˈbevəridʒ] n. 饮料
incorporate [inˈkɔːpəreit] v. (使)合并,并入, 合编
Coca Cola 可口可乐
Tsingtao Brewery Group 青岛啤酒集团
bottle-opener 起瓶器
Guangzhou Fair 广州商品交易会

Notes

1. As a rule, when packing these small bottles of beer, we pack them six bottles in one carton, and four cartons in one box. Besides, all these boxes should be lined with shockproof cardboard from inside and reinforced with straps from outside. 一般来说,我们在包装这些小瓶啤酒时,6瓶为一盒,4盒装一箱。并且,这些箱子都需要里面内衬防震板,外加加固条。

2. I don't think glass-bottles are popular nowadays for liquids. The shortcomings are obvious: first, they can easily be broken in transit even though you put 24 bottles in a well-lined box; second, glass-bottles are too heavy and it would increase the cost of

freight; third, it is not convenient to drink the beer packed in bottles because you have to use a bottle-opener to open them. 我认为现在用玻璃瓶子装饮料已不太时兴,其缺陷是很明显的:第一,运输途中易破,即使你在纸箱里装上 24 瓶,衬垫得很好,也会是这样;第二,玻璃太重,这必然增加运费;第三,酒装在瓶子中喝起来不方便,因为你得用一把起瓶器来开瓶盖子。

3. The paper tins can only be used to pack liquids like tea and milk, but not beer perhaps, because there is some gas as well as the pressure from inside of the container when the container is opened. So, I'm afraid paper tins cannot stand the pressure. 纸质罐头壳只能用于茶、牛奶之类的饮料,恐怕对啤酒不太合适,因为啤酒打开后会出现气体,从容器内部就会产生压力,纸质壳子恐怕经受不住压力。

 Exercises

Ⅰ. **Oral practice**: Practice the above dialogue with your partner until you can learn the lines by heart.

Ⅱ. **Team work**: Make up a dialogue according to the following situation and practice it with your partner.

Situation:

Richard is a businessman from England, Mr. Liu is a marketing manager of a textile company. Now they are talking about packing style of silk blouses.

Tips:

1. We have unique ways of packing …

2. As to silk blouses, we use …, all ready for window display.

3. I hope the packing will be …

4. We have here a sample packing …

5. Do you mind if I give you a little suggestion?

6. Your packing needs improvement. I mean …

7. Your suggestion on packing is welcome as well.

8. What's your outer packing?

9. Cardboard boxes are light to handle and less expensive while wooden cases are clumsy and cost more.

Ⅲ. **Write an E-mail to your customer, telling them about the following information.**
Contents:

1. 向有合作意向的客户介绍你的公司及产品。

2. 详细介绍公司产品的销售包装情况。

3. 询问产品的销售包装是否能迎合对方国家消费者的口味。

4. 欢迎对方提出好的建议。

Unit 5 Packaging

IV. Fill in the blanks with the words in the following box. Change the forms if necessary.

| fall into love | eye-catching | handle | go ahead | attractive |
| reinforce | improvement | suggestion | function | lost |

(*Mr. Fred is a distributor in America, Mr. Chen is the marketing manager of a company in China, Now they are talking …*)

F: Do you mind if I give you a little _____?

C: No, I don't mind. _____.

F: Your products are good, and there's no question of that. But your packing needs _____. I mean your packing does not look _____ enough to the buyer. We both know that one important _____ of packing is to stimulate the buyer's desire to buy. He should _____ with your product at the first sight.

C: That's a good suggestion. Could you be more specific?

F: I feel your cartons are not thick and sturdy enough. They're kind of flimsy; therefore, the feeling of expensiveness is _____. And the color of the design of your packing really should be more _____. My opinion is that packing should give the buyer an idea of what is packed inside.

C: That's really a good idea. I'll pass it onto our designers and ask them to improve on it.

F: About the outer packing then, how are you going to _____ that?

C: Well, we'll _____ all those cardboard cartons with straps from outside; and mark them with the words such as "handle with care" and other general markings for transportation.

F: That really sounds good. Thanks.

V. Put the following mail into Chinese.

From: SES SHA/Warren warren.wong@ses.com

To: bill.clinton@wirginnet.co.uk

Cc: Johnson.smith@ses.com

Date: Mon. Mar. 30, 2010 10:30 AM

Subject: Developing Sino-UK Market

Dear Bill,

Your message is noted with thanks. I hope you had a nice weekend.

I note with great interest the conclusion you made after visiting some clients in UK.

Some importers in UK have no language skill and can not communicate directly with Chinese manufacturers (by the same token most Chinese manufacturers do not speak nor write English), but, we do.

Importers in UK may not be fully aware of the true manufacturing cost—it is their weak point where we can strike. By assisting them to find out the true cost here, even assisting them with supplier sourcing, price negotiation etc. (look at these additional attractive benefits), they probably betray their current freight partners and turn to us. I believe few FF here is willing and able to assist them in this regard. As for some large prospect, we do not care to go further to help them.

With our joint effort, I believe SES will be enjoying a much larger share in Sino-UK freight market.

Warren

 Supplementary Reading

Development of Packaging

Prior to World War II, packaging was used primarily to surround and protect products during storage, transportation, and distribution. Some packages were designed with aesthetic appeal and even for ease-of-use by the end consumer, but package design was typically left to technicians. After World War II, however, companies became more interested in marketing and promotion as a means of enticing customers to purchase their products. As a result, more manufacturers began to view packaging as an integral element of overall business marketing strategies to lure buyers.

This increased attention to packaging coincided with socio-economic changes taking place around the world. As consumers became better educated and more affluent, their expectations of products—and their reliance on them—increased as well. Consequently, consumers began to rely much more heavily on manufactured goods and processed food items. New technologies related to production, distribution, and preservatives led to a massive proliferation in the number and type of products and brands available in industrialized nations. Thus, packaging became a vital means of differentiating items and informing inundated consumers.

The importance of consumer packaging was elevated in the United States during the late 1970s and 1980s. Rapid post-war economic expansion and market growth waned during that period, forcing companies to focus increasingly on luring consumers to their products or brand at the expense of the competition. Package design became a marketing science. And, as a new corporate cost-consciousness developed in response to increased competition, companies began to alter packaging techniques as a way to cut production, storage, and distribution expenses. Furthermore, marketers began to view packaging as a tool to exploit existing product lines by adding new items and to pump new life into maturing products.

Today, good package design is regarded as an essential part of successful business practice. Since many potential customers first notice a new product after it has arrived on the shelves of a store, it is vital that the packaging provide consumers with the information they need and motivate them to make a purchase. But packaging decisions involve a number of tradeoffs. While making a product visible and distinctive may be the top priority, for example, businesses must also comply with a variety of laws regarding product labeling and safety. Protecting products during transport is important, but businesses also need to keep their shipping costs as low as possible.

Ⅰ. **Answer the following questions.**
1. Prior to World War Ⅱ, what was packaging primarily used to?
2. After World War Ⅱ, what did manufacturers begin to view packaging as?
3. When was the importance of consumer packaging elevated in the United States?
4. During the late 1970s and 1980s, what happened to the economic environment?
5. Today, what is good package design regarded as?

Ⅱ. **Tell whether the following statements are true or false.**
1. Prior to World War Ⅱ, packaging became a vital means of differentiating items and informing inundated consumers. ( )
2. After World War Ⅱ, package design was typically left to technicians. ( )
3. During the late 1970s and 1980s, marketers began to view packaging as a tool to exploit existing product lines by adding new items and to pump new life into maturing products. ( )
4. Today, good package design is regarded as an essential part of successful business practice. ( )
5. Today, companies are free to design their own package, they don't have to comply with any laws. ( )

Unit 6

International Logistics

> ◆ Knowledge Learning Objectives 知识学习目标 ◆
> - To understand what is containerization
> - To know the shipping documents
> - To learn the inter-modal transportation
>
> ◆ Skill Developing Objectives 技能培养目标 ◆
> - Communication skill in talking about the loading and unloading port
> - Communication skill in changing the port of destination
> - Writing skill in changing the post of loading and destination

Ⅰ. Containerization

1. Container Transportation(集装箱运输)

With the expansion of international trade, the container service has become popular. The transportation of international trading is nowadays frequently carried out in containers. The usage of containers provides a highly efficient form of  transport by road, rail and air though its fullest benefits are felt in shipping, where cost may be reduced by as much as one half.

2. Sizes of Containers(集装箱的尺寸)

Containers are constructed of metal and are of standards lengths from ten to forty feet. 20-foot container and 40-foot container have become more common. The 20-foot container has become the standard unit of measure quoted in terms of "TEUs" or 20-foot equivalent units. One 40-foot container equates to two TEUs.

3. The Advantage of Containers(集装箱的优势)

The advantage of containers from the shipper's point of view is that freight can be loaded and the box sealed before it leaves the warehouse. The goods themselves are not touched again until the customer receives the container and opens it.

- There is no risk of goods getting lost or mislaid in transit.
- Manpower in handling is greatly reduced, with lower costs and less risk of damage.
- Overall transportation cost can be reduced since container shipment offers the economy of mass transportation and minimizes the need for transshipment.
- Usage of container reduces the time ships spend in port and greatly increases the number of sailings.
- Temperature-controlled containers are provided for the types of cargo that need them.

4. The Disadvantage of Containers(集装箱的劣势)

Containers have a restricted application in inland transportation. Because containers on ships must be stacked, they must be sturdy in construction. In turn, this makes them heavy—too heavy for road transport since they unduly restrict payloads.

5. The FCL Service(整箱服务)

If the exporter intends to fill a full container load (FCL), the forwarder of shipping line will be prepared to send an empty container to the exporter for loading. The container is sealed with the carrier's seal, this is sometimes done by the shipper.

6. The LCL Service(拼箱服务)

If the cargo is less than a full container load (LCL), the exporter sends it to the container freight stations (CFSs), where it will be consolidated with the goods of other exporters in a group container.

7. Inter-modal Transportation(多式联运)

Inter-modal transportation refers to the movement of a shipment from origin to destination utilizing two or more different modes of transport. It involves a variety of shipment, transshipment and warehousing activities. The whole intent of inter-modal transport is to allow the shipper to take advantage of the best characteristics of all modes: the convenience of road, the long-distance movement efficiency of rail, and the capacity of ocean shipping. Therefore, inter-modal transportation offers the opportunity to combine modes and find a less costly alternative than a single transport mode. Numerous technical improvements, such as river/sea shipping and better rail/road integration, have been established to reduce interchange cost, but containerization remains the most significant achievement so far.

New Words and Phrases

container [kən'teinə] n. 容器,集装箱
containerization [kən,teinərai'zeiʃən] n. 集装箱化
expansion [iks'pænʃən] n. 扩充,开展
construct [kən'strʌkt] v. 建造,建立
quote [kwəut] v. 引用,提出,提供
mass [mæs] adj. 大规模的,集中的
restrict [ris'trikt] v. 限制,约束
application [,æpli'keiʃən] n. 应用,运用
stack [stæk] v. 堆放,堆叠
sturdy ['stə:di] adj. 坚固的,坚定的
unduly ['ʌn'dju:li] adv. 过度地,不适当地
fill [fil] v. 装满,充满,填充
forwarder ['fɔ:wədə] n. 货运公司,货运代理商
seal [si:l] n. 封铅,封条,印；v. 封,密封
consolidate [kən'sɔlideit] v. 装货,配货
origin ['ɔridʒin] n. 出发地,生产地
destination [,desti'neiʃən] n. 目的地
utilize [ju:'tilaiz] v. 利用
characteristic [,kærikə'ristik] n. 特性,特征
convenience [kən'vi:njəns] n. 便利,方便

efficiency [i'fiʃənsi] n. 效率,功效
capacity [kə'pæsiti] n. 容量,装载量
combine [kəm'bain] v. (使)结合
alternative [ɔ:l'tə:nətiv] n. 二中择一,可供选择的办法
integration [,inti'greiʃən] n. 综合
significant [sig'nifikənt] adj. 有意义的,重大的
achievement [ə'tʃi:vmənt] n. 成绩,成就,完成,达到
carry out 履行,执行
standard unit 标箱
TEUs＝twenty-foot equivalent units 20英尺的标箱
equate to 相当于,相等于
temperature-controlled 温控
FCL＝ a full container load 整箱服务
LCL＝ less than a full container load 拼箱服务
CFSs＝ container freight stations 集装箱运输站
inter-modal transportation 多式联运
so far 迄今为止

Notes

1. The usage of containers provides a highly efficient form of transport by road, rail and air though its fullest benefits are felt in shipping, where cost may be reduced by as much as one half. 集装箱的使用为道路、铁路和航空提供了一种高效的运输方式,它的全部优势在海运中体现得淋漓尽致,在海运中使用集装箱可以将成本降低一半。

2. Containers are constructed of metal and are of standards lengths from ten to forty feet. 集装箱由金属制造,包括10英尺到40英尺各种标准尺寸。

3. Overall transportation cost can be reduced since container shipment offers the economy of mass transportation and minimizes the need for transshipment. 由于使用了集装箱运输,提供了运输的规模经济并将转运需求降到最低,全面的运输成本得以降低。

4. Because containers on ships must be stacked, they must be sturdy in construction. 因为在船上集装箱必须叠放,所以必须建造得足够坚固。

5. Therefore, inter-modal transportation offers the opportunity to combine modes and find a less costly alternative than a single transport mode. 因此,与单一运输方式相

比,多式联运将适当的运输方式结合在一起,为降低成本提供了机会。

6. Numerous technical improvements, such as river/sea shipping and better rail/road integration, have been established to reduce interchange cost, but containerization remains the most significant achievement so far. 许多技术进步,如水运/海运和更完善的铁路/公路的结合,使运输方式转换时成本降低,但是迄今为止,集装箱化运输仍是意义最重大的进步。

Exercises

Ⅰ. Pair work: Discuss the following questions.
1. What is containerization?
2. What basic sizes do containers have?
3. What are the advantages of container transportation?
4. What is the multi-modal transportation?
5. Why would a shipper choose multi-modal transportation?
6. What is the FCL?
7. What is the LCL?
8. Why is container suitable to inter-modal transportation?

Ⅱ. Cloze test.

Containerization

The __1__ cargo transport volume has been on the rise together with the world's economic growth since the third quarter of last decade. Also we are living in a rapidly __2__ industry society. There have been a number of major changes in the shipping __3__, but the one that has the most far-reaching __4__ is the development of the container system.

This is referred to as "containerization", by which various general cargoes are stuffed __5__ big containers for the purpose of quick loading on __6__ ships and unloading from ships both for inbound and __7__ transport. By this measure, loading and unloading time at __8__ is reduced to one tenth of the time length on the average compared with the conventional handling method where general cargoes were, being much diversified in __9__ and size, handled on a two-ton sling unit basis.

Containerization has also implemented quick transit between ships and other modes of transportation, such as road and railway transport. Therefore, container transport is __10__ efficient not only for the marine transportation but also for the inland transportation.

1. A. international   B. bulk   C. inventory   D. domestic
2. A. changing   B. changed   C. changeable   D. exchange
3. A. enterprise   B. company   C. terminal   D. industry

4. A. aftermath	B. influence	C. suggestion	D. impact
5. A. from	B. for	C. into	D. down
6. A. board	B. our	C. bond	D. behind
7. A. side	B. bound	C. outbound	D. bounding
8. A. point	B. berth	C. port	D. terminal
9. A. color	B. type	C. material	D. shape
10. A. high	B. highly	C. far	D. quite

Ⅲ. Translate the following sentences into Chinese.

1. Inter-modal transportation is seen as a solution that could work in certain situations.

2. Temperature-controlled containers are provided for the types of cargo that need them.

3. With the improvement of international trade, the container service has become popular.

4. Before containerization, economies of scale were difficult to achieve with breakbulk cargo.

5. Maersk Sealand is one of the largest liner shipping companies in the world, serving customers all over the world.

Ⅳ. Translate the following sentences into English.

1. 经济全球化对多式联运的基础设施提出了更多的挑战。

2. 我建议采取多式联运。先用火车把货运到宁波，再用船运到伦敦。

3. 集装箱的使用极大地提高了物流效率。

4. 整箱运输的费率低于拼箱运输。

5. 这家国际货代公司可以提供拼箱服务。

Ⅴ. Read the following passages and answer the questions.

All over the world, more and more ocean freights are carried out with containers. This trend will continue because containerized shipment offers so many advantages. Among them are:

1. Economy. Overall transportation costs can be reduced by the container shipment. In the case of general cargo of 10000 tons, it takes 48 hours to load and unload, but for the container ship of 35000 tons, only 6~8 hour needed to load and unload.

2. Safety. The cargo can be handled in any weather and is efficiently protected from theft and damage, because it is completely enclosed.

3. Large scale. Container ship has become giant from 10000 tons in 1970 to 100000 tons, now it continues to grow bigger and bigger.

There are two kinds of containers, 20' and 40', mostly adopted. 20' container is called TEU, Twenty-feet Equivalent Unit, and standard container. One 40' container is equals two 20's.

Containers are used in ocean, railway and highway transportation. In recent years, many container terminals have been established. The continental bridge transport is introduced to load containers by trains. The road transportation follows this tendency, the tractors pull the container with the speed in 100km per hour in highway.

1. What is container shipment? (　　)
    A. To load goods in container.
    B. Container is only choice for transportation.
    C. Containerized transportation.
    D. Container ship, container train and container track.
2. What is containerization shipment? (　　)
    A. To load goods in container.
    B. Container is only choice for transportation.
    C. Containerized transportation.
    D. Container ship, container train and container track.
3. Only 20' and 40' container are available. Is it a fact? (　　)
    A. Correct.   B. Wrong.
    C. Not mentioned.   D. I don't know.
4. 20' container is standard container. Is it true or not? (　　)
    A. Yes.   B. No.
    C. It is an old concept. D. It is a new kind of container.
5. Container ships need the container terminal to load and unload goods. Is it correct or not? (　　)
    A. Correct.   B. Wrong.   C. Depend.   D. No mention.

Dialogue 1　Talking About the Unloading Port

(*The following is a conversation between Mr. Geng, a clerk in a logistics company and Mike, a customer of a company.*)

Geng: Mike, are you tired today after your visit to the Great Wall yesterday?
Mike: No, not at all. I am very interested in the visit.
Geng: What are your impressions about the Great Wall?
Mike: It's just too great, and it has made an everlasting impression on me.
Geng: Well, do you think now we should talk a bit about the port of discharge?
Mike: I'm ready.
Geng: Our offer is CIF European main ports. The time of shipment is August.

What's your unloading port please?

Mike:Hamburg.

Geng:But as I know, sailings to Europe in August only call at London and Antwerp.

Mike:Our customers are all located near Hamburg. It's not reasonable to have the goods unloaded at London.

Geng:I see.

Mike:We do hope you'll contact the shipping company once again to make sure that the shipment will arrive in Hamburg.

Geng:Sure and I will do that, there is a vessel sailing to Hamburg in July. But I'm afraid it's too late to book the shipping space.

Mike:Please try your best, and I trust that you can make it.

Geng:All right. But the question we have at the moment is whether the manufactures can get the goods ready in July.

Mike:You can contact the factory again to hurry them up. It will be marvelous if the goods can be shipped in July.

Geng:I'll certainly try my best, but if we fail to do that, there will be another chance. The next early available chance will be the Hamburg ships in September. There will be two of them. What do you think if the shipment is effected in September, a month later than the schedule?

Mike:We'd like the shipment to be made in July, but if nothing can be done about it, the goods can be shipped in September. There should be no more changes in the schedule, anyway.

Geng:I'm sure there will be no more changes.

New Words and Phrases

impression [im'preʃən] *n.* 印象,感想
everlasting [,evə'lɑ:stiŋ] *adj.* 永恒的,持久的
Hamburg ['hæmbə:g] *n.* 汉堡(欧洲主要港口)
Antwerp ['æntwə:p] *n.* 安特卫普(欧洲主要港口)
reasonable ['ri:znəbl] *adj.* 合理的
marvelous ['mɑ:vələs] *adj.* 令人惊异的,不可思议的
effect [i'fekt] *v.* 实现,达到
schedule ['skedʒjul] *n.* 时间表;*v.* 确定时间
port of discharge 卸货港
CIF 到岸价(成本,保险加运费)

Notes

1. Our offer is CIF European main ports. 我们的报价是欧洲主要港口的到岸价。

2. It's not reasonable to have the goods unloaded at London. 在伦敦港卸货不太合理。

Unit 6 International Logistics

 Exercises

Ⅰ. **Oral practice**: Practice the above dialogue with your partner until you can learn the lines by heart.

Ⅱ. **Team work**: Make up a dialogue according to the following situation and practice it with your partner.

Situation:

Jerry is a clerk of a logistics company. Now he is talking with his customer about the loading and unloading port.

Tips:

1. We should talk about the port of loading and discharging.
2. I think Dalian is suitable to us.
3. What's your unloading port please?
4. We'd better have a brief talk about the loading port.
5. We'd like to designate Shanghai as the loading port because it is near the producing area.
6. As most of our clients are near London, we'd like to appoint London as the unloading port.
7. An early reply from you will help us to speed up shipment.
8. You may depend on what I promise you.

Ⅲ. **Write an E-mail to your customer, telling them about the following information.**

Contents:

1. 就货物装运推迟之事进行道歉。
2. 由于恶劣天气造成装运推迟。
3. 保证3日内再次发运。

Ⅳ. **Read the dialogue and translate into Chinese.**

A: Hello. Welcome to Bumbles.

B: Can I speak to James Chen.

A: Yes, James is Speaking.

B: This is Zhaoyang Electronics Co. of Suzhou.

A: Have you received the request from the Shanghai Hongqiao Customs House regarding the survey of your cargo?

B: Yes. But is it a condition to go through the custom clearance procedures?

A: Why, of course. The Customs House must make sure that the goods you sent to be exported conform to what is stated on the air waybill.

B: But the consignment is very small, only 100 kilograms of CDs.

A: It is the rule that each and every consignment for export shall be inspected before leaving China.

B: Can you not put in a word for us? You are our freight forwarder for so many years and …

A: Sorry. But that is not the rules of the game. You had better send someone here as soon as possible. Otherwise, warehousing expense will incur.

B: OK. Xiao Wang from our export department will be with you this afternoon.

A: I will be in my office then. Bye-bye.

B: Bye-bye.

Ⅴ. Put the following mail into Chinese.

Fast Freight Forwarding Ltd. (3F) was established in Hong Kong in 1975 and is one of the loading agents in the territory. Active in both sea and air freight, 3F has expertise in warehousing, cargo logistics, cargo consolidation and project shipments. 3F has been accredited IATA agent and member of both FIATA and HAFFA. 3F has been granted ISO 9002 certification.

3F has been developing the China market over many years and has licensed offices in Guangzhou, Shanghai, Ningbo etc. A full range of services is being offered from these locations. With a worldwide network of professional agent, 3F operates services to and from major centers on all continents.

SEA FREIGHT

Weekly groupage and NVOCC services to and from major centers in Europe, USA, Australia, as well as Eastern Bloc countries, are being offered, in conjunction with our reliable worldwide agency network.

Further services offered include (both sea and air)

—Consolidation for Overseas Buyers

—Warehousing and Inventory Control

—Cartage and Delivery Services

—Distribution

—Customs Clearance

—Packing

—Purchase Order Processing

—Shipment Tracking

—EDI with Clients and Carriers

3F is a member of both FIATA (The International Federational of Freight Forwarding Agents) and HAFFA (the Hong Kong Assosiation of Freight Forwarding Agents)

AIR FREIGHT

Regular scheduled consolidation services to major world centers are being offered.

3F has been an approved and certified agent of IATA since 1985, having met the high professional standards Air Transport Association(IATA).

Ⅱ. Main Logistics Documents

1. Introduction to Logistics Documents(物流单据介绍)

Logistics documents refer to all documents involved in the course of logistics. Generally speaking, logistics documents contain two kinds of documents: cargo documents and transport documents. They are applied for various purposes in the whole process of transport of goods. The following paragraphs are introduction to bill of lading, air waybill, packing list, commercial invoice, insurance policy and certificate of origin.

2. Bill of Lading(提单)

One of the most important documents in maritime is the bill of lading (abbreviated to B/L). It is used primarily in international sales of goods where the carriage of goods is by sea. It must be presented at the port of final destination by the importer in order to claim goods. A B/L is nearly always prepared on a pre-printed form. Whatever its form, a B/L may contain some main elements, such as quantity of goods, accurate cargo description and condition, date of the B/L, names of shipper and consignee, party to be notified, name of vessel, ports of loading and discharge, terms and conditions of carriage and payment of freight.

The functions of the maritime B/L can be classified into three categories:

- a receipt for the goods shipped
- evidence of the contract of carriage
- document of title for the goods

3. Air Waybill(空运运单)

An air waybill is a form of B/L used for the air transport of goods. It is an evidence of a transportation contract. The air waybill is approximately equivalent to the sea B/L, but it is not a document of title to goods or a negotiable document.

Each air waybill has 3 originals and at least 6 copies. The air waybill must be accurately completed, clear forwarding instruction must be given to the airline or agent. The air waybill is used as a receipt of the goods for dispatch and evidence of the contract of carriage between the carrier and the consignor.

4. Multi-modal Transport Document(多式联运单)

When goods are carried by more than one mode of transport (usually in containers), a combined (multi-modal) transport document is recommended as the multi-modal transport operator accepts liability for carriage of the goods throughout the entire journey. Where part of the journey is undertaken by sea, some types of multi-modal transport document can convey title to the goods.

5. Packing List(装箱单)

A packing list is a document prepared by the shipper at the time the goods are shipped, giving details of the invoice, buyer, consignee, country of origin, vessel or flight details, port or airport of loading and discharge, place of delivery, shipping marks, container number, weight and cubic of goods, etc. Its prime purpose is to give an inventory of the shipped goods and is required by the customs clearance.

6. Commercial Invoice(商业发票)

The commercial invoice is a document offered by the seller to the buyer regarding the sold goods. The commercial invoice is issued by the exporter. It provides details of a transaction between the importer and the exporter. Its main function is a check for the importer against charges and delivery. Besides, it is used as determination of value of goods for the assessment of customs duties, preparation for consular documentation, insurance claims and packing purposes.

7. Insurance Policy(保险单)

An insurance policy is a document confirming insurance of cargo and indicating the type and amount of insurance coverage. This document is usually issued to the party buying the insurance.

The details on the policy must match those on the bills of lading-voyage, ship, marks and numbers, etc. It must also be in the same currency as the credit and endorsed in blank. The amount covered should be at least the invoice amount; credits usually call for invoice value plus 10 per cent. The policy must be dated not later than the date of shipment as evidenced by the bill of lading. The risks covered should be those detailed in the credit. If coverage against "all risks" is called for (which is obtainable), a policy which states that it covers all insurable risks will be acceptable.

8. Certificate of Origin(原产地证书)

A certificate of origin is a document issued by a certifying authority such as a chamber of commerce in the exporter's country stating the country of origin of the goods. It is usually required by countries to set the appropriate duties for the imports.

New Words and Phrases

cargo [ˈkɑːɡəu] n. 货物
invoice [ˈinvɔis] n. 发票
carriage [ˈkæridʒ] n. 运输,运费
destination [ˌdestiˈneiʃən] n. 目的地

element [ˈelimənt] n. 要素,成分,元素
description [disˈkripʃən] n. 描述,形容
consignee [kɔnsaiˈniː] n. 收货人,收件人
category [ˈkætiɡəri] n. 种类,分类

approximately [əprɔksi'mətli] adv. 近似地,大约
equivalent [i'kwivələnt] adj. 相当的,相等的
negotiable [ni'gəuʃjəbl] adj. 可流通的,可转让的
dispatch [dis'pætʃ] n. 派遣,发送
consignor [kən'sainə] n. 委托者,发货人,交付人
cubic ['kju:bik] n. 体积
transaction [træn'zækʃən] n. 处理,交易
assessment [ə'sesmənt] n. 评估,估价
insurance [in'ʃuərəns] n. 保险,保险业
authority [ɔ:'θɔriti] n. 权威,权力机关
appropriate ['prəupriit] adj. 适当的,恰当的

duty ['dju:ti] n. 义务,责任,关税
bill of lading(B/L) 提单
air waybill 空运运单
packing list 装箱单
insurance policy 保险单
certificate of origin 原产地
port of loading 装货港
port of destination 目的港
document of title 物权凭证
customs clearance 通关,清关
chamber of commerce 商会

Notes

1. Generally speaking, logistics documents contain two kinds of documents: cargo documents and transport documents. 通常来讲,物流单据包括两类:货物单据和运输单据。

2. It must be presented at the port of final destination by the importer in order to claim goods. (提单)是进口商为在目的地港领取货物时提交的单据。

3. Whatever its form, a B/L may contain some main elements, such as quantity of goods, accurate cargo description and condition, date of the B/L, names of shipper and consignee, party to be notified, name of vessel, ports of loading and discharge, terms and conditions of carriage and payment of freight. 不论形式如何,提单一般包括一些主要的元素,如货物的数量、商品准确的名称和状况、提单的日期、托运人和收货人的名称,通知方、船名、装/卸货港、运输合同的条款和运费的支付方式。

4. document of title for the goods 货物的物权凭证

5. The air waybill is approximately equivalent to the sea B/L, but it is not a document of title to goods or a negotiable document. 空运运单的内容与海运提单大概相似,但是空运运单不是物权凭证,也不能转让和流通。

6. Each air waybill has 3 originals and at least 6 copies. 每份空运运单有三份正本以及至少六份副本。

7. Besides, it is used as determination of value of goods for the assessment of customs duties, preparation for consular documentation, insurance claims and packing purposes. 除此之外,商业发票还用作货物价值评估、关税估价、准备领事文件、保险索赔以及包装目的。

Exercises

Ⅰ. Team work: Discuss the following questions.
1. How many kinds of shipping documents do you know?
2. What is B/L?
3. What are the functions of B/L?

4. What is air waybill?

5. What is the purpose of packing list?

6. How many types of invoices do you know?

Ⅱ. Fill in the blanks with the words in the following box. Change the forms if necessary.

insurance	receipt	cargo	destination	function
amount	document	transport	negotiable	exporter

1. A certificate of origin is a _____ issued by a certifying authority.

2. The shipping company will tell you when your _____ is loaded on board the ship.

3. Logistics documents contain two kinds of documents: cargo documents and _____ documents.

4. B/L must be presented at the port of final _____ by the importer.

5. B/L is a _____ for the goods shipped.

6. Air waybill is not a _____ document.

7. The bill of lading performs a number of _____.

8. The commercial invoice is issued by the _____.

9. An insurance policy is a document confirming _____ of cargo.

10. An insurance policy is a document indicating the type and _____ of insurance coverage.

Ⅲ. Translate the following sentences into Chinese.

1. One of the most important documents in maritime trade is the bill of lading.

2. A cargo manifest provides information regarding cargoes on board.

3. The shipping note is a commitment on the shipper to ship the goods and serves as the basis for the preparation of the bill of lading.

4. The main parties on a bill of lading are shipper, consignee, party to be notified and carrier.

5. A mate's receipt is the receipt issued by the carrier in the acknowledgement of the goods received on board.

Ⅳ. Translate the following sentences into English.

1. 提单显示船公司收到货时,货物外表良好。

2. 第二份提单没有注明为正本。

3. 副本提单不可以流通。

4. 提单从不同角度分很多类别。

5. 国际物流中使用着大量单据。

Ⅴ. Read the following passages and answer the questions.

Now, we discuss the relation between the international trade and logistics. As you know, trading involves several steps:

1. Making deal. In this stage, the buyer and seller should negotiate the price of the goods, the way to pay, finally sign the contract.

2. Payment. It is a core step in the trading. General speaking, buyers can't pay to sellers directly. They usually ask their bank to write the Letter of Credit (L/C) to the sellers. L/C is the promise to pay from the buyer, transferred to sellers' band under the conditional articles.

3. Transportation. After receiving qualified L/C, the seller begins to deliver the goods. Then transportation takes the main place of the trading. So, international transportation is similar word to international logistics. Logistics can move the commodities form one country to another with ships, trucks and air. Logistics may fix the cost of transportation to the trading partners with the terms of FOB and CIF. FOB means the deal price without insurance and freight. CIF contains cost of goods, insurance and freight. Transportation as the main function of the logistics has the very close relationship with foreign trade.

4. Customs clearance and Inspection. In the final step, logistics helps customers and customs in two ways, on one hand, arrangement of goods to be cleared on the other, handing in the documents to be examined.

1. There is not close relationship between international trade and logistics. Is it correct? (   )
    A. Correct.　　　　　　　　　　　　B. Wrong.
    C. This is not the main topic in the page.　D. I don't know.
2. What is contract? (   )
    A. Paper.　　　　　　　　　　　　　B. Arrangement.
    C. Arrangement by both sides of deal.　D. Memo.
3. What does the customs do? (   )
    A. Inspecting goods and collecting duty.　B. Government organ.
    C. Collecting tax.　　　　　　　　　D. Inspecting commodities.
4. Does the author talk about the transportation equipment? (   )
    A. Yes.　　　　　　　　　　　　　　B. No.
    C. Only a little.　　　　　　　　　　D. Dropping a hint.

Dialogue 2　Change the Port of Destination

(*Jane is talking to the customer, Wangjian, who came into the office in a hurry.*)

Jane: Hey, Mr. Wang, what's the matter? Why are you soaking wet?

Wang: I have something urgent to ask you. But as it is raining so hard, I couldn't find any taxi.

Jane: Then tell quickly so that you can go home and change into dry clothes.

Wang: I have just received a fax from our customer in Germany, who wants us to change destination of our cargo.

Jane: Which cargo?

Wang: The dresses to Toulouse. I remember the consignment consists of twenty TEU.

Jane: Where do you wish the cargo to go now?

Wang: Our customer now wishes to land it at Marseilles. Can you do it?

Jane: Let me see. (*After checking his computer*) The ship that carries your containers is still at Suez, waiting for the transit of the Suez Canal. It will not pass the canal in 48 hours. We can send a cable to the ship and the port of Marseilles and tell them.

Wang: Thank you very much.

Jane: But I must have the three original Bills of Lading.

Wang: Oh, they are now on their way to the consignee. Why do you want them?

Jane: We want to make sure that no third party will claim the cargo with any of the original B/L.

Wang: Do you accept Letter of Indemnity?

Jane: As a rule, we have to make a commercial decision and take the risk ourselves if we do so. But considering you are our long time customer, we accept it.

Wang: Thank you. I will go back to the company and ask the bank to provide you with a Letter of Indemnity.

Jane: Wait a moment. Who will pay for the extra expense that may incur when the containers are moved?

Wang: Of course we will contact the customer and ask them to pay.

Jane: Well, that is not our business. You'll have to advance the expenses, I'm afraid.

Wang: Of course. All the expense incurred for this purpose will be for our account. Now, see you later.

Jane: See you later.

New Words and Phrases

destination [ˌdestiˈneiʃən] *n.* 目的地
Toulouse [tuˈluːz] *n.* 图卢兹(法国南部港口)
consignment [kənˈsainmənt] *n.* 委托之货物
Marseilles [mɑːˈseilz] *n.* 马赛(法国东南部港口)
transit [ˈtrænsit] *n.* 通过,通行

original [əˈridʒənəl] *adj.* 最初的,正本的
incur [inˈkəː] *v.* 引起,导致
TEU 20 英尺的标箱
Suez Canal 苏伊士运河
Letter of Indemnity 补偿信

Notes

1. I remember the consignment consists of twenty TEU. 我记得这批货物包括20个标箱。

2. I must have the three original Bills of Lading. 我必须拿到三份正本提单。

3. Who will pay for the extra expense that may incur when the containers are moved? 谁来支付货物转运引起的额外费用?

4. All the expense incurred for this purpose will be for our account. 所有由此引起的费用从我们账户中支付。

 Exercises

Ⅰ. **Oral practice**: Practice the above dialogue with your partner until you can learn the lines by heart.

Ⅱ. **Team work**: Make up a dialogue according to the following situation and practice it with your partner.

Situation:

Jenny is planning to import the goods. She needs the help of the Xinxing International Logistics Co., Ltd. on the customs clearance.

Tips:

1. Nice to meet you.
2. We need to talk about …
3. We can provide all types of services on the international logistics.
4. Our core business is the customs clearance.
5. You can depend on us.
6. We specialize in …
7. You need to provide all relative documents.
8. All expenses will be on our account.

Ⅲ. Write an E-mail to your customer, telling them about the following information.

Contents:

1. 该批出口货物必须检验,这是海关的规定。
2. 我们可以找检验师检验货物。
3. 在两天内做完。
4. 所有的费用由你们支付。

Ⅳ. **Read the dialogue and translate into Chinese.**

Xiaoyang, a business representative of A company, negotiates with Mr. Jackson, a business representative of B company, concerning shipment of wrong goods.

Xiaoyang: Upon the examination of your delivery, we find it does not contain the goods we ordered. No doubt, you have made an error.

Jackson: Would you please tell us in detail?

Xiaoyang: We ordered tablecloths, whereas the contents are towels. Evidently, the goods are wrong. We're holding the goods for your disposal in our warehouse.

Jackson: The mistake is entirely on our side. We'll try to bring the case to a speedy close and arrange to send you replacement immediately, but it is preferable if you can dispose of them at your end.

Xiaoyang: Let me think.

Jackson: We are prepared to allow 15% off the invoice price if you would accept the wrong delivery.

Supplementary Reading

Types of Marine B/L

B/L are of many kinds, and can be classified into the following categories.

1. In terms of whether or not the goods are on board: On Board B/L and Received for Shipment B/L

On Board B/L is issued by the carrier or its agent when all the goods are loaded on board of the ship, and must bear the name of the ship and the date of shipment. Received for Shipment B/L is issued by the carrier or its agent when the goods are under his control before loaded on boarded the shipment. The buyer does not favor it, and usually the L/C will require the seller to present shipped B/L for negotiation at the bank. However, with development of containers, received for Shipment B/L are being increasingly applied.

2. On the basis of the apparent condition of goods noted: Clean B/L and Unclean (or Foul) B/L

When the shipping company writes on the B/L "The goods loaded are in apparent good order", this B/L is a clean one. When the shipping line gives such an indication as "The goods loaded are not in apparent good order" or "The packing is broken or ... is polluted, etc.", this B/L is a foul one and non-negotiable at the bank.

3. In the light of different characteristics of consignees: Straight B/L, Order B/L and Open (or Bearer) B/L

Straight B/L has a specified name in the column of consignee, which means that the goods can only be received by the specified person and the B/L cannot be transferred to a third person. So it is not negotiable. Order B/L does not have a specified name but the phraseology of "To order", or "To the order of ..." in the column of consignee. This kind of B/L can be transferred to others by endorsement. Open B/L has neither the consignee's name nor the phraseology of "To order" fill in the column of consignee. This type of B/L is negotiable without endorsement, and ownership of the goods passes when the B/L is handed over to anyone.

4. In terms of modes of transport: Direct B/L, Transshipment B/L, Through B/L and Combined Transport (or Container) B/L

Under Direct B/L, the goods will be directly carried to the port of destination without transshipment, while with transshipment under Transshipment B/L. Through B/L is a development of these two B/L. Under Through B/L, the goods will at least be carried by two different modes of transport before arriving at the port of destination. A multi-modal operator responsible for the whole voyage issues combined Transport B/L, involving two or more different kinds of transport. This kind of B/L is usually used in container transport and may be a Received for Shipment B/L, but a Through B/L must be a Clean Shipped B/L.

5. In conformity with the form and clauses: Long Form B/L and Short Form B/L

A Long Form B/L has detailed clauses printed on its back concerning the transport of goods so as to solve any possible disputes. While a Short Form B/L does not have such clauses on its back. However, if such wording as "all transport clauses are based on the Long Form B/L of our company" is stamped on the back of a Short Form B/L, this B/L is equal to a long form one and will be accepted by the bank for negotiation.

Questions:
1. How many types of B/L are mentioned in this text?
2. How should they be distinguished from each other?
3. Why is a Straight B/L not negotiable?

Unit 7

Purchasing

- ◆ Knowledge Learning Objectives 知识学习目标 ◆
  - Understand the role of purchasing
  - Be familiar with the purchasing process
  - Learn the benefits of outsourcing
- ◆ Skill Developing Objectives 技能培养目标 ◆
  - Communication skill in ordering goods
  - Communication skill in introducing the product
  - Communication skill in purchasing
  - Writing skill in purchasing

Ⅰ. Purchasing

1. Definition of Purchasing(采购的概念)

Purchasing is not simply buying goods and services, and it is a group of functional activities associated with buying the goods and services required by organizations. These activities include supplier identification and selection, buying, negotiation and contracting, supply market research, supplier measurement and improvement, and purchasing systems development, etc.

2. The Role of Purchasing(采购的作用)

The most important and traditional role of purchasing is to meet the requirements of internal users. In the past, the emphasis was laid to buy what firms need from the right source, at the right price, in the right quantity, to the right internal customer and at the right specifications. However, with the increase of outsourcing, firms are more and more relying on external suppliers to provide not only just materials and products, but also information technology, service, and even logistics. Therefore, to ensure the uninterrupted flow of high-quality goods and services is becoming more critical for modern enterprises.

Purchasing department must develop and maintain close relationships with other functional groups within the organization which may include manufacturing, marketing, technology and finance. Effective communication with these departments is essential and necessary for the whole organization to keep as competitive. For example, if a supplier's components are defective and causing problem for manufacturing, then the purchasing department must work with the supplier to improve their quality.

In order to ensure the current suppliers are competitive, purchasing must identify new suppliers and improve or replace the existing suppliers who are not meeting the requirements. That means that purchasing needs to keep abreast of the newest conditions in supply market.

3. The Need of Purchasing(采购需求)

Nowadays the need for purchasing to be involved in corporate strategy has received a great deal of attention. The reason is that the amount of money spent on purchasing has increased significantly, and the potential savings from strategic management of purchasing are considerable. Another factor is the trend toward outsourcing, which means firms must manage their suppliers effectively. Now it is believed that suppliers play a critical role in supporting a firm's competitive strategy, whether it is cost leadership, differentiation, or a mixed strategy.

4. Decision of Purchasing(采购决策)

Purchasing those products and services which firms can not produce is necessary and easily understood, but if they can make or provide these products and services in-house, what will they do? Decisions about whether a producer of goods or services will insource or outsource are also called make-or-buy decisions. Answering such questions is often not as obvious as black and white. To make it clear, management needs to answer the question: What is the difference in relevant costs between the alternatives? Therefore, it is necessary to calculate costs among alternatives and consider its resources and opportunity cost. Finally, some other strategic issues also need to be taken into account.

5. Centralized and Decentralized Purchasing(集中采购和分散采购)

When a firm has several facilities, management must decide whether to buy centrally or respectively.

Centralized purchasing is where all material purchasing responsibility is at the top level of the operation. It is practiced when the purchasing activity affects the entire operation, such as buying steel for steel strap manufacturing. The advantages of centralized purchasing are greater power to influence the suppliers, abilities to coordinate with other members in the whole supply chain, and deep knowledge of suppliers market. Companies with a single plant or small companies usually have centralized purchasing.

When there is more than one manufacturing plant or separate product divisions, the purchasing responsibility may be separated and moved from corporate control to local control. This arrangement is an example of decentralized purchasing. The advantage of decentralized control is that responsibility and authority are closer to the operation allowing for greater flexibility. Another advantage is the reduced reaction time in emergencies.

New Words and Phrases

functional ['fʌŋkʃənl] adj. 功能的
internal [in'tə:nl] adj. 内部的
specification [,spesifi'keiʃən] n. 规格，规范
outsourcing ['aut,sɔ:siŋ] n. 外包，外购
ensure [in'ʃuə] v. 确保
uninterrupted [ʌnintə'rʌptid] adj. 不间断的，连续的
enterprise ['entəpraiz] n. 企业，商业机构
finance [fai'næns] n. 财务，金融
essential [i'senʃəl] adj. 基本的，必需的
competitive [kəm'petitiv] adj. 有竞争力的，竞争的
component [kəm'pəunənt] n. 零件，部分

defective [di'fektiv] adj. 有缺陷的
differentiation [,difə,renʃi'eiʃən] n. 差异化
relevant ['relivənt] adj. 相关的，相应的
alternative [ɔ:l'tə:nətiv] adj. 选择性的，二中选一的
strategic [strə'ti:dʒik] adj. 战略上的，关键的
laid to 把……归于
rely on 依赖，依靠
keep abreast of 保持与……并列
cost leadership 成本领先
opportunity cost 机会成本
take into account 重视，考虑

Notes

1. These activities include supplier identification and selection, buying, negotiation and contracting, supply market research, supplier measurement and improvement, and purchasing systems development, etc. 这些活动包括供应商的认定和选择、采购、谈判、合同签订、供应市场调研、供应商的考核和改进以及采购系统的开发等。

2. That means that purchasing needs to keep abreast of the newest conditions in supply market. 这就意味着采购需要与供应市场的最新情况同步。

3. Suppliers play a critical role in supporting a firm's competitive strategy, whether it is cost leadership, differentiation, or a mixed strategy. 供应商在支持企业的竞争战略上扮演极其重要的角色，不管这种战略是成本领先、差异化还是二者的混合。

4. Decisions about whether a producer of goods or services will insource or outsource are also called make-or-buy decisions. 有关一个生产者会自己生产或者外包其产品或服务的决策也称为生产或购买决策。

5. Therefore, it is necessary to calculate costs among alternatives and consider its resources and opportunity cost. Finally, some other strategic issues also need to be taken into account. 因此,有必要在不同的可选项之间计算各自的成本,考虑其资源和机会成本。最后,一些其他的战略因素也需要考虑在内。

Exercises

Ⅰ. **Pair work: Discuss the following questions.**
1. What is purchasing?
2. What are the main tasks for a purchasing manager?
3. Price is the only variable concerned by purchasing managers, isn't it?
4. Can purchasing play a role in supporting a firm's strategic success?
5. What requires that purchasing assume more responsibility?
6. How do you understand the role of purchasing?
7. How to manage the suppliers effectively?
8. How to reduce the purchasing cost?

Ⅱ. **Comprehension: True/False/Not mentioned.**
1. Purchasing is simply buying the goods needed by firms or organizations.
2. Meeting the requirements of internal users is the traditional role of purchasing.
3. Nowadays price is not important any more for purchasing.
4. It is necessary to develop and maintain close relationships with other functional groups within the organization.
5. Purchasing needs to know the latest condition in supply market.
6. When a supplier's components are defective, the purchasing department will solve the problems solely.
7. Suppliers do not play a role in supporting a firm's competitive strategy.
8. Firms will only purchase goods or service which they cannot produce or provide.
9. Make-or-buy decisions are usually obvious and clear to answer for managers.
10. Comparing the difference in relevant cost between the alternatives is helpful to make outsourcing decisions.

Ⅲ. **Choose the best answer to each of the following questions.**
1. What is the passage mainly about? (   )
    A. How to purchase goods and services.
    B. What is purchasing?
    C. Purchasing is important.
    D. Make-or-buy decisions.
2. What activities are included in purchasing? (   )
    A. Supplier selection.   B. Negotiation.

C. Supplier measurement.   D. All of above.

3. With the increase of outsourcing, firms are more relying on external suppliers to provide(　　).

    A. materials   B. information technology

    C. logistics   D. all of above

4. Nowadays, which of the following is more critical for modern enterprises? (　　)

    A. Buying from the right source.

    B. Buying at the right price.

    C. Buying in the right quantity.

    D. Uninterrupted flow of high-quality goods.

5. Outsourcing is (　　).

    A. to buy goods or services outside   B. to make goods or service inside

    C. to buy materials outside   D. none of above

Ⅳ. Translate the following sentences into Chinese.

1. One of the most important duties of purchasing is the right to select suppliers.

2. Most firms include purchasing as a major supply chain activity.

3. The purchasing department performs many activities to ensure it delivers great value to the organization.

4. Suppliers can help differentiate a producer's final goods or service.

5. A supplier that performs well can help our organization be more efficient, produce higher quality products or services, reduce costs, and increase profits.

Ⅴ. Translate the following sentences into English.

1. 采购有助于提升公司在许多方面的效率和有效性。

2. 购买商品和服务是许多公司最大的成本因素之一。

3. 这家公司为构建数据库采购了新的硬件。

4. 采购已经成为供应链管理重要的一部分。

5. 采购绝不仅仅是够买原材料。

Dialogue 1　What Is Purchasing

(*Mr. Wang, the purchasing manager in a multinational company, is talking with Miss Li, a new graduated university man.*)

Li: Good morning, Mr. Wang. My major is marketing, so I know little about purchasing. Could you tell me more about it?

Wang: OK. Purchasing is an important function for firms and even non-profit organizations. It is just as important as marketing, and it requires a lot of tactics and rich experience.

Li: Really? I thought purchasing was simply to buy something you need, and it will be easier to do.

Wang: In fact, purchasing consists of many tasks, for example, to identify the internal needs, find the suitable suppliers, negotiate contract, and make sure what you purchase will be delivered on time.

Li: May I say that cost control is the most important for you?

Wang: Yes. Price, together with quality and delivery are the most obvious and important factors for purchasing managers to consider.

Li: Are there any other things related to purchasing?

Wang: Yes. Such as make-or-buy decision, supplier technology, and how purchasing can support the firm's competitive strategy.

Li: Well, I know some of them. But how can purchasing support a firm's competitive strategy?

Wang: The movement toward global sourcing, rapid changes in technology, and increased competition require purchasing to assume more responsibility in the planning and implementation of strategies to support corporate strategy.

Li: It sounds reasonable.

Wang: Now considerable focus is placed on ensuring supply, inventory minimization, quality improvement, supplier development, and the lowest total cost of ownership.

Li: Exactly, all of these are connected with purchasing.

Wang: That means good purchasing can make the corporate more profitable.

Li: I know much about purchasing now. So what is the current situation in most firms?

Wang: Unfortunately, most organizations have not fully understood the role of purchasing. It is clear that the attitudes of top management and purchasing managers themselves must change before purchasing playing a strategic role in organizations.

Li: It must be a long way.

Wang: Yes. Besides, purchasing skills also need to be developed.

Li: Definitely.

Wang: So have you got the rough picture of purchasing now?

Li: Yes. Now I fully understand what you said. Purchasing is really important.

Wang: We welcome you to join the purchasing profession in the future.

Li: Thanks a lot. I will consider it seriously.

New Words and Phrases

major ['meidʒə] *n.* 专业,主修方向
function ['fʌŋkʃən] *n.* 功能
tactics ['tæktiks] *n.* 战术,策略

identify [ai'dentifai] *v.* 确定
negotiate [ni'gəuʃieit] *v.* 商议,谈判
assume [ə'sjuːm] *v.* 承担

reasonable ['ri:znəbl] adj. 有道理的
role [rəul] n. 任务，角色
management ['mænidʒmənt] n. 管理
rough [rʌf] adj. 大致的
profession [prə'feʃən] n. 职业，专业

non-profit 非营利的
consist of 由……组成
make-or-buy 生产或购买
competitive strategy 竞争策略

Notes

1. Purchasing is an important function for firms and even non-profit organizations. 采购是企业甚至非营利性组织的一个重要功能。

2. Such as make-or-buy decision, supplier technology, and how purchasing can support the firm's competitive strategy. 比如，生产或购买的决策，供应商的技术，以及采购如何支持企业的竞争策略。

3. The lowest total cost of ownership 最低总拥有成本

4. Unfortunately, most organizations have not fully understood the role of purchasing. It is clear that the attitudes of top management and purchasing managers themselves must change before purchasing playing a strategic role in organizations. 遗憾的是，大多数组织还没有完全理解采购的功能。只有高层管理者以及采购经理的态度发生改变，采购才可能在组织中发挥战略作用。

Exercises

Ⅰ. **Oral practice**: Practice the above dialogue with your partner until you can learn the lines by heart.

Ⅱ. **Team work**: Make up a dialogue according to the following situation and practice it with your partner.

Situation:

Mary is a retailer of daily necessities. Now some of her goods that sell well are out of stock, so she is phoning her supplier Mr. Smith asking for more supplies.

Tips:

1. Hi, this is … speaking.

2. Is there anything I can do for you?

3. I need some …

4. There is a great need of …

5. I'm in urgent need of …

6. What else do you need?

7. I'm not sure if you have …

8. How soon can I get it?

9. I'm afraid you have to wait until …

10. Sorry, we don't have the goods you need right now, but we can …

Ⅲ. **Write an E-mail to a website to order goods, telling them about the following information.**

Contents:

1. 向某网站订购你所需要的商品。
2. 说明商品的名称和型号。
3. 说明送货的时间和地点。

Ⅳ. **Give the English words or phrases according to the meanings provided.**

1. _____ the activity of buying things, especially for a company or an organization
2. _____ to find or discover somebody/something
3. _____ the main subject or course of a student at college or university
4. _____ to try to reach an agreement by formal discussion
5. _____ a plan that is intended to achieve a particular purpose
6. _____ that is likely to make money
7. _____ a particular situation or fact that makes you sad or disappointed
8. _____ the people who run and control a business or similar organization
9. _____ fair, practical and sensible
10. _____ a situation in which people or organizations compete against each other

Ⅴ. **Read the following passages and answer the questions.**

The basic principles to make business are to open market and control cost. Usually, it is easier for cost reduced than market developing because the credit of any company decides its market share, it needs a long time to build it up. But sometimes, we face another headache. For example, if you are the manager of a company making sales to two firms. One of them makes purchase once a year but the volume is relatively big, and the payment comes in time. Meanwhile, the other one hopes to reduce its inventory and buy your goods many times and in small lots with low price. Moreover, the latter one is very strict to quality, you have to spend a lot of energy and money to meet its bargaining.

1. Which one is the bigger buyer to you? (   )
   A. Second one.   B. First one.   C. None of them.   D. The same.
2. How is the quality demand of the first one? (   )
   A. No mention in the article.   B. Very low.
   C. Very high.   D. We don't know.
3. What is the meaning of "reduce inventory"? (   )
   A. Low level of goods in warehouse.   B. Low buyer.
   C. Low level of warehouse.   D. Low price of goods.

4. Which one is the same meaning of purchase? (   )
   A. Get something.   B. Selling something.
   C. Making order.   D. Buying goods.
5. What increases a company's market share? (   )
   A. Capital.   B. Credit.
   C. Money.   D. None of them.

Ⅱ. Purchasing Process

The purchasing process usually consists of six stages:
- Identify user need for product or service
- Evaluate potential suppliers
- Supplier selection
- Purchase approval
- Release and receive purchase requirements
- Measure suppliers' performance

However, these stages may vary in different organizations, depending on whether purchasing is to buy a new or repeat item, and also whether there is an approval process for purchases that exceed a specific amount. New items require that purchasing spend much more time evaluating potential sources. Repeat items usually have approved sources already available.

1. Identify User Need for Product or Service(确认产品或服务的用户需求)

The purchasing process begins with identifying materials or services needed by an internal user. Material requirements might include equipment, components, raw materials, or even completely finished products. Examples of service can be a need for computer programmers, transportation carriers, or maintenance service providers. Users may use different ways to communicate with purchasing, such as by phone, word-of-mouth, or through the internal computer networks.

2. Evaluate Potential Suppliers(评估潜在的供应商)

Once a firm identifies potential items to be purchased, it must gather and evaluate information on potential suppliers, and this is the case particularly for a new purchase. A list of potential suppliers can be generated from a variety of resources, including market representatives, trade shows, trade journals, the current suppliers, and the Internet. Although the traditional ways are still widely used and helpful, more and more firms are utilizing the Internet as an aid to search business opportunities since it is effective, efficient and inexpensive.

3. Supplier Selection(选择供应商)

Selecting suppliers is one of the most important activities performed by companies, since mistakes made during this stage can be damaging and long-lasting. When price is a main criteria and the required item or service has clear specifications, competitive bidding is the commonly used method. Generally the lowest bidder receives the contract; otherwise, the buyer must explain why it did not get the contract. However, when non-price variables exist, then the buyer and seller usually negotiate directly. Finally, the purchasing team will select a supplier based on the bids received, or the negotiation result, and then move on to the next stage.

4. Purchase Approval (采购实施)

After the supplier is selected, purchasing grants an approval to purchase the product or service. This is accomplished through issuing a purchase order (PO), also called a purchase agreement. The purchase order will specify the details agreed by the buyer and seller, such as quantity, price, delivery date, method or delivery, and so on. It should be noted that nowadays more and more firms are using computerized databases to perform these tasks and are moving to a "paperless" office.

5. Release and Receive Purchase Requirements(发送和接收采购需求)

At this stage, purchasing or other functional groups must monitor the process carefully. Lots of potential conflicts may occur at this period, since the supplier and buyer are two separated groups in traditional sense and their goals may be in conflict. For example, the supplier wants to produce and ship in an economic size, while the buyer's goal is to minimize inventory and expect small orders and short lead time.

6. Performance Measurements(业绩衡量)

Suppliers' performance is critical to an organization, and evaluation should be conducted on a continuous basis. A supplier that performs well can help organizations be more efficient, produce higher quality products or services, reduce costs, and increase profits. However, very few companies have developed systems to measure their suppliers' performance.

New Words and Phrases

stage [steidʒ] *n.* 阶段,时期
approval [ə'pru:vəl] *n.* 同意,批准
exceed [ik'si:d] *v.* 超过
maintenance ['meintinəns] *n.* 维护
particularly [pə'tikjuləli] *adv.* 特别地,独特地
journal ['dʒə:nl] *n.* 期刊
utilize ['ju:tilaiz] *v.* 利用

aid [eid] *n.* 帮助,辅助
effective [i'fektiv] *adj.* 有效的
efficient [i'fiʃənt] *adj.* 有效率的
grant [grɑ:nt] *v.* 同意,准予
accomplish [ə'kɔmpliʃ] *v.* 完成,实现
issue ['isju:] *v.* 发布
monitor ['mɔnitə] *v.* 监控

conflict ['kɒnflikt] n. 冲突
conduct ['kɒndʌkt] v. 实施,进行
depending on 取决于,视……而定
finished product 成品
word-of-mouth 口头的

trade show 贸易展览
long-lasting 持续长时间的
non-price 非价格
on a continuous basis 持续地

Notes

1. These stages may vary in different organizations, depending on whether purchasing is to buy a new or repeat item, and also whether there is an approval process for purchases that exceed a specific amount. 在不同的组织中,这些阶段可能会有所不同,取决于是重复还是全新的采购,还有是否规定了超过一定限额的采购需要一个批准程序。

2. Material requirements might include equipment, components, raw materials, or even completely finished products. 物料需求可能包括设备、零部件、原材料,甚至是完全的制成品。

3. Although the traditional ways are still widely used and helpful, more and more firms are utilizing the Internet as an aid to search business opportunities since it is effective, efficient and inexpensive. 虽然传统的方法仍然被广泛地使用,也很有帮助,但越来越多的组织逐渐使用互联网来辅助搜寻商业机会,因为它不但有效,效率高而且也不昂贵。

4. Finally, the purchasing team will select a supplier based on the bids received, or the negotiation result, and then move on to the next stage. 最后,采购团队将根据收到的标书或是谈判的结果来选定一家供应商,然后转向下一个阶段。

5. It should be noted that nowadays more and more firms are using computerized databases to perform these tasks and are moving to a "paperless" office. 应该注意到,今天越来越多的企业开始采用计算机数据库来完成这些工作,逐渐走向"无纸化"办公。

6. Suppliers' performance is critical to an organization, and evaluation should be conducted on a continuous basis. 供应商的表现对一个组织来说极为重要,因此应该经常性地进行评价。

Exercises

Ⅰ. Comprehension: True/False/Not mentioned.

1. For any organization, the purchasing process consists of six stages.

2. Repeat items usually have approved sources already available.

3. The purchasing department communicates with internal users by the internal computer networks only.

4. The purchasing department usually uses the Internet as the main source to search suppliers.

5. Bidding is the commonly used method for buyers.

6. Ninety percent of firms now use computerized databases to perform approval tasks and moving to a "paperless" office.

7. Monitoring the purchasing process is necessary and important.

8. Many companies have developed systems to measure their suppliers' performance.

Ⅱ. Fill in the blanks with the words in the following box. Change the forms if necessary.

| identify | maintenance | negotiate | accomplish | goal |
| performance | efficient | effective | bidding | minimize |

1. _____ inventory is one of the goals set by management.

2. Purchasing process begins with by _____ internal needs.

3. With today's technology you can absolutely _____ the dream of a paperless office.

4. Suppliers' _____ is critical for your organization's success in today's competitive environment.

5. The website uses an automatic system to make _____ more convenient and less time-consuming for buyers.

6. The school pays for heating and the _____ of the buildings.

7. _____ communication skills are essential for success in today's knowledge-based society.

8. I was really impressed by their _____ management system.

9. Our _____ is to develop successful, long-term partnerships where our services integrate with your specific needs.

10. _____ contracts requires a lot of skills and rich experience.

Ⅲ. Translate the following sentences into Chinese.

1. Purchasing is slowly but surely receiving greater attention from top management.

2. The purchasing process is a cycle consisting of several stages.

3. The process that buyers use to select suppliers can vary widely depending on the required items.

4. Buyers use different performance criteria when evaluating potential suppliers.

5. Online ordering systems involve direct electronic links from a buyer's system to a seller's system.

Ⅳ. Translate the following sentences into English.

1. 每个公司都有适合自己的采购方法和流程。

2. 这家超市集团每年要从中国购买400个TEU的货物。

3. 利用互联网进行采购已经成为企业采购的常见手段。

4. 采购部门通常负责合同和供应商的管理。

5. 中国官方的采购经理人指数——制造业的一个关键指标——六月跌至50.9。

Ⅴ. Read the following passages and answer the questions.

Unless your company only uses one vendor for each item they purchase, there will inevitably be occasion when a decision has to be made as to which vendor gets our business. There are many different scenarios when this will occur, for example when the item is purchased for the first time and when an item is no longer singly sourced.

Purchasing An Item For The First Time:

When a decision has to be made between vendors, the purchasing department will use some vendor evaluation method to be their tool in the decision. If the item is to be bought for the first time, the purchasing department may have contacted a number of vendors and sent them a Request for Quotation (RFQ). Each vendor would then complete the RFQ with the information that was required. The purchasing department would then use these completed quotations, in conjunction with other information they have collected on the vendors, to make short list for further evaluation or make a final selection. The purchasing department would evaluate the vendors based on a number of criteria they had decided upon which may include objective criteria such as price and warranty and subjective data which would include past experience with the vendor. Based on the weighting given to these criteria the purchasing department would be able to fairly evaluate each vendor.

Choosing Between Vendors:

If the sourcing of an item has been from a single vendor but another vendor has been approved to supply the same item, a decision would need to be made on vendor selection when a requisition has been received by the purchasing department. Many companies use a vendor evaluation tool that allows transaction data to be analyzed to give a comparison between vendors. The vendor evaluation uses criteria that have been determined by the purchasing department to compare vendors such as price, delivery reliability, delivery date adherence and quality of the item. There are many numbers of criteria that can be used in a comparison and these are usually weighted so that important criteria are given more credence(信任).

Conclusion:

Vendor evaluation is important as it can reduce supply chain costs and improve the quality and timeliness of the delivery of items to your company. The skill in evaluating vendors is to determine which criteria are important and the weighting that these criteria are given. It is important to remember that these criteria may be different for each item you are sourcing and possibly different between regions or countries. Objective data is useful to compare the information that you can obtain from each purchase order and goods receipt, but sometimes the subjective data that your purchasing agents can provide such as customer service and the willingness of the vendor to accommodate your requirements, is as or more important in a vendor evaluation.

1. According to the passage, customer service belongs to (   ).
   A. subjective criteria
   B. objective criteria
   C. the most important criterion
   D. the last criterion that should be considered
2. Why does the purchasing department send vendors a Request for Quotation (RFQ)? (   )
   A. The purchasing department needs to prove that they have contacted more than one vendor.
   B. The purchasing department uses RFQ as a tool so that the department staff does not need to go to the vendor for information.
   C. The purchasing department will rely on the information from RFQ to decide which vendor is the best choice.
   D. The purchasing department has contracts with vendors.
3. Which of the following is the definition of "adherence" in Paragraph 3? (   )
   A. To follow the rule decided by both parties.
   B. When someone behaves according to a particular rule, belief, principle etc.
   C. To finish something before headline.
   D. Timeless.
4. Why is vendor evaluation important? (   )
   A. It saves cost.
   B. It guarantees the quality of the items bought.
   C. It guarantees that the delivery time is alright.
   D. All of the above.
5. When evaluating vendors, you should know that (   ).
   A. criteria may vary
   B. RFQ is a must
   C. comparisons should be quantitative
   D. purchasing department need have no direct contact with vendors

Dialogue 2 Ordering Equipment

(*Mr. Li, the purchasing officer in a University is talking with Miss Zhang, the marketing representative of an IT company.*)

Zhang: Good morning. Mr. Li.

Li: Hello. Miss Zhang.

Zhang: We know that the University will build a new computer laboratory. Could you give me some details about that?

Li: Yes. The project will need hundreds of computers, relevant software and accessories.

Zhang: That's great. How will you do that?

Li: Bidding. Companies should provide documents for initial evaluation, such as a copy of financial accounts for the previous three years, etc.

Zhang: I see.

Li: All responses will be fully evaluated according to the agreed criteria, including price, lead-time, quality and suitability of equipment, reputation of supplier, etc.

Zhang: OK. That must include many documents and tables.

Li: Yes. You can get that in our office, or download from our website.

Zhang: Great. May I ask the payment terms?

Li: Payment will be within 45 days of receipt of invoice and goods, but during this period installation and provision of training must be finished.

Zhang: OK. When should we submit the tender document?

Li: No later than 12:00 a.m. on July 21. And you may send it to the address on the invitation in a sealed envelope.

Zhang: That will be no problem for us.

Li: Please note that one printed copy of the tender document must be submitted, together with an electronic one.

Zhang: All right.

Li: You can provide companies or organizations, which have previously purchased the same equipment from you as a reference.

Zhang: That is fine for us. We have sold the similar products to several universities in the past few years.

Li: University contracts offer companies a marketing advantage, as those provide them a showcase to the students, who are potential buyers in the future.

Zhang: That depends. It may or may not work.

Li: Anyway, Please consider this and the University looks forward to receiving a substantial educational discount.

Zhang: OK. I will talk this to my boss.

Li: For more details, you can see from the documents.

Zhang: Thank you very much. We will work on it and submit it on time.

Li: We look forward to seeing it soon. See you.

Zhang: See you soon.

New Words and Phrases

accessory [ækˈsesəri] n. 零件，附件
bidding [ˈbidiŋ] n. 招标
evaluation [iˌvæljuˈeiʃən] n. 评价
criteria [kraiˈtiəriə] n. 标准

receipt [ri'si:t] n. 收到,收据
invoice ['invɔis] n. 商业发票
installation [,instə'leiʃən] n. 安装
envelope ['enviləup] n. 信封,信袋
reference ['refrəns] n. 参考,证明

showcase ['ʃəukeis] n. 展示
substantial [səb'stænʃəl] adj. 真实的
discount ['diskaunt] n. 折扣
financial account 财务报告
tender document 标书

Notes

1. The project will need hundreds of computers, relevant software and accessories. 该项目需要几百台计算机以及相关的软件和零配件。

2. Payment will be within 45 days of receipt of invoice and goods, but during this period installation and provision of training must be finished. 在收到货物和发票之后的 45 天内我们会付款,但在此期间安装与培训必须完成。

3. Please note that one printed copy of the tender document must be submitted, together with an electronic one. 请注意需要上交一份打印的标书,还有一份电子版的。

4. University contracts offer companies a marketing advantage, as those provide them a showcase to the students, who are potential buyers in the future. 大学的合同给公司提供了营销的优势,因为它们提供了一个向学生展示的平台,而这些学生都是将来的潜在购买者。

5. Please consider this and the University looks forward to receiving a substantial educational discount. 请考虑这一点,而且学校期待着实实在在的教育折扣。

Exercises

Ⅰ. **Read the dialogue carefully again and discuss the following questions.**

1. What does the university plan to purchase?
2. How does the university intend to select suppliers?
3. When is the deadline for submitting the tender?
4. Does the university prefer to get references from companies or organizations which have previously bought the same equipment?
5. Does the university ask for installation and training?
6. Why does the university expect substantial discount from suppliers?

Ⅱ. **Brainstorming: Work with your partner, list things which you may concern if you are a purchasing manager.**

| price, installation,_____, _____,_____ |
| delivery,_____,_____,_____ |

Ⅲ. **Write an E-mail to your supplier based on the following information provided.**

1. 确定所需要购买的计算机数量为 50 台。

2. 明确交货时间为两周之内。

3. 付款时间为交货后的一个月之内。

Ⅳ. Give the English words or phrases according to the meanings provided.

1. _____ an extra piece of equipment that is useful but not essential
2. _____ connected with money
3. _____ a list of goods that have been sold, showing what you must pay
4. _____ to offer to pay a particular price for something
5. _____ the act of receiving something
6. _____ a thing you say or write that mentions somebody/something else
7. _____ an amount of money that is taken off the usual cost of something
8. _____ the act of fixing equipment or furniture in position

Supplementary Reading

Buying Overseas

As the growth of international trade continues, the professional standards of buying overseas rise. In many situations such company involvement has arisen due to force of circumstances and has not resulted from any preconceived policy. The end result is sometimes that the company's resources are not always used cost effectively nor are the strategies well conceived. Hence, senior management must devote adequate time and energy to effective planning and the evolvement of sound realizable strategies.

When a company is committed to a policy of buying overseas, it must earmark adequate resources in terms of personnel, finance and accommodation for production, assembly and storage. Such data will feature in the company's budget. Personnel should be professionally qualified in the area of international business with sound linguistic, negotiating and product knowledge skills. Additionally, the executive must be culturally focused with logistic and high-tech computer skills. Furthermore, the buyer must have a good technical knowledge of the product sought and all the ingredients of the overseas contract embracing finance, import duty and documentation.

The buyer must take a keen interest in the supplier's product and company and technical development to ensure it is competitive in the marketplace and cost effective to buy. Regular visits should be exchanged. Company policy on product sourcing overseas requires continuous review in terms of suppliers, price, technical development, general competitiveness and the market environment. Market research should play a major role. The important area is planning.

Planning is the processing of regulating and coordinating activities on a time basis together with the resources necessary to carry out these activities in order to achieve set objectives. Essentially it is a management function and has a strategic focus. Planning is especially important for the complex and diverse process of international purchasing. It yields a great many benefits.

Directions: Read the passage and answer the following Yes/No questions.

1. Do the professional standards of buying rise as the growth of international trade continues? (   )

2. Is the end result sometimes that the company's resources are always used cost effectively and strategically? (   )

3. Must senior management devote some time and energy to effective planning? (   )

4. When a company is committed to a policy of buying overseas, must it earmark adequate resources in terms of personnel, finance and accommodation for production, assembly and storage? (   )

5. Should personnel be professionally qualified in the area of international business with sound linguistic, negotiating and product knowledge skills? (   )

6. The buyer doesn't need to take a keen interest in the supplier's product and company's technical development to ensure it is competitive in the marketplace, does he?
(   )

7. Should regular visits be exchanged? (   )

8. Does market research play a major role? (   )

9. Does planning have a strategic focus? (   )

10. Does Planning yield some benefits? (   )

Unit 8

The Third Party Logistics

◆ Knowledge Learning Objectives 知识学习目标 ◆
- To understand the nature of the third party logistics
- To know the advantages and disadvantages of the 3PL
- To learn situation of 3PL in China

◆ Skill Developing Objectives 技能培养目标 ◆
- Communication skill in searching the 3PL companies
- Communication skill in cooperating with the 3PL companies
- Writing skill in cooperating with the 3PL companies
- Communication skill in evaluating the 3PL companies

Ⅰ. The Nature of the Third Party Logistics

1. What Is the Third Party Logistics(什么是第三方物流)

The most accepted definition of the third party logistics is from the Council of Supply Chain Management Professionals (CSCMP) in America. It defines the term as outsourcing all or much of a company's logistics operations to a specialized company. The Third Party Logistics (3PL) provider is a firm which provides multiple logistics services for use by customers. These firms facilitate the movement of parts and materials from suppliers to manufacturers, and finished products from manufacturers to distributors and retailers. Among the services which they provide are transportation, warehousing, cross-docking, inventory management, packaging, and freight forwarding. So we can see 3PL has the following features at present:

- Integrated (or multi-modal) logistics service provider
- Logistics' consulting service provider

2. Integrated Logistics Service Provider(提供物流整合)

A 3PL provider is regarded as an integrated logistics service provider. Preferably, these services are integrated, or "bundled" together by the provider. Even IT-related activities, which control goods flow such as order processing and inventory management, are also included in the function of the 3PL provider. However, the 3PL provider needs not provide all the services solely, and it can outsource some activities to sub-contractors.

3. Logistics' Consulting Service Provider(提供物流咨询)

Offering consulting services to the firms is an important feature of the 3PL. Many third-party logistics companies have been found to offer services such as logistics information systems, shipment consolidation, warehouse management, carrier selection, rate negotiations, product returns, order fulfillment, and purchasing, etc. In the meantime, the 3PL provider may provide advice and answer customers' requirements concerned with these services.

4. Advantages of 3PL(第三方物流的优势)

One of advantages 3PL users generally agree that it costs less to use contract logistics firms than to carry out the same functions in-house. Logistics being their core business, 3PL firms can lower costs resulting from economies of scale and economies of scope. Likewise, by outsourcing logistics activities, firms can save on capital investments, and thus reduce financial risks. Another advantage of using 3PL is that it enables users to gain competitive advantage, adding measurable value to products, enhancing customer service and assisting in opening new markets. Use of contract logistics enables firms to spend more time pursuing strategic planning and management issues, and focus on their core business, rather than on logistics. The third advantage of using 3PL is that they can provide their clients with expertise and experience that otherwise would be difficult to acquire, or costly to have in-house. Their expertise gained from working with other clients allows users to lower costs and improve customer service.

5. Disadvantages of 3PL(第三方物流的劣势)

Although there are several advantages of using 3PL, some disadvantages also exist. One of them is that firms will lose control over the logistics function, and it may be critical to some firms. Another concern is that there will be more distance from clients, and it is not beneficial to building a close customer relationship. The most uncertain factor is that problem may rise in cooperation with the third party companies, and that may lead to many difficulties.

6. The Future of 3PL(第三方物流的未来)

Without question the future of third party logistics is in the midst of rapid global expansion. Undoubtedly the growth will be a result of the marketplace. Logistics requirements are shaping the market direction, this is fueled by the growth in outsourcing. As logistics capabilities of 3PL providers improve, higher expectations of the services are provided. Higher expectations such as speed remain the same or decline. All 3PL providers will not only meet these expectations, but also need to exceed them. In order for 3PL providers to continue to grow and be competitive they must demonstrate a clear market or cost advantage. Users are looking for logistics expertise, improved service, and lower cost, not outsourcing for the sake of outsourcing. In many organizations such higher expectations can best be met by the use of a 3PL provider. Certainly never before has the logistics industry had the number of major corporations seeking logistics excellences.

New Words and Phrases

council ['kaunsil] n. 委员会
multiple ['mʌltipl] adj. 多样的
facilitate [fə'siliteit] v. 帮助,推动
integrated ['intigreitid] adj. 综合的
consulting [kən'sʌltiŋ] adj. 咨询的
solely ['səuli] adv. 独自地,单独地
enhance [in'hɑ:ns] v. 提高,增强
pursue [pə'sju:] v. 追求,从事

expertise [ˌekspə'ti:z] n. 专门知识
otherwise ['ʌðəwaiz] adj. 另外的; adv. 另外, 不同地
economies of scale 规模经济
sub-contractors 分包商
core business 核心业务
competitive advantage 竞争优势

Notes

1. The most accepted definition of the third party logistics is from the Council of Supply Chain Management Professionals (CSCMP) in America. 最广为接受的第三方物流的定义来自美国供应链管理专业协会。

2. These firms facilitate the movement of parts and materials from suppliers to manufacturers, and finished products from manufacturers to distributors and retailers. 这些企业帮助将零部件和原材料从供应商交付生产者,将制成品由生产者交付分销商或零售商。

3. Offering consulting services to the firms is an important feature of the 3PL. 向企业提供咨询服务也是第三方物流企业一个重要的特点。

4. Logistics being their core business, 3PL firms can lower costs resulting from economies of scale and economies of scope. 物流是3PL的核心业务,他们可以通过规模经济以及区域经济来降低成本。

5. Use of contract logistics enables firms to spend more time pursuing strategic

planning and management issues, and focus on their core business, rather than on logistics. 使用合同物流使企业可以有更多的时间来进行战略策划、从事管理事务，以及集中精力于核心业务而不是物流。

6. The third advantage of using 3PL is that they can provide their clients with expertise and experience that otherwise would be difficult to acquire, or costly to have in-house. 第三个优势是他们可以提供给客户专门的知识和经验，而客户如果想通过另外的方式来获得这些是非常困难的，自己去做成本又很高。

7. Another concern is that there will be more distance from clients, and it is not beneficial to building a close customer relationship. 另外一个担心是疏远客户，这对建立紧密的客户关系是不利的。

 Exercises

Ⅰ. **Pair work: Discuss the following questions.**

1. What is 3PL?
2. What services does the 3PL company often provide?
3. How do you integrate the logistics activities?
4. What are the advantages of 3PL?
5. What are the disadvantages of 3PL?
6. How do you use the advantages of 3PL?

Ⅱ. **Comprehension: True/False/Not mentioned.**

1. The third party logistics provider is a company which provides transportation service only.
2. It costs less to use contract logistics firms than to carry out the same functions in-house.
3. The third party logistics company usually offers consulting service to the firms.
4. The expertise and experience provided by 3PL companies are useful to their clients.
5. The 3PL providers must accomplish all the provided services by themselves.
6. By outsourcing logistics activities, firms can save on capital investments.
7. The use of 3PL is not helpful to building a close customer relationship.
8. Problems will certainly rise in cooperation with the 3PL companies.

Ⅲ. **Fill in the blanks with the words in the following box. Change the forms if necessary.**

| facilitate | define | outsource | multiple | integrated |
| pursue | in-house | result from | expertise | economies of scale |

1. The Internet has been used to _____ the flow of information between 3PL companies and their clients.
2. Speed and cost are key drivers for our customers seeking to _____ their 3PL logistics activities.

3. The _____ and experience from 3PL providers are vital for some companies which are not familiar with the international regulations.

4. The 3PL companies can achieve substantial cost saving due to _____.

5. The 3PL companies usually can provide _____ logistics services for their clients.

6. Manufacturers usually face decisions whether to make the product _____ or not.

7. Clients generally hope that 3PL suppliers can provide _____ services.

8. Sometimes it is difficult to _____ a term in a few words since it usually has too many things.

9. Cost reduction _____ outsourcing is not so obvious, and it varies from industry to industry.

10. Cost saving is one of the important goals for managers to _____.

Ⅳ. Translate the following sentences into Chinese.

1. The Third Party Logistics industry has entered a period of rapid expansion and transformation.

2. We can increase your profits with our expertise in logistics management.

3. We will keep you up to date on both domestic and international shipping requirements.

4. Third Party Logistics providers are commonly classified into the asset-based and the non-asset-based companies.

5. Sometimes the lowest cost is not necessarily the best choice.

Ⅴ. Translate the following sentences into English.

1. 近几年，物流业创造了大量的就业机会。
2. 与其他电子商务企业相比，京东商城的优势是它强大的物流系统。
3. 政府应采取各种有效政策措施，促进物流产业的精细化发展。
4. 电商的迅猛发展，对物流业提出更大的挑战。
5. 有的第三方物流公司专注于为客户提供供应链管理服务。

Dialogue 1　Searching the 3PL Companies

(*Mr. Wang, the logistics officer in a factory, is talking with Miss Zhang, the customer service representative in an international logistics company.*)

Zhang：Hello, what can I do for you?

Wang：Hello. Our company is growing fast in recent years. So we need a logistics company helping us distribute goods to other countries.

Zhang：Well, that is just our strength. Our company provides comprehensive international logistics services.

Wang：Can you introduce your company in brief?

Zhang: Sure. Our company is one of the leading logistics companies in the world, and our global network can help you manage your goods efficiently.

Wang: What are specific features of your service?

Zhang: OK. Our shipping service runs 7 days a week, and it is more time guaranteed than any other company.

Wang: How about your tracking service? Our customers sometimes want to know exactly when the goods can reach their warehouse.

Zhang: That's quite simple. You may track your goods anywhere in the world just on our website.

Wang: Since our business is expanding, many international rules are new to us.

Zhang: We can also provide many value-added services. I think it will be very useful to your company.

Wang: What are they?

Zhang: Such as delivery confirmation, delivers the COD package and collects from the consignee.

Wang: Great, we often use this kind of method, since lots of customers are new.

Zhang: OK. We also provide information based service. It can make your international business easier.

Wang: Really? How does it work?

Zhang: We provide trade information about different countries, such as trade agreement, customs regulations, duty rates, etc.

Wang: Yes. They are very important to us.

Zhang: Usually non-compliance with these government regulations can lead to potential fines or legal actions.

Wang: Exactly.

Zhang: Our strength can help to turn your international trade into a competitive advantage.

Wang: Great. I hope we can have a long-term partnership in future.

Zhang: You can count on us.

New Words and Phrases

strength [streŋθ] *n.* 实力,力量
comprehensive [ˌkɔmpriˈhensiv] *adj.* 全面的,广泛的
leading [ˈliːdiŋ] *adj.* 领先的,最主要的
guarantee [ˌgærənˈtiː] *v.* 保证,担保
track [træk] *v.* 跟踪
compliance [kəmˈplaiəns] *n.* 依从,顺从

fine [fain] *n.* 罚款
in brief   简单扼要地
value-added   增值的
COD (Cash on Delivery)   货到付款
duty rate   税率
long-term   长期的
count on   依靠,指望

Notes

1. Our shipping service runs 7 days a week, and it is more time guaranteed than any other company. 我们的运输服务每周工作七天,比其他任何一家公司更有时间保证。

2. Such as delivery confirmation, delivers the COD package and collects from the consignee. 比如收货确认,货到付款运输并且代收货款。

3. We provide trade information about different countries, such as trade agreement, customs regulations, duty rates, etc. 我们提供各个国家的贸易信息,如贸易协定、海关规定及关税税率等。

4. Usually non-compliance with these government regulations can lead to potential fines or legal actions. 违反这些规定可能会导致罚款或者法律上的诉讼。

 Exercises

Ⅰ. **Read the dialogue carefully again and discuss the following questions.**

1. What kinds of logistics companies Miss Zhang is looking for?
2. What are specific features about the services mentioned in the dialogue?
3. Why does the company need the logistics company helping them collect money from the consignee?
4. Is the information based service helpful to the company?
5. Is Miss Zhang happy with the logistics company so far?

Ⅱ. **Team work: Make up a dialogue according to the following situation and practice it with your partner.**

Situation:

Jim is willing to transport ten cartons of dresses from Dalian to London. He is talking with Peter, a clerk in the transport department of Sino International Logistics Company.

Tips:

1. Shall we discuss the shipment now?
2. As to shipping, there is a problem we have to face …
3. Is it possible for you to …?
4. As for the shipment, the sooner, the better.
5. Can you manage to ship the goods in May?
6. That's the best we can do right now.
7. I see your point, but …, it's really beyond our power.
8. We'll try our best to help you.

Ⅲ. **Write an E-mail to one 3PL provider based on the following information provided.**

Contents:

1. 你所需要的物流服务是国际快递运输。

2. 你需要货到付款服务。

3. 需要他们上门提货。

Ⅳ. **Give the English words or phrases according to the meanings provided.**

1. _____ including all the items, details, facts, or information
2. _____ in a few words, without details
3. _____ most important or most successful
4. _____ to promise to do something
5. _____ to follow the movements of somebody or something
6. _____ a statement that shows something is true, correct or definite
7. _____ the practice of obeying rules or requests made by people in authority
8. _____ to trust somebody to do something

Ⅴ. **Read the following passages and answer the questions.**

Is the freight market still declining, stabilizing or possibly even recovering? The answer seems to vary with every analyst and report that is published. Some analysis see the US economy still suffering with almost ten percent unemployment and the Chinese economy still rather volatile(反复无常的), which of course impacts into the US.

On the other hand, the larger US transportation companies are doing their best to talk their way into a recovery by announcing that freight volumes are somewhat stable and they expect that trend to continue through the third and fourth quarters of 2009. However, is this a result of smaller companies being squeezed out, effectively reducing capacity which in turn increases the bottom line for the larger carriers.

The US freight market is tied to consumer confidence and until spending increases the freight companies will have to look to cost cutting to increase profits or reduce losses. A recent from the US Commerce Department shows that retail sales in May increased by 0.5% over April, but this single indicator does not mean an end to the recession. With the variety of reports showing there is no overall upward trend, the freight companies are still going to have to wait a bit longer for that real good news.

1. In the view of the author, it seems that US economy (   ).

   A. is closely related to Chinese economy

   B. has nothing to do will Chinese economy

   C. is independent from all other economic

   D. is now recovering

2. The unemployment rate in the US nowadays is (   ).

   A. less than 10%   B. exactly 10%

   C. more than 10%   D. far more than 10%

3. Larger transportation companies announced than (   ).

   A. their freight volumes are declining

   B. their freight volumes are stabilizing

C. their freight volumes are recovering

D. their freight volumes of smaller companies are being squeezed out

4. What is the "real good news"? (　　)

A. Is the Freight Market up or down?

B. Freight Market.

C. The Freight Market is decided by larger companies.

D. The US commerce department report.

Ⅱ. 3PL in China

1. 3PL Market Is Growing Rapidly(第三方物流发展迅速)

According to a study conducted recently, the 3PL market is growing significantly in China. Compared to overall logistics services, Outsourcing logistics services in China are reported to be growing by 25 percent per year. In fact, several of the most promising providers in the Chinese market say that they have experienced annual doubling of revenues in the past couple of years.

2. Outsourcing Logistics Activities to Reduce Costs(外包物流为了降低成本)

Chinese respondents are more likely to outsource transportation, warehousing, customs clearance and brokerage, forwarding transportation management and shipment consolidation services to 3PL providers. Conversely, they are less inclined to outsource activities such as freight bill auditing and payment, unlike U. S. respondents. Outsourcing cross-docking activities is not prevalent in China.

Nearly a third of all shippers surveyed cited pressure to reduce logistics costs as a key challenge, and this is the top reason given for outsourcing logistics. As one director of white goods manufacturing noted, "Competition is fierce, and margins are decreasing. So we are looking to external logistics providers to reduce our logistics costs in order to maintain profitability." Other logistics challenges cited by shippers—depending on industry—include the need to shorten cycle time, reduce inventory levels, and improve service/reliability. Some other reasons mentioned are to be able to focus attention on the core business, improve service levels, and simplify complex operations.

3. Multinational Corporations Need Logistics Cooperation(跨国公司需要物流合作)

Most demand for 3PL services in China currently comes from multinational corporations. Multinational manufacturers and importers active in China are more likely to outsource logistics because they have sophisticated logistics needs. The light-asset nature of many importers also means that they must rely heavily on 3PL providers. In contrast, traditional state-owned enterprises are the least likely to use 3PL services, as they have the in-house assets and people to handle logistics. They also lack experience in managing external vendors and can be slow to realize the benefits of outsourcing.

4. Some 3PL Provide Unsatisfying Services(一些第三方物流公司的服务让人不满意)

Some shippers believe that high-quality, well-established providers are few and the industry credibility is also a problem. Although thousands of companies claim to be logistics providers, only half a dozen players are considered reliable, high-quality providers with the scope and scale to fully meet shippers' requirements. "All providers are good at sales and marketing," said one shipper interviewed, "but not so good at operations. They promise much more than they can deliver." Shippers saw most 3PL providers as "trucking companies with poor IT systems".

Generally, shippers tend to see foreign 3PL providers as strong in IT systems, industry/operational expertise, standardized operating processes, and international networks. Chinese 3PL providers are viewed as offering lower prices and as having strong local knowledge and domestic network coverage. Currently, foreign 3PL providers receive nearly all of their revenues from multinationals, primarily because their role has been limited mostly to serve the import/export-related logistics needs of their global clients. For Chinese 3PL providers, revenues are nearly evenly split among Chinese and multinational clients.

New Words and Phrases

study ['stʌdi] n. 研究
promising ['prɔmisiŋ] adj. 有希望的
annual ['ænjuəl] adj. 每年的
respondent [ris'pɔndənt] n. 回答者
prevalent ['prevələnt] adj. 普遍的,流行的
survey [sə:'vei] n./v. 调查
multinational [mʌlti'næʃənəl] adj. 多国的,跨国公司的,多民族的
margin ['mɑ:dʒin] n. 利润

simplify ['simplifai] v. 使简化
sophisticated [sə'fistikeitid] adj. 复杂的
vendor ['vendə] n. 卖主
credibility [,kredi'biliti] n. 可信性
reliable [ri'laiəbl] adj. 可靠的,可信赖的
revenue ['revinju:] n. 收入,税收
split [split] v. 分开,划分
state-owned 国有的

Notes

1. According to a study conducted recently, the 3PL market is growing significantly in China. 据一份最近的研究表明,第三方物流在中国的发展非常迅猛。

2. Competition is fierce, and margins are decreasing. So we are looking to external logistics providers to reduce our logistics costs in order to maintain profitability. 竞争激烈,利润下降。因此为了维持收益,我们希望外部的物流服务提供者可以帮助我们降低物

流成本。

3. Multinational manufacturers and importers active in China are more likely to outsource logistics because they have sophisticated logistics needs. 因为活跃于中国市场的跨国生产企业和进口商有复杂的物流需求，他们更有可能使用外包物流。

4. The light-asset nature of many importers also means that they must rely heavily on 3PL providers. 很多进口商"轻资产"的特性也意味着他们必须更多地依赖于第三方物流服务提供者。

5. Shippers saw most 3PL providers as "trucking companies with poor IT systems". 托运者视这些第三方物流提供者为"缺乏IT系统支持的卡车公司"。

Exercises

Ⅰ. Pair work: Discuss the following questions.

1. How do you understand the situation of 3PL in China?

2. Why do the companies outsource the logistics activities?

3. Multinational companies are more likely to cooperate with the 3PL providers, aren't they?

4. Why are the traditional state-owned enterprises the least likely to use 3PL services?

5. What advantages do the foreign 3PL providers have?

6. Are the shipper satisfied with the 3PL services?

Ⅱ. Comprehension: True/False/Not mentioned.

1. The 3PL market in China is growing significantly in recent years.

2. The Chinese respondents have the similar outsourcing pattern with U.S. firms surveyed.

3. All shippers surveyed cited pressure to reduce logistics cost as a key challenge.

4. To improve service level is not the challenge mentioned by firms.

5. Currently multinational corporations are the main users of 3PL services in China.

6. Many importers with light-asset nature rely heavily on 3PL providers.

7. Most 3PL companies are good at sales and marketing but with poor operations.

8. Reliable and high-quality 3PL providers are nearly half of the total logistics companies.

9. Both foreign 3PL providers and Chinese 3PL providers have their own strengths and weaknesses.

10. Some 3PL providers are "tracking companies with poor IT systems".

Ⅲ. Fill in the blanks with the words in the following box. Change the forms if necessary.

| conduct | benefit | promising | survey | simplify |
| rely on | good at | network | revenue | focus |

1. More and more logistics companies _____ the Internet to transfer information electronically.

2. In order to maintain proper partnerships, supplier evaluation shall be _____ at the end of each year.

3. China is viewed as the most _____ logistics market with huge potentials.

4. A business _____ can be defined as a group of people that have some kind of commercial relationship.

5. Outsourcing logistics will allow manufacturers to be able to _____ on their core business, rather than complicated logistics operations.

6. One of the assumptions underlying outsourcing is that firms are _____ their core business.

7. That company nearly doubled its _____ last year due to the fast growing logistics market.

8. The _____ of outsourcing has not been fully recognized by many firms.

9. E-commerce will greatly _____ businesses processes such as stock control and payment.

10. Customer satisfaction _____ can deliver powerful information and provide ways to gain a competitive advantage.

Ⅳ. **Translate the following sentences into Chinese.**

1. Identify what you are trying to achieve before entering into a relationship with a third party logistics provider.

2. Outsourcing frees them up to concentrate on their core businesses, and the cost savings can be remarkable.

3. If you haven't considered the advantages of third party logistics, you may be missing an opportunity.

4. It is important to find the right-sized 3PLs which are large enough to provide the level of service required, yet small enough to focus on your customer's needs.

5. A contract usually defines the relationships between two parties.

Ⅴ. **Translate the following sentences into English.**

1. 第三方物流被称作合同物流或者外包物流。
2. 第三方物流应根据客户的不同需求提供个性化服务。
3. 京东将与江苏省的商家共享京东物流资源,提供网络店铺、专业市场等。
4. 第三方物流应能为客户提供更多的增值服务。
5. 菜鸟物流整合了众多快递公司的资源为客户服务。

Ⅵ. **Put the following into Chinese.**

Translink Logistics (China) Ltd.

A Brief Timeline

....

October, 2002 "Class A" License Approval

July, 2003 Shanghai Branch Grand Opening

Our Mission
....

1. As a neutral 3PL, we provide total logistics solutions to our clients.
2. We strive to add more value to our customers.
3. To be amongst the leading Logistics Services Providers (LSPs) in China.

Translink Logistics directly engages in all of below activities:
....

- Booking Space
- Stuffing and Unstuffing Containers
- Issuing Cargo Receipts
- Collecting Freight and Other Charges for Authorized Services
- Repairing and Maintaining Containers and Other Equipments
- Arranging and Concluding Contracts with Trucking Companies for Trucking Services
- Inland Transportation
- Direct Contract with Licensed Customs Broker

What We Can Do
....

Import—Booking—Documentation—Warehousing—Trucking—Customs Declaration—Order Tracing—Air Freight—Ocean Freight—NVOCC

Value-added Service

Tallying and Stuffing Supervision—Free Storage (15 days) —Palletizing—Shrinking—Labeling—Fumigation—CFS GOH Handling—Quality Inspection—Vendor Education Program Assembling/Dis-assembling—Inventory Management—Pick and Pack—Barcode Scanning—Customized Reporting—Q. A. Center

Strengths
....

- Strong ties with the Chinese authorities
- Single contact point for the customer—"One-Stop-Stop"
- Strong management support and commitment
- Highly skilled and qualified team
- Solution tailored for customers' needs
- Competitive price

Advantages
....

Compared with other freight forwards, consolidators or logistics companies without "Class A" license, Translink has the advantages of—Issuing own invoices—Issuing cargo receipts—Collecting freight and other charges—Booking with carriers directly and legally—Extending services scope, e. g. distribution—Investing in logistics industry.

Dialogue 2   Evaluating 3PL Companies

(*The following is a conversation between Mr. Lin, the logistics manager in a factory, and Miss Guo, his assistant.*)

Lin: I guess we need some measures to manage those 3PL companies.

Guo: Yes. Sometimes I feel difficult to choose one company. We must set criteria to get a clear result.

Lin: OK. So in your point, how to establish this system?

Guo: There are many 3PL companies we have used, and there are dozens of aspects which are important and should be measured.

Lin: But we don't need to include all companies, and the rule of 20-80 is perhaps still useful.

Guo: Do you mean we only need to consider those companies we often use?

Lin: Yes. We measure companies which we spend much, and those which have the most impact on us.

Guo: OK. I see. And what kinds of measures should be included?

Lin: Cost and delivery performance will be necessary, such as on-time delivery of goods, responsiveness, and resolution of problems.

Guo: Shall we take continuous improvement in service levels into account?

Lin: Yes, that's critical, if we are going to establish long term relationship with those companies.

Guo: Right.

Lin: Next, we must determine the raters who participate in the evaluation process.

Guo: I guess that should be people in our department.

Lin: Yes. But it will be better to include people from other relevant departments. In that way, we can get a deep understanding about these 3PL companies' performance from a broad sense.

Guo: Great.

Lin: So try to work on these three aspects: 3PL companies needed to evaluate, elements for rating and raters for each element.

Guo: OK, I'll do it and give you for correction later.

Lin: Be sure to use quantitative measures if possible.

Guo: Sure.

Lin: OK, please give me before next Friday.

Guo: No problem.

New Words and Phrases

measure ['meʒə] n. 方法,措施   rater ['reitə] n. 评分者
impact ['impækt] n. 影响   quantitative ['kwɔntitətiv] adj. 定量的
must [mʌst] n. 绝对必需的(东西)   dozens of   许多的
responsiveness [ris'pɔnsivnəs] n. 快速反应   continuous improvement   不断改进
resolution [,rezə'lju:ʃən] n. 解决   take into account   考虑,重视

Notes

1. I guess we need some measures to manage those 3PL companies. 我想我们需要一些办法来管理那些第三方物流公司。

2. We must set criteria to get a clear result. 为了获得确切的结果,我们必须设定标准。

3. But we don't need to include all companies, and the rule of 20-80 is perhaps still useful. 但是我们不必包括所有的公司,"二八原则"也许仍然有用。

4. We measure companies which we spend much, and those which have the most impact on us. 我们只评定那些我们花费多的,以及对我们有重要影响的公司。

5. Be sure to use quantitative measures if possible. 如果可能的话,尽量使用定量的方法。

Exercises

Ⅰ. Read the dialogue carefully again and discuss the following questions.

1. Why do they plan to establish an evaluation system?
2. When do they do the evaluation, do they include all companies used? Why?
3. What kinds of measures are mentioned in the dialogue?
4. Who will be the raters participating in the evaluation process?

Ⅱ. Brainstorming: Work with your classmates, and list things which you may consider when establishing an evaluation system.

Ⅲ. Team work: Make up a dialogue according to the following situation and practice it with your partner.

Situation:

Jack shipped his goods a few days ago. Now he wants to know the position of the goods, then he calls the shipper to inquire about his goods.

Tips:

1. I'm willing to check the position of goods.
2. I want to know where my container is.
3. You can use my tracing system to check.
4. The only thing you will do is to connect your computer to the Internet, enter the number of the container, and you will know where your container is.
5. You can call the customer department to check the position.
6. Your goods are in good condition.
7. Your goods are in bad condition.
8. You will get your goods before June 5.

Ⅳ. Write an E-mail to your supplier based on the following information provided.

1. 你对他们近期的服务不满意。
2. 希望他们可以提高改进服务，特别是沟通方面的不足。
3. 告知他们你会经常地对其服务进行监督评价。

Ⅴ. Give the English words or phrases according to the meanings provided.

1. _____ a standard or principle by which something is judged
2. _____ in large numbers, a lot of (people or things)
3. _____ the powerful effect that something has on somebody/something
4. _____ to consider particular facts, circumstances, etc. when making a decision
5. _____ to take part in or become involved in an activity
6. _____ a change that makes something more accurate than it was before
7. _____ connected with the amount or a number of something
8. _____ an official action that is done in order to achieve a particular aim

Ⅵ. Put the following into English.

北京快捷货运代理有限责任公司是主要从事国际货运代理业务的一级专业公司。公司主要承办海运、空运进出口货物的国际代理业务，包括揽货、订舱、仓储、中转、集装箱拼装拆箱、结算运杂费、报关、报检、保险、相关的短途运输服务及咨询业务等。

快捷公司设在北京，自1997年6月成立以来，取得了长足的发展，现设有深圳、广州、上海、天津、大连等九个分公司，以及宁波、连云港、青岛、太原等办事处，并与中国许多内陆地区的货运企业建立了伙伴关系。快捷公司现拥有海运、空运、陆运、报关、销售、计算机、财务等各类技术人员400余人，拥有自己的货运站、海关监管库、车队，能够在中国绝大多数地区为客户提供"门到门"的服务。

快捷公司努力拓展国际货运市场，与世界上知名的海运、空运或物流企业建立了亲密的合作关系，并在中国的某些地区成为它们的指定货运代理。目前快捷公司的国际货运网络已遍及欧、亚、美、非等地区，如与中远、中集、日邮、马士基、东方海外等大中型船公司签订了代理协议，并成功地成为国航、东航、南航、加航、联邦快递、韩亚航空等国内外航空公司的代理。基于上述国内、国际的货运网络，快捷公司可以为中、外客户提供全方位的海、空运输及陆运配送服务。

Ⅶ. Read the following passages and answer the questions.

WASHINGTON-Earlier today, the United States Postal Service and FedEx Express said they have renewed their Global Express (CXG) alliance.

Terms of the agreement were not disclosed. USPS officials said that GXG is comprised of its date-certain international delivery service to more than 190 countries and territories, adding that CXG shipping labels and packaging feature both USPS and FedEx logos.

USPS and FedEx began offering this joint service in July 2004 Prior to that, USPS had a similar arrangement with DHL with GXG, customers drop off packages at their local at which point FedEx picks up those packages sorts them, and handles the country-to-country line haul and final delivery.

USPS and FedEx said that GXG is available at thousands of participating postal retail locations and through Click-N-Ship online at usps.com.

"This partnership make sense, because FedEx does a good job on international shipments and charges a reasonable price", said Doug Caldwell, executive vice president of ParcePool, a parcel consultancy.

A nice feature of GXG cited by Caldwell is that "the price you pay is the price you pay" as there are not as many add-on charges-or accessorial-which can often be extensive with international shipments. And oftentimes, he said shipping internationally with the USPS can be more cost-beneficial than a private carrier due to negotiated discounts. He added if shippers have a clear understanding of their delivery COSTS between point A and point B, particularly if they are subject to an extended area surcharge, shipping with the USPS can be less expensive.

1. Which of the following statements about USPS is NOT correct? ( )
    A. USPS is the abbreviation for the United States Postal Service.
    B. USPS had the CXG alliance with FedEx Express for the first time.
    C. Shipping internationally with the USPS can save money, in accordance with to an executive vice president of a parcel consultancy.
    D. Shipping with the USPS can be less expensive.
2. USPS and FedEx began joint service in ( ).
    A. 2002   B. 2004   C. 2006   D. 2008
3. Why does USPS have partnership with FedEx? ( )
    A. FedEx has Click-N-Ship online.
    B. FedEx has good reputational shipments.
    C. FedEx charges a reasonable price.
    D. Both B and C.

4. In Paragraph 4, the phrase of "prior to" means (   ).
   A. due to   B. before
   C. as a result of   D. in addition to
5. This article must be adapted from (   ).
   A. a science fiction   B. a leaflet
   C. a piece of news   D. a notice

Supplementary Reading

Lloyd's Today

Lloyd's clients, numbered in their millions and located in almost every corner of the world, expect the market to provide a first class service. Indeed, the key role played by Lloyd's in the global reinsurance industry means that the smooth functioning of that industry is dependant upon the market's efficiency and service.

The new leadership of Lloyd's is committed to raising the standards of professionalism and client service and reducing costs throughout the market. During 1993, the chairman, chief executive officer and key people in the market traveled extensively to consult with brokers and clients. They explained the changes under way and the strong future that lies ahead.

Policy production is a critical area. The programs now in progress, to introduce full electronic processing will ensure the fast, accurate production of policies and produce major savings. Lloyd's long-term goal is to create a unified processing structure for the London market thereby providing superior service to clients.

Lloyd's has also formed a specialist claims unit to act on behalf of the whole market in dealing with asbestos, pollution and health hazard claims. The unit's concentration of expertise will enable it to take a leading role in the resolution of the legacy of these industry-wide, long-tail claims for the benefit of clients and insurers alike.

A powerful, well-resourced team is working on the creation of NewCo, which is designed to solve the problems of old, long-tail liabilities and to lay firm foundations for the market's secure and prosperous future. NewCo is committed to meeting the legitimate claims of policy-holders in a fair and equitable manner.

As the Society's capital base has grown, Lloyd's has intensified its efforts to offer the benefits of its expert underwriting skills to hitherto undevelopment markets.

Ⅰ. Read the passage and give a brief answer to each question.
1. Use one or two phrases you've heard to describe that Lloyd's has many clients.
2. How important is Lloyd's in the global reinsurance industry?
3. During 1993 who travelled extensively and why?
4. What is Lloyd's long-term goal?

Ⅱ. **Supply the missing words.**

Lloyd's has also formed a _____ claims unit to act on _____ of the whole market in dealing with _____, _____ and _____ hazard claims. The unit's _____ of expertise will enable it to take a leading role in the resolution of the _____ of these industry-wide, long-tail claims for the _____ of clients and _____ alike.

Unit 9

Supply Chain Management

◆ Knowledge Learning Objectives   知识学习目标 ◆
- To understand the definition of supply chain management
- To know the reason for developing supply chains
- To learn the goal of supply chain management

◆ Skill Developing Objectives   技能培养目标 ◆
- Communication skill in developing a supply chain
- Writing skill in solving the supply chain problem
- Writing skill in establishing the business relationship

Ⅰ. Supply Chain Management

1. Overview of Supply Chain(供应链概述)

Supply chain (also called value chain or demand chain) is the network of the involved companies, through upstream and downstream linkages, in the different processes and activities that produce value in the form of products and services in the hands of the ultimate consumer.

There are five components in the supply chain involving supplier, producer, wholesaler, retailer and customer. Each of the components is called member enterprise of supply chain. The member enterprises must cooperate with each other in order to make the effectiveness maximum in the supply chain management.

For example, a shirt manufacturer is part of a supply chain that goes upstream through the weavers of fabrics to the manufacturers of fibers, and downstream through distributors and retailers to the final consumer. Each of these organizations in the chain is dependent upon each other.

2. The Definition of Supply Chain Management(供应链管理的定义)

There are various definitions of different edition. But in general, supply chain management means the management of upstream and downstream relationships with suppliers and customers to deliver superior customer value at less cost to the supply chain as a whole. The supply chain arrangement links a firm and its distributive and supplier network to end customers. The integrated value-creation process must be managed from material procurement to end-customer product delivery. The integrated supply chain management shifts traditional channel arrangements from loosely linked groups of independent businesses that buy and sell inventory to each other toward a coordinated initiative to increase market impact, overall efficiency, continuous improvement, and competitiveness.

Successful supply chain management requires companies to apply the systems approach across all organizations in the supply chain. When applied to supply chains, the systems approach suggests that companies must recognize the interdependencies of major functional areas within, across, and between firms. In turn, the goals and objectives of individual supply chain participants should be compatible with the goals and objectives of other participants in the supply chain. For example, a company that is committed to a high level of customer service might be out of place in a supply chain comprised of companies whose primary value proposition involves cost containment.

3. Reasons for Developing Supply Chains(供应链发展的原因)

- Greater competitive advantage
- Greater value to consumers
- Reduces the lead time gap
- Faster and smaller deliveries to intermediate customers
- Introduces the concept of increased shareholder value

These reasons give rise to the notion that in future, we will see supply chains competing with supply chains rather than competition between organizations.

4. The Goal of Supply Chain Management(供应链管理的目标)

Since World War II, with the development of the operations research and management science, there has been an increasing interest in supply chain planning and management. Working together, supply chain planners/managers and all members of the front, middle and back end of the supply chain may enhance revenue, cost control, and asset utilization as well as customer satisfaction. Furthermore, software for optimization has been embraced by all of these parties, as it offers mathematical modeling solutions to supply chain problems. For example, a software package might provide an optimum delivery route of the products, from supplier to manufacture. In conclusion, the goal is to optimize efficiency through supply chain management.

Optimization promises to improve a company's supply chain performance in a variety of areas:

- Reducing supply costs
- Improving product margins
- Increasing manufacturing throughput
- Better return on assets

New Words and Phrases

overview ['əuvəvju:] n. 概要
upstream ['ʌp'stri:m] adj. 上游的,溯流而上的
downstream ['daunstri:m] adj. 下游的
linkage ['liŋkidʒ] n. 连接
ultimate ['ʌltimit] adj. 最终的
fabric ['fæbrik] n. 织物,布
fiber ['faibə] n. 纤维
channel ['tʃænl] n. 渠道
arrangement [ə'reindʒmənt] n. 排列,安排
distributive [dis'tribjutiv] adj. 分发的,分配的
integrated ['intigreitid] adj. 综合的,完整的
procurement [prə'kjuəmənt] n. 获得,取得
coordinate [kəu'ɔ:dnit] adj. 协调的,综合的,并列的

initiative [i'niʃiətiv] n. 初步,开始
efficiency [i'fiʃənsi] n. 效率
competitiveness [kəm'petitivnis] n. 竞争力
shareholder ['ʃɛəhəuldə] n. 股东
utilization [,ju:tilai'zeiʃən] n. 利用
optimization [,ɔptimai'zeiʃən] n. 最佳化,最优化
mathematical [,mæθi'mætikəl] adj. 数学的,精确的
modeling ['mɔdliŋ] n. 建模,造型
margin ['mɑ:dʒin] n. 盈余,利润,毛额
throughput ['θru:put] n. 生产量,生产能力
give rise to   引起,导致

Notes

1. But in general, supply chain management means the management of upstream and downstream relationships with suppliers and customers to deliver superior customer value at less cost to the supply chain as a whole. 但概括起来,供应链管理是指以整体供应链的较低成本提供较高顾客价值的、对供应商和客户之间的上下游关系的管理。

2. The integrated supply chain management shifts traditional channel arrangements from loosely linked groups of independent businesses that buy and sell inventory to each other toward a coordinated initiative to increase market impact, overall efficiency, continuous improvement, and competitiveness. 整合的供应链管理改变了传统的渠道安排,从互相买卖存货、联系松散的独立的商业行为,转向能提高市场影响力、整体效率、获得持续增长、增强竞争力的协调的主动行为。

3. Reduces the lead time gap   减少订货至交货的时间间隔

4. Working together, supply chain planners/managers and all members of the front, middle and back end of the supply chain may enhance revenue, cost control, and asset utilization as well as customer satisfaction. 通过协同工作,供应链的计划者或管理者以及供应链的前端、中间和后端的所有成员都能在满足顾客需要的同时增加收入、增强

成本的控制并且使资产得到合理的利用。

 Exercises

Ⅰ. **Pair work：Discuss the following questions.**

1. What is supply chain?
2. What is the definition of supply chain management?
3. As a consumer, are you part of supply chain?
4. What are the disadvantages of the traditional supply chain?
5. What are the reasons for developing supply chains?
6. What is the goal of supply chain management?

Ⅱ. **Fill in the blanks with the words in the following box. Change the forms if necessary.**

| competitiveness | utilization | shareholder | optimization | linkage |
| procurement | throughput | downstream | modeling | margin |

1. The river departed from its original course several miles _____.
2. It now provides a _____ to more than 60 home pages of government agencies and related organizations.
3. We'll try to work as _____ agent on behalf of IBM.
4. _____ is also about the quality and creativity of the people.
5. He resigned in the face of mounting pressure from the _____.
6. We expect to increase _____ of the helicopters.
7. Hi-tech industry has been driving the _____ of the economic structure.
8. She would like to be a film actress, but at present she is _____.
9. The general price level declined by small _____.
10. We have the busiest container port in the world and the busiest international air freight _____.

Ⅲ. **Translate the following sentences into Chinese.**

1. Traditionally, marketing, distribution, planning, manufacturing, and the purchasing organizations along the supply chain operated independently.
2. Supply chain management is "… an integrative philosophy to manage the total flow of a distribution channel from supplier to the ultimate user."
3. The supply chain arrangement links a firm and its distributive and supplier network to end customers.
4. Leading companies are using other tactics in addition to just-in-time and "lean manufacturing" practices.
5. Since World War Ⅱ, with the development of the operations research and management science, there has been an increasing interest in supply chain planning and management.

Ⅳ. **Translate the following sentences into English.**

1. 我们一直都在供应链管理中平衡这两者。
2. 供应链是一个包含供应商、制造商、运输商、零售商以及客户等多个主体的系统。
3. 供应链通常有一家核心企业。
4. 供应链是全过程的战略管理。
5. 成功的供应链管理能够协调并整合供应链中所有的活动。

Ⅴ. **Put The following mail into Chinese.**

Sinolink Express Services Co., Ltd. was set up in 1988 and has become the market leader in China's freight forwarding and logistics industry today. Its business scope covers sea, air, rail freight forwarding, express services and shipping agency services with access to a worldwide network.

Sinolink Ocean Freight Department furnishes Door to Door services to our customers covering Door Pickup, Domestic and Overseas Space Booking, Insurance Covering, Charter Brokerage, Application for Commodity Inspection and Quarantine, Warehouse, Trucking, Door Delivery and other logistics related services. It has the absolute predominance in the routes of Shanghai-Southeast Asia/Australia & New Zealand/America & Canada.

Sinolink air freight forwarding business involves air transportation of import and export cargoes, road-feeder services, customs declaration and clearance, space booking (including charter services), preparation of the relevant transportation documentation, consolidation and distribution.

Sinolink Shanghai Airfreight Department is to implement a quality management system for the whole operation procedures strictly in accordance with the ISO 9002 standards. Its operation procedures are automatically controlled and recorded by computers so that business queries and accounting settlements could be done conveniently and accurately. The personnel of each functional department has passed the professional training courses of CAAC and IATA.

Dialogue 1 Developing a Supply Chain

(*Mr. Li, a local manager of Pacific Department Store, is speaking to Mr. Gao, a district manager of the retail chain.*)

Li: In the past three months, the distributor for our small appliances has often issued back orders. Sometimes we do not receive our goods of the orders for as much as 20 days.

Gao: Really? We're probably losing customers!

Li: Yes, most of them probably don't wait that long. They probably go somewhere else for their appliances.

Gao: Have you any idea how often the customer has to be told the items are out of stock?

Li: I've asked the clerks to write me a note when they have that kind of conversation with a customer.

Gao: We've been using the same distributor for some time. I wonder what's causing the delays.

Li: Have other districts been having these delays? I think they're really costing us some money.

Gao: It's not been mentioned in our meetings; but I'll certainly check on it. Order-to-shelf delays are always costly.

Li: I've been attempting to call the distributor very promptly with our orders, but I haven't always been able to get through by phone during working hours.

Gao: Well, then that's not efficient. If other districts are having similar problems, it's probably time we developed a supply chain very soon.

Li: Do you think it might be time we got our ordering system on-line?

Gao: That would certainly allow our distributor to immediately realize the demand for each item.

Li: Could that kind of communication channel be installed while we're working up the agreements of the supply chain?

Gao: I think so. Then we'd be all the more ready for other companies to join the chain.

Li: That's right. Although from what we've been learning about supply chains, there are some start-up costs in time and capital, it would solve a problem like this one.

Gao: On-line ordering is certainly something to consider. Let me talk to the other managers on our conference call tomorrow and get back to you.

New Words and Phrases

district ['dɪstrɪkt] n. 区域
appliance [ə'plaɪəns] n. 电器,设备
clerk [klɑːk] n. 店员,职员
promptly ['prɒmptli] adv. 迅速地,敏捷地
capital ['kæpɪtəl] n. 资本,资金
department store 百货公司

back order 待发货订单,延期交货
out of stock 无货,断货
check on 核实,核对
get through 打通(电话),到达
on-line 在线的,即时的,在网上的
start-up 启动

Notes

1. In the past three months, the distributor for our small appliances has often issued back orders. 过去三个月里,我们的小家电经销商经常延期交货。

2. Although from what we've been learning about supply chains, there are some

start-up costs in time and capital, it would solve a problem like this one. 据我们所知,虽然建立供应链需要时间和资金方面的启动成本,但供应链管理可以解决这类问题。

 Exercises

Ⅰ. **Oral practice**: Practice the above dialogue with your partner until you can learn the lines by heart.

Ⅱ. **Team work**: Make up a dialogue according to the following situation and practice it with your partner.

Situation:

Mr. Gary is a district manager of the retail chain in America. Mr. Chen is the marketing manager of a textile company in China. Mr. Chen wants to become a supplier to the retail chain. Now they are talking …

Tips:

1. Nice to meet you.

2. I'm really glad to have the opportunity to visit your company.

3. I have brought some catalogues of …

4. We are suppliers of …

5. I think your end-users will be interested in some of our new products.

6. We are thinking of ordering …

7. Our prices compare most favorably with quotation you can get from other manufacturers.

8. We hope to establish regular business relations with you.

9. We'll consider it carefully then we will give you a reply.

Ⅲ. Write an E-mail to your customer, telling them about the following information.

Contents:

1. 为有合作意向的客户介绍你的公司及产品。

2. 附上公司产品的详细资料。

3. 表达成为其供应商的意愿。

Ⅳ. Fill in the blanks with the words in the following box. Change the forms if necessary.

catalogue	favorably	subject to	discount
negotiate	indication	supplier	according to

(Mr. Zhang, a marketing manager of Beijing Machine Tool Products Corporation, is coming to a machinery agency company in Canada. He is talking to Miss Wright, the secretary …)

Z: May I see the manager?

W: I'm afraid he isn't in. Is there anything I can do for you?

Z: Yes, I have brought some _____ of machine tools. I wonder if any of your end-users would like to have a look at them.

W: They certainly would. Would you leave them with me?

Z: We are _____ of machine tools of various types. I think your end-users will be interested in some of our new products.

W: We're thinking of ordering some special kinds of machine tools. We would be interested in your products if they are of the types we want.

Z: As you probably know, we also take orders for machine tools made _____ specifications.

W: How long would it take you to deliver the orders?

Z: About three months after receipt of the covering L/C. It would take longer to deliver the special orders, though never longer than six months.

W: Very well, I'll send your catalogues to those who are interested in. Meanwhile, may I have an _____ of the price? Can I have your price sheet?

Z: Yes, of course, here you are. Our prices compare most _____ with quotations you can get from other manufactures. You'll see that from our price sheet. The prices are _____ our confirmation, naturally.

W: All your quotations are on an F.O.B Vancouver basis. May I ask if you allow any _____?

Z: Please tell me what you have in mind.

W: From European suppliers we usually get a 5% discount, and sometimes 10%.

Z: If your order is large enough, we'll consider giving you some discount.

W: Fine! We'll _____ after we decide how many machine tools we are going to order from you.

Z: When shall I hear from you?

W: Next Friday.

Ⅴ. Read the following passages and answer the questions.

Managers in the last two decades have witnessed a period of change unparalleled in the history of the world, in terms of advances in technology, globalization of markets and stabilization of political economies. With the increasing number of "world-class" competitors both domestically and abroad, organizations have had to improve their internal processes rapidly in order to stay competitive. In the 1960s and 1970s, companies began to develop detailed market strategies, which focused on creating and capturing customer loyalty. Organizations also realized that strong engineering, design and manufacturing functions were necessary in order to support these market requirements. Design engineers had to be able to translate customer needs into product and service specifications, which then had to be produced at a high level of quality and at a reasonable cost. As the demand for new products escalated in the 1980s, manufacturing organizations were required to become increasingly flexible and responsive to modify existing products and processes or to develop new ones in order to meet ever-changing customer needs. As manufacturing capabilities improved in the 1990s, managers realized that material and service input from suppliers had a major impact on their organization's ability to meet customer needs. This led to an increased focus on the supply base and the organization's sourcing strategy. Managers also realized that producing a quality product was not enough. Getting the products to customers when, where, how, and in the quantity that they want, in a cost-effective manner, constituted an entirely new type of challenge. More recently, the era of the "Logistics Renaissance" was also born, recreating a whole set of time-reducing information technologies and logistics network aimed at meeting these challenges.

As a result of these changes, organizations now find that it is no longer enough to manage their organizations. They must also be involved in the management of to manage their organizations. They must also be involved in the management of the network of all upstream firms that provide inputs (directly or indirectly), as well as the network of downstream firms responsible for delivery and after-market service of the product to the end customer. From this realization emerged the concept of the "supply chain".

1. When did the great changes take for the world economy? (　)
   A. 1970.　　　　　　　　　　B. Last 20 years or more.
   C. Last century.　　　　　　　D. Long time ago.
2. What is the meaning of "customer loyally"? (　)
   A. The most important customers for any firm.
   B. Loyal to company.
   C. The customers to buy a lot.
   D. The long term customers.
3. What is the meaning of "Logistics Renaissance"? (　)
   A. Logistics began a new period.
   B. Logistics is reborn.
   C. Logistics has taken economic functions much more before.
   D. Logistics is developing.
4. What is the meaning of "Upstream" for supply chain? (　)
   A. Customers.　　　　　　　　B. Suppliers.
   C. Buyers.　　　　　　　　　　D. A and B.
5. What is the meaning of "Downstream" for supply chain? (　)
   A. Customers.　　　　　　　　B. Suppliers.
   C. Sellers.　　　　　　　　　　D. B and C.

II. Developing Trends in Supply Chain Management

Globalization, price deflation, supply chain competitiveness and customer service are the most prominent trends in the supply chain industry in the 21st century.

1. Globalization(全球化)

We've all heard about this one. Companies close down their operations in Canada or the US and set up or outsource to a company in India, China, Mexico, Africa, etc. While unit labor costs are lower and offer a competitive advantage, the lead time to replenish goods has increased. As a consumer, are you willing to wait another 3~4 weeks for a bicycle that is 20% cheaper than the competition price, or buy a competitor's bicycle now for your long weekend excursion? To minimize stock-outs, these companies often must carry larger inventories which entail higher holding, or carrying costs.

While there may not be a right or wrong answer, what is true is with the advent of trade liberalization and more countries opening their borders to foreign companies. This trend will continue. The challenge, of course, is to manage this more complex supply chain.

2. Price Deflation(价格降低)

The globalization causes more companies flood the market with their lower-priced goods. More enterprises must be processed in the supply chain for the same level of sales. This will result in higher operating costs which in turn will decrease profitability.

3. Supply Chain Competitiveness(供应链竞争)

There is a new notion for how companies must now compete. They can no longer do so in isolation, but must collaborate with their supply chain partners to reduce overall supply chain costs. This requires the management of efficient processes.

For example, a supplier that packs and sends a box of men's shirts to a retailer folds the shirts with a dimension of 10 inches across. The retailer, upon receiving the shirts uses store labor to utilize a folding table to re-fold the shirts at 8 inches across to better accommodate its shelving configuration, as it can display 3 shirts across in their 24 inches display area. If it did not re-fold, only two shirts would fit on the shelf (2×10 inches) and would leave 4 inches as wasted space. If the retailer receives 100 boxes of shirts (and each box contains 24 shirts) it has to fold 2400 shirts! If the average store employee can fold 60 shirts per hour, this represents 40 hours (or 1 week) of labor. At $15 per hour, the cost to do this is $600. Of course, the consumer ultimately pays for this as it is part of the shirt's cost, however it is an unnecessary cost as the supplier can be told to re-fold at 8 inches. The new competitive frontier is across supply chains as they have the potential to significantly reduce costs and increase profitability for companies.

4. Perfect Customer Service(完美的客户服务)

Customer service level measures the performance of the logistics process in an organization; for example, the percentage in-stock for an item or the on-time delivery performance of a transportation provider, etc. While companies like Dell have capitalized on adding value through customer service by offering after-sales support for their products, the basic level of customer service is having the right product available for the customer at the right time. This is achieved by carefully determining a customer service strategy that is linked to the overall logistics and supply chain strategy. As with improving quality, 80% of quality is built into the systems and processes that produce the product, the other 20% is during the production/testing process. Employees at the end of the product line are not likely to increase quality at that point. Similarly, the design of the logistics system is responsible for the level of customer service in an organization.

New Words and Phrases

globalization [ˌgləubəlaiˈzeiʃən] n. 全球化
deflation [diˈfleiʃ(ə)n] n. 降低,缩小,通货紧缩,物价低廉
competitiveness [kəmˈpetitivnəs] n. 竞争
prominent [ˈprɔminənt] adj. 卓越的,突出的
outsource [ˈautsɔːs] v. 外包
replenish [riˈpleniʃ] v. 补充,装满
excursion [iksˈkəːʃən] n. 远足,游览,短程旅行
entail [inˈteil] v. 使必需,使蒙受,使承担,遗传给
advent [ˈædvənt] n. 出现,到来
liberalization [ˌlibərəlaiˈzeiʃən] n. 自由主义化,使宽大
challenge [ˈtʃælindʒ] n. 挑战

flood [flʌd] v. 涌入,进入
profitability [ˌprɔfitəˈbiliti] n. 收益性,利益率
isolation [ˌaisəˈleiʃən] n. 隔离,独立
collaborate [kəˈlæbəreit] v. 合作
dimension [diˈmenʃən] n. 尺寸,尺度
accommodate [əˈkɔmədeit] v. 使适应,容纳
configuration [kənˌfigjuˈreiʃən] n. 构造,结构,配置,外形
measure [ˈmeʒə] v. 衡量
performance [pəˈfɔːməns] n. 履行,表现
similarly [ˈsimiləli] adv. 同样地,类似于
stock-out 断货,缺货

Notes

1. Globalization, price deflation, supply chain competitiveness and customer service are the most prominent trends in the supply chain industry in the 21st century. 21世纪供应链产业发展最突出的趋势是经济全球化,价格降低,供应链之间的竞争及客户服务。

2. While unit labor costs are lower and offer a competitive advantage, the lead time to replenish goods has increased. 企业降低单位劳动成本从而提供了具有竞争力的价格,

但同时补货所需的前置时间却增加了。

3. To minimize stock-outs, these companies often must carry larger inventories which entail higher holding, or carrying costs. 为了将缺货的可能性降到最低,公司必须经常持有更大的库存,但这样导致了更高的持有或处理成本。

4. This will result in higher operating costs which in turn will decrease profitability. 这样会引起更高的运营成本,反过来将会降低利润率。

5. They can no longer do so in isolation, but must collaborate with their supply chain partners to reduce overall supply chain costs. 他们不再孤军奋战,而是与供应链成员共同合作来降低全面的供应链运营费用。

6. The new competitive frontier is across supply chains as they have the potential to significantly reduce costs and increase profitability for companies. 由于供应链具备为企业极大降低成本和增加收益的潜能而成为企业新的竞争领域。

7. Customer service level measures the performance of the logistics process in an organization; for example, the percentage in-stock for an item or the on-time delivery performance of a transportation provider, etc. 在一个组织内部,物流流程的运转程度是用客户服务水平来衡量的,例如,某一商品可供货的百分比或者一个运输供应商能否及时供货等。

8. As with improving quality, 80% of quality is built into the systems and processes that produce the product, the other 20% is during the production/testing process. 就提高产品质量来说,80%的产品质量取决于生产产品的流程和系统,另外20%则取决于产品的生产和检验过程。

 Exercises

Ⅰ. Team work: Discuss the following questions.

1. What are the most prominent trends in the supply chain industry in the 21st century?

2. Why do some companies close down their operations in Canada or the US and set up or outsource to a company in India, China, Mexico, Africa, etc. ?

3. With the advent of trade liberalization and more countries opening their borders to foreign companies, what will happen?

4. The new competitive frontier is across supply chains, isn't it? Why?

5. What is responsible for the level of customer service in an organization?

6. How can the supply chain cost be reduced effectively?

Ⅱ. Fill in the blanks with the words in the following box. Change the forms if necessary.

| deflation | ultimately | advent | accommodate | turbulence |
| prominent | configuration | impeccable | collaborate | entail |

1. I think I'll be all right as soon as the plane gets out of this _____.

2. People are much better informed since the _____ of television.

3. Vendors could charge between $190 and $375 per computer, depending on _____.

4. Every value they created _____ redounded to his boss.

5. As your company's representative, your phone manners should be _____.

6. Tax became a powerful policy instrument to tackle monetary _____.

7. He is a _____ scholar in the field of linguistics.

8. I would ask you to _____ with us in this work.

9. We must _____ ourselves to circumstances.

10. Her intemperance will _____ the curse of insanity upon her innocent children.

Ⅲ. **Translate the following sentences into Chinese.**

1. Dynamic markets, characterized by turbulence from changing consumer demands, lower costs and reduced margins means organizations must reengineer their processes to remain competitive.

2. It requires a great deal of management effort and cooperation to achieve a successful supply chain.

3. The concept of supply chain management is relatively new, however, it is in fact an extension of the logistics.

4. With the numerous advantage of supply chain integration, its management can be a complex challenge.

5. For most manufacturers, the supply chain looks less like a pipeline or chain than an uprooted tree where the branches and roots are the extensive network of customers and suppliers.

Ⅳ. **Translate the following sentences into English.**

1. 供应链管理的目标是提升客户的最大满意度和降低公司的成本。

2. 供应链管理中,一切围绕"以客户为中心"的理念运营。

3. 供应链更加注重围绕核心企业的网链关系。

4. 通过供应链管理,打造企业的核心竞争力。

5. 供应链管理把所有节点企业看作一个整体。

Ⅴ. **Read the following passages and answer the questions.**

Supply Chain is a management tools which is based on the following facts:

1. All products are made by linked suppliers, just like a kind of chain.

2. Every supplier is customer at the same time and controlled by its up supplier, then again controls its customer at the same time.

3. The relation between the two suppliers is competitive and cooperation. If not, no longer term business or deal can be existed. In other words, "they are on the same boat".

4. All the members in the Supply Chain should get profit more or less. If the up suppliers earn total profit, rest of the supplier must loss. All the suppliers in the supply chain should be managed by a specific rule, that is Supply Chain Management (SCM). SCM is a management method, also a software.

SCM has several characters:

1. SCM is single way process, not cycle system.

2. SCM links all the members, including suppliers and end customers, with computer procedure and math.

3. SCM try to get the highest profit on the whole chain. SCM can be used in huge company, or a city economy. General Electronics and Singapore are good examples on adopting SCM.

1. Is SCM a real chain, or a software? (   )

    A. Both yes.   B. Both not.   C. The latter.   D. The former.

2. Every supplier in the supply chain is customer. Is it true or not? (   )

    A. Yes.   B. No.

    C. Yes, but not same time.   D. Not mentioned.

3. SCM can't earn the biggest profit to every member, but a whole chain can. What is your opinion? (   )

    A. I don't think so.   B. Wrong.

    C. Depend.   D. Correct.

4. Is the logistics same as SCM? (   )

    A. Yes.   B. No.

    C. Depend.   D. No mention here.

Dialogue 2   The Possibility of Creating a Supply Chain

(*In an executive board meeting costs of storage are being discussed. The possibility of creating a supply chain is mentioned. The following is a conversation between Mr. Gao and Mr. Huang.*)

Gao: Our marketing department has developed relations with two American companies which are attracted to our product line for their Christmas market. There's a big problem of storing the products as they come to us from the manufacturers. Mr. Huang, what should we do?

Huang: What size orders do we expect to ship?

Gao: They're each ordering two large containers.

Huang: That's a considerable amount of product. We don't want to lose these orders.

Gao: Yes, and I think we ought to have the product all in one place for final shipping.

Huang: How long will we need to store the product?

Gao: There will be a lead-time of 6~8 weeks between early production and actual shipping.

Huang: And for Christmas we'll need to get it shipped to New York by September 1 at the latest.

Gao: Yes, that means storing the product in the hottest part of the summer. We'll need storage that's well ventilated.

Huang: I suppose our manufacturers are concerned that their capital for raw materials will not be replenished until the order is filled; therefore, their ability to rent space for storage is very limited.

Gao: We need some insurance against losses during the storage period.

Huang: I'm concerned about damage and pilferage during the lead-time.

Gao: We need warehouses that are well managed against damage and are secure.

Huang: Can the cost of storage be passed along (become part of the retail price) so that the customer actually contributes to it? (An expense of operating a business is shared by each member of the distribution chain.)

Gao: I think we've been absorbing too much of the storage costs on most of our products. The usual plan, as you know, is that the overhead is shared at each step of manufacturing and distribution. You know, manufacturing, warehousing, shipping, wholesaling each adds 1.6% to the price of the production.

Huang: We need some contractual negotiations regarding these handling costs, including storage and some insurance to cover damage and pilferage while the products are stored.

Gao: Didn't you attend training about supply chain advantages and disadvantages?

Huang: Yes, I did. I'll review my notes. The instructor said we could call him for advice if we wished.

Gao: Get your notes together and meet with me in the morning. I'll make some time in the next 48 hours to research what other companies are doing.

New Words and Phrases

ventilated ['ventileitid] *adj.* 通风的
replenish [ri'pleniʃ] *v.* 补充,补给
rent [rent] *v.* 租,租借,出租
pilferage ['pilfəridʒ] *n.* 偷窃
contribute [kən'tribju:t] *v.* 捐助,捐献,贡献

overhead ['əuvəhed] *n.* 经常性支出,管理经费
contractual [kən'træktjuəl] *adj.* 契约的
executive board 执行委员会
retail price 零售价

Notes

1. There will be a lead-time of 6~8 weeks between early production and actual shipping. 开始生产至实际运输之间的时间有6~8个星期。

2. I suppose our manufacturers are concerned that their capital for raw materials will not be replenished until the order is filled; therefore, their ability to rent space for storage is very limited. 我认为我们的制造商关心的是他们用于采购原材料的资金在订单完成之前将不会得到补充,因此,他们租赁储存仓库的能力是非常有限的。

3. I think we've been absorbing too much of the storage costs on most of our products. The usual plan, as you know, is that the overhead is shared at each step of manufacturing and distribution. 我认为我们在产品上已经花费了太多的储存成本,你知道,按照通常的计划,生产和分销每个环节都应分摊这笔费用。

 Exercises

Ⅰ. Oral practice: Practice the above dialogue with your partner until you can learn the lines by heart.

Ⅱ. Team work: Make up a dialogue according to the following situation and practice it with your partner.

Situation:
Mary is the manager of Pacific Department Store in America. Mr. Tan is the marketing manager of a textile company in China. Now they are talking about the establishment of the supply chain partnership.

Tips:
1. The purpose of my trip this time is mainly to visit our old friends.
2. Thank you for coming all the way to China to visit me.
3. In the past couple of years the business relationships between us have been good.
4. We really appreciate your cooperation.
5. We still got a small problem … out of stock.
6. It's probably time we developed a supply chain.
7. It might be time we got our ordering system on-line.
8. That would certainly allow you to immediately realize the demand for each item.
9. It sounds like a good suggestion, let me …

Ⅲ. Write an E-mail to your customer, telling them about the following information.

Contents:
1. 对双方的长期合作表示肯定和赞许。
2. 探询双方成为供应链合作伙伴的可能性。

3. 征求双方对组建供应链的看法。

Ⅳ. **Fill in the blanks with the words in the following box. Change the forms if necessary.**

| communication | so that | in order to | fork-lift | transportation |
| individually | stack | unless | pile up | mold |

(*An assembly-line producer has changed the packaging of some toys without consulting a distributing company. Miss Zhou, in the receiving department of the distributing company, is speaking with Mr. Xie, the plant manager.*)

Z: Mr. Xie, we have a serious problem in receiving today.

X: What is that?

Z: We just received a large order of toys from ABC Company. They're not in boxes.

X: What problem does that create?

Z: They won't _____ on the pallets for easy movement.

X: What do you mean?

Z: They're in these new plastics _____ to the shape of the toys which are different sizes. I can't stack them in large quantities to be carried by the _____.

X: Can you put them in bags?

Z: Bags! Bags of toys _____ in the trucks will crush each other and cause a lot of damage. They will probably take longer to load and unload too. The bags will have to be handled _____ and those workers have just demanded higher wages.

X: I'll call ABC Company and see why they changed their packaging. I'll let them know this packaging creates problems for _____.

Z: I don't see any immediate solution _____ we buy some large boxes that can be loaded and unloaded with our fork-lifts.

X: Before you buy boxes, let me know what they'll cost.

Z: It seems we need direct _____ up and down the line of production, assembly, and distribution _____ avoid these kinds of problems in the future.

X: This situation definitely shows that we need a supply chain arrangement _____ from begin to end we understand each other's systems.

Z: Sounds like we need another meeting with the District Manager as soon as possible.

Supplementary Reading

Development of Supply Chain Management

In the 1980s the term Supply Chain Management (SCM) was developed, to express the need to integrate the key business processes from end user through original suppliers that provide products, services and information that add value for customers and other stakeholders. The basic idea behind the SCM is that companies and corporations involved in a supply chain by exchanging information regarding market fluctuations, production capabilities etc. can rationalize the processes involved in the supply chain resulting in mutual gains.

If all relevant information is accessible to any relevant company, every company in the supply chain has the possibility to and can seek to help optimizing the entire supply chain rather than sub optimize based on a local interest. This will lead to better planned overall production and distribution which can cut costs and give a more attractive final product leading to better sales and better overall results for the companies involved.

Incorporating SCM successfully leads to a new kind of competition on the global market where competition is no longer of the company versus company form but rather takes on a supply chain versus supply chain form.

The primary objective of supply chain management is to fulfill customer demands through the most efficient use of resources, including distribution capacity, inventory and labor. Various aspects of optimizing the supply chain include cooperating with suppliers to eliminate bottlenecks; implementing JIT techniques to optimize manufacturing flow; and using location/allocation, vehicle routing analysis, dynamic programming and, of course, traditional logistics optimization to maximize the efficiency of the distribution side.

Starting in the 1990s several companies choose to outsource their supply chain management by partnering with a 3PL, Third-party logistics provider.

Ⅰ. **Answer the following questions.**

1. When was the term Supply Chain Management developed?
2. What is the basic idea behind SCM?
3. According to the text, what is the new kind of competition on the global market?
4. What is the primary objective of supply chain management?
5. What is 3PL?

Ⅱ. **Tell whether the following statements are true or false.**

1. The term Supply Chain Management (SCM) was developed in the 1980s. (   )
2. If all relevant information is accessible to any relevant company, every company in the supply chain has the possibility to sub optimize based on a local interest. (   )
3. Nowadays competition on the global market is no longer of the company versus company form but rather takes on a supply chain versus supply chain form. (   )
4. The primary objective of supply chain management is to fulfill customer demands through the most efficient use of resources. (   )
5. Starting in the 1990s several companies choose to outsource their supply chain management by partnering with a 4PL. (   )

Unit 10

Logistics Information Management

♦ **Knowledge Learning Objectives** 知识学习目标 ♦
- To understand the definition of information
- To know the role of the information in logistics
- To get to know the components of information decisions

♦ **Skill Developing Objectives** 技能培养目标 ♦
- Communication skill in receiving the customer
- Communication skill in introducing the present MIS
- Communication skill in introducing the supply chain management information system

---

Ⅰ. The Role of Information Management

1. Importance of Information in Logistics Management(物流管理中信息的重要性)

According to some examples, timely and accurate information is more critical now than at any time in the history of American business. Three factors have strongly impacted this change in the importance of information. Firstly, satisfying, in fact pleasing, customers has become something of a corporate obsession. Serving the customer in the best, most efficient and effective manner has become critical, and information about issues such as order status, product availability, delivery schedule, and invoices has become a necessary part of the total customer service experience. Secondly, information is a crucial factor in the managers' abilities to reduce inventory and human resources requirements to a competitive level. Finally, information flows play an essential role in the strategic planning for and deployment of resources.

A key notion in the essential nature of the information systems in the development and maintenance of successful logistics is the need for virtually seamless bonds within and between organizations. This means creating inter organizational processes and links to facilitate delivery of seamless information between marketing, sales, purchasing, finance, manufacturing, distribution and transportation internally, as well as inter organizationally to customers, suppliers, carriers, and retailers across the logistics. Perhaps more importantly, it means alteration of perspective at the firm's highest levels. Changes in thinking that become necessary include aligning corporate strategies to the paradigm, providing incentives for functions to achieve common goals through the sharing of information, and implementing the technologies to redesign the movement of goods to maximize channel value and lower cost.

2. Role in the Supply Chain(在供应链中的角色)

Information could be overlooked as a major supply chain driver because it does not have a physical presence. Information, however, deeply affects every part of the supply chain in many ways. Consider the following:

Information serves as the connection among the supply chain's various stages, allowing them to coordinate their actions and bring about many of the benefits of maximizing total supply chain profitability.

Information is also crucial to the daily operations of each stage in a supply chain. For instance, a production scheduling system uses information on demand to create a schedule that allows a factory to produce the right products in an efficient manner. A warehouse management system uses information to give the warehouse's inventory visibility. The company can then use this information to determine whether new orders can be filled.

3. Role in the Competitive Strategy(在竞争策略中的角色)

Information is a driver whose importance has grown as companies have used it to become both more efficient and more responsive. The tremendous growth of the importance of information technology is a testimony to the impact information can have on improving a company. Like all the other drivers, however, even with information, companies reach a point where they must make the trade-off between efficiency and responsiveness.

Another key decision involves what information is most valuable in reducing cost and improving responsiveness within a supply chain. This decision will vary depending on the supply chain structure and the market segments served. Some companies, for example, target customers who require certain customized products that carry a premium price tag. These companies might find that investments in information allow them to respond more quickly to their customers. The following examples illustrate this kind of investment.

4. Example 1: Andersen Windows(案例 1：爱德森制窗公司)

Andersen Windows, a major manufacturer of residential wood windows located in Bayport, Mmnesota, has invested an information system that enables it to get customized products to the market rapidly. This system, called "Window of Knowledge", allows distributors and customers to actually design windows to custom-fit their needs. Users can select from a library of more than 50000 components that can be combined in any number of ways. The system immediately gives the customer price quotes and automatically sends the order to the factory if the customer decides to buy. This information investment not only gives the customer a much wider variety of products, but it allows Andersen to be much more responsive to the customer as it gets the customer's order to its factory as soon as the order is placed.

5. Example 2: Dell(案例 2：戴尔公司)

Dell operates differently from most personal computer(PC) manufacturers in that it has invested in building up its own channel—a direct channel to the customer. Most PC manufacturers sell their product to a distributor, who then either sells it to a dealer or a corporate customer. Dell takes orders directly from consumers over the phone and via the Internet. This direct channel required an investment to build, given the added functions Dell must perform. A large part of that cost can be attributed to information. However, with the direct channel model, Dell is able to view the actual consumer demand much sooner than most PC manufactures, and therefore, the company can respond more quickly to changes in consumer needs. Dell can then modify its product offering to meet these new needs. Dell is not the low-cost provider. The company is, however, the most responsive provider, and a large part of its responsiveness is due to the information flow between Dell and its customers' Dell and its suppliers that is made possible by its investment in information.

New Words and Phrases

role [rəul] n. 角色,任务
overlook [,əuvə'lu:k] v. 没注意到,忽视
driver ['draivə] n. 驱动因素
physical ['fizikəl] adj. 物质的,自然的,物理的
presence ['prezns] n. 本质,属性
coordinate [,kəu'ɔ:dineit] v. 调整,整理
crucial ['kru:ʃəl] adj. 至关紧要的
inventory ['invəntri] n. 存货,库存
visibility [,vizi'biliti] n. 可见性,明显度

responsive [ris'pɔnsiv] adj. 响应的,作出响应的
testimony ['testiməni] n. 证词(尤指在法庭所作的),宣言,陈述
segment [segmənt] n. 段,节,片段; v. 分割
customized ['kʌstəmaizd] adj. 定制的
distributor [dis'tribjutə] n. 分销商
channel ['tʃænl] n. 渠道
dealer ['di:lə] n. 经销商,商人

supply chain 供应链
trade-off 交换，协定，交易，平衡
premium price 溢价
information flow 信息流

Notes

1. Information could be overlooked as a major supply chain driver because it does not have a physical presence. 由于不具备具体的表现形式，所以信息作为供应链的一个主要的驱动因素可能被忽略了。

2. Information is a driver whose importance has grown as companies have used it to become both more efficient and more responsive. 信息作为一个驱动因素，它的重要性在于公司运用信息使公司的工作效率和反应速度越来越快。

3. Dell operates differently from most personal computer(PC) manufacturers in that it has invested in building up its own channel—a direct channel to the customer. 戴尔公司与许多个人计算机制造商运作的不同之处在于，它投资建立自己的渠道——一种直接面向顾客的渠道。

Exercises

Ⅰ. **Comprehension questions.**

1. What is the role of information?
2. What's the advantage of the company who has invested in information?
3. What can you get from the cases?
4. Is it possible to build a direct channel to the customer? How can it be done?

Ⅱ. **Cloze test.**

Information is crucial __1__ supply chain performance because it provides the facts that supply chain managers use to make decisions. Without information, a manager will not know what customers want, how much inventory is __2__ stock, and when more products should be produced and shipped. In short, without information, a manager can only make decisions blindly. __3__, information makes the supply chain visible to a manager. __4__ this visibility, a manager can make decisions to improve the supply chain's performance. Without information, it is impossible for a supply chain to deliver products __5__ to customers. With information, companies have the visibility they need to make decisions that improve company and overall supply chain performance. In this sense, information is the most important of the supply chain drivers because without it, none of the other drivers can be used to deliver a high level of performance.

1. A. to   B. for   C. of   D. from
2. A. out of   B. from   C. in   D. at
3. A. Whereas   B. Therefore   C. However   D. Nevertheless
4. A. To be given   B. Giving   C. Given   D. To give

5. A. effective B. effectiveness C. effected D. effectively

Ⅲ. **Translate the following sentences into Chinese.**

1. According to some examples, timely and accurate information is more critical now than at any time in the history of American business.

2. With the goal of reducing total supply chain assets, managers realize that information can be used to reduce inventory and human resource requirements.

3. In this way, information availability can reduce operating and planning uncertainty.

4. Automating and integrating the order process frees time and reduces the likelihood of information delays.

5. In the development and maintenance of the logistics' information systems, both hardware and software must be addressed.

Ⅳ. **Translate the following sentences into English.**

1. 我们公司有一个十分完善的客户服务信息系统。
2. 一个信息系统通常包括硬件和软件。
3. 我们可以通过条形码实现对商品的全程实时跟踪。
4. 近年来,信息流的地位日益提高。
5. 我在这家物流公司的信息技术部门工作。

Ⅴ. **Read the following passages and answer the questions.**

In supply chain management software, the forecast is a calculation that is fed data from real time transactions and is based on a set of variables that are configured(配置) for a number of statistical forecast situations. Planning professionals are required to use the software to provide the best forecast situation possible and often this is left unchecked without any review for long periods. To best use the forecasting techniques in the supply chain software, planners should review their decisions with respect to the internal and external environment. They should adjust the calculation to provide a more accurate forecast based on the current information they have.

Statistical forecasts are best estimates of what will occur in the future based on the demand that has occurred in the past. Historical demand data can be used to produce a forecast using simple linear regression(回归). This gives equal weighting to the demand of the historical periods and projects the demand into the future. However, forecasts today give greater emphasis on the more recent demand data than the older data. This is called smoothing and is produced by giving more weight to the recent data. Exponential(指数的) smoothing refers to ever-greater weighting given to the more recent historical periods. Therefore a period two months ago has a greater weighting than a period six months ago. The weighting is called the Alpha Factor and the higher the weighting, or Alpha factor the fewer historical periods are used to create the forecast. For example, a high Alpha factor gives high weighting to recent periods and demand from periods for a year or two years ago are weighted so lightly that they have no bearing on the overall forecast. A low Alpha factor means historical data is more relevant to the forecast.

Historical periods generally contain demand data from a fixed month, i.e. June or July. However, this introduces error into the calculation as some months have more days than other months and the number of workdays can vary. Some companies use daily demand to alleviate(减轻) this error, although if the forecaster understands the error, monthly historical periods can be used along with a tracking indicator to identify when the forecast deviates(偏离) significantly from the actual demand. The level at which the tracking signal flags the deviation is determined by the forecaster or software and vary between industries, companies and products. A small deviation may require intervention when the product being forecasted is high-value, whereas a low-value item may not require the forecast be scrutinized(细察) to such a high level.

1. Based on this passage, the function of forecast in supply chain management software (   ).

    A. is complaint-free

    B. includes variables that can be and should be updated

    C. is accurate

    D. is not welcomed by the customer

2. "They" in Paragraph 1 refers to (   ).

    A. the forecasting techniques   B. planners

    C. long periods   D. transactions

3. Paragraph 2 focuses on (   ).

    A. the definition of statistical forecasts

    B. linear regression

    C. why statistical forecasts are adopted

    D. how statistical forecasts work

4. The last paragraph tells us (   ).

    A. the history of statistical forecasts

    B. the duration that statistical forecasts work

    C. some circumstances, like problems, of statistical forecasts

    D. the future development of statistical forecasts

5. When writing the passage, the author seems to be (   ).

    A. optimistic about the future of the software

    B. biased to statistical forecasts

    C. objective in introducing statistical forecasts

    D. confident in telling the theory of statistical forecasts

Dialogue 1 Difference between Legacy System and Present System

(Michael, a logistic manager with rich experience in information management, is now talking in his office with Mr. Hunter, a client who wishes to get acquainted with information system.)

Hunter: Hello! Michael. Sorry to trouble you.

Michael: Never mind. Welcome to our company.

Hunter: Today I'd like to know something about the difference between legacy system and present system on information management.

Michael: Oh! It's like this. Legacy systems are older information systems based on mainframe technology that usually work at an operation level on only one stage or even one function within a stage of the supply chain.

Hunter: What's the advantage of the present system ERP?

Michael: Enterprise resource planning, ERP, systems are operational information systems that gather information from across all of a company's functions, resulting in the entire enterprise having a broader scope.

Hunter: A broader scope?

Michael: Yeah! Legacy systems can range from order entry to manufacturing scheduling to delivery, but present systems' scope allows ERP systems to track orders through the entire company from procurement to delivery.

Hunter: Does that mean legacy systems tend to focus solely on a particular function and are built as independent entities with little regard for other systems?

Michael: That's it! For instance, a legacy system might deal only with inventory levels in a particular warehouse in a distributor's network. This system would monitor inventory levels in that warehouse but would likely have difficulty communication with the legacy system that handled transportation for the same distributor; ERP systems monitor material, orders, schedules, finished goods inventory, and other information throughout the entire organization.

Hunter: Thank you! Now I feel I know something about the legacy system and present system.

Michael: It's my pleasure. If you have any more questions about it, don't hesitate to let me know.

Hunter: Sure, I will. See you later.

Michael: See you later.

New Words and Phrases

legacy ['legəsi] n. 遗赠（物），传统
mainframe [meinfreim] n. [计]主机，大型机
range [reindʒ] n. 山脉，行列，范围，射程；
   v. 排列，归类于，使并列，放牧
operational [ˌɔpə'reiʃənl] adj. 操作的，运作的
entry ['entri] n. 登录，条目，进入，入口，[商] 报关手续
track [træk] v. 追踪，跟踪

procurement [prə'kjuəmənt] n. 获得，取得
entity ['entiti] n. 实体
monitor ['mɔnitə] v. 监控
get acquainted with 了解，开始知道
enterprise resource planning (ERP) 企业资源计划
manufacturing scheduling 制造计划
finished goods 制成品

Notes

1. Legacy systems can range from order entry to manufacturing scheduling to delivery, but present systems' scope allows ERP systems to track orders through the entire company from procurement to delivery. 传统的系统涉及从订单录入、生产制造计划到配送，而如今的系统范围允许 ERP（企业资源计划）系统跟踪从采购到配送整个过程的订单。

2. ERP systems monitor material, orders, schedules, finished goods inventory, and other information throughout the entire organization. ERP 系统监控整个组织内部的物料、计划、成品库存以及其他信息。

Exercises

Ⅰ. **Oral practice**：Practice the above dialogue with your partner until you can learn the lines by heart.

Ⅱ. **Team work**：Make up a dialogue according to the following situation and practice it with your partner.

Situation：
Cherry is a clerk of a logistics company. At the moment, she is getting herself acquainted with the inventory system with the help of Mr. White, the assistant to the warehouse manager.

Tips：
1. So good to see you again.
2. Would you please …?
3. Don't you think …?
4. I quite agree with you on that point.
5. I'm not sure about …, but I think …
6. Could you tell me how …?

7. You'd better do ...

8. Take it easy.

Ⅲ. Write an E-mail to your customer, telling them about the following information.
Contents:

1. 邀请你的客户来公司参观并现场演示你公司开发的物流信息管理系统。

2. 表示你合作的诚意,竭诚满足客户对系统功能的要求并提供良好的售后服务。

3. 希望能与客户建立长期的业务关系。

Ⅳ. Fill in the blanks with the words in the following box. Change the forms if necessary.

| district | than | through | building |
| hold | room | module | road |

(*Mr. Zhang, a clerk of transportation department, is making a reservation with one staff of Red Star Information consultation corporation.*)

Operator: Hello. This is Red Star Information Consultation Corporation.

Zhang: Would you please put me _____ to your Technology Service Center?

Operator: _____ the line, please.

(*The line's through now.*)

Zhang: Hello. Is this Technology Service Center?

Clerk: Yes. Can I help you?

Zhang: Can you come to our corporation to show your software on logistical information system, especially the transportation _____?

Clerk: Sure. May I have your name, address and telephone number, please?

Zhang: Yes. Zhang Tao, _____ 201, _____ C, 196 Dalian _____, Hongkou _____, Shanghai. My telephone number is 66678555.

Clerk: Oh, yes, Mr. Zhang, you can expect us no later _____ tomorrow afternoon.

Zhang: Thank you.

Clerk: You're welcome.

Ⅱ. Pick-to-Light Basics

1. What Is Pick-to-Light? (什么是电子标签辅助拣选)

Light-directed order fulfillment systems use light indicator modules mounted to shelving, flow rack, work benches, pallet rack or other storage locations. Whenever product is needed from a particular location, the right indicator turns on, drawing attention where action is required. The operator picks the product quantity displayed. The operator then confirms the pick by pressing the lighted button.

2. Pick-to-Light Is Fast（电子标签辅助拣选迅速）

By lighting the exact location or locations needed, pick-to-light is acknowledged to be the fastest operator-based picking strategy available. In the time it takes to hear and interpret a location number or read a location number from a pick list of an RF terminal screen, the pick-to-light operator is already making the pick.

3. Pick-to-Light Is Accurate（电子标签辅助拣选准确）

By getting the operator to the right location each time the picking process is greatly simplified. Task simplification and replication produces accuracy.

4. Pick-to-Light Is Paperless（电子标签辅助拣选无纸化）

No more pick sheets to handle and tally marks to record. Pick-to-light operators simply scan an order number on the carton or tote and the system does the rest. Paperless picking reduces costs, reduces errors and streamlines operations.

5. Pick-to-Light Is Simultaneous（电子标签辅助拣选同时性）

Other computer-based solutions like RF terminals and voice terminals are sequential in nature. The equipment is only capable of showing what the computer thinks should be the next pick. In a pick-to-light system all locations required in an area light up at once. This allows the operator to choose the best pick path and even pick in both directions.

6. Pick-to-Light Is Team-Based（电子标签辅助拣选以组为单位）

Operators work in assembly line fashion. Each worker's area is called a zone. Orders are passed from zone to zone on a conveyor, cart or other transportation mechanism. This assembly line approach further enhances productivity by reducing walking.

7. Pick-to-Light Is Cost Effective（电子标签辅助拣选节省成本）

Pick-to-light has been around for nearly 20 years. Originally, only the largest facilities with the fastest processing requirements could afford it. Recent advances in technology and the advent of Windows-based computer systems have brought the cost within reach of nearly all order fulfillment operations.

Unit 10 Logistics Information Management

New Words and Phrases

directed [di'rektid] *adj.* 有指导的,定向的
indicator ['indikeitə] *n.* 指示器
module ['mɔdju:l] *n.* 模数,模块,指令舱
mount [maunt] *v.* 爬上,使上马,装上,设置,安放
shelving ['ʃelviŋ] *n.* 架设棚架,作棚架用的材料
rack [ræk] *n.* 架,行李架
pallet ['pælit] *n.* 扁平工具,货盘
accurate ['ækjurit] *adj.* 正确的,精确的
simplify ['simplifai] *v.* 单一化,简单化
tote [təut] *n.* 手提
scan [skæn] *v.* 扫描

streamline [stri:mlain] *adj.* 流线型的
simultaneous [ˌsiməl'teinjəs] *adj.* 同时的,同时发生的
sequential [si'kwinʃəl] *adj.* 连续的,相续的,有顺序的
mechanism ['mekənizəm] *n.* 机械装置
enhance [in'ha:ns] *v.* 提高
advent ['ædvənt] *n.* （尤指不寻常的人或事）出现,到来
tally mark 骑缝号
pick-to-light 电子标签辅助拣选
work bench 工作台

Notes

1. Light-directed order fulfillment systems use light indicator modules mounted to shelving, flow rack, work benches, pallet rack or other storage locations. 灯光指示命令完成系统应用灯光指示器模组置于货架、传送带、工作台、托盘及其他储存地之上。

2. By lighting the exact location or locations needed, pick-to-light is acknowledged to be the fastest operator-based picking strategy available. 通过打开所需货物所在确切位置的指示灯,电子标签辅助拣选被认为是目前可供选择的最快捷的操作员分拣方法。

3. In the time it takes to hear and interpret a location number or read a location number from a pick list of an RF terminal screen, the pick-to-light operator is already making the pick. 在需要花时间从无线射频终端显示屏上的分拣列表中听到和译出一组位置号或读出一组位置号时,电子标签辅助拣选的操作员已经在做分拣了。

Exercises

Ⅰ. **Team work：Discuss the following questions.**

1. What is pick-to-light?
2. What are the features of pick-to-light?
3. Can you speak out the process of using pick-to-light?

Ⅱ. **Study the following words and fill each of the blanks with one of them in right form.**

strategy	higher	individual	key	maximize
entire	enable	craft	broad	affect

The Importance of Information in a Supply Chain

Information is the __1__ to the success of a supply chain because it __2__ management to make decisions over a __3__ scope that crosses both functions and companies. Successful supply chain __4__ results from viewing the supply chain as a whole rather than looking only at the __5__ stages. By taking a global scope across the entire supply chain, a manager is able to __6__ strategies that take into account all factors that __7__ the supply chain rather than just those factors affecting a particular stage or function within the supply chain. Taking the __8__ chain into account __9__ the profit of the total supply chain, which then leads to __10__ profits for each individual company within the supply chain.

Ⅲ. Fill in the blanks with the words in the following box. Change the forms if necessary.

| capture | gather | serve | process | analyze | utilize |
| understand | optimal | electron | combine | install | transfer |

1. IT _____ as the eyes and ears of management in a supply chain.

2. By _____ a supply chain IT system, the company was able to gather and analyze data to produce recommended stocking levels.

3. Wal-Mart has been a pioneer not only in _____ information, but also in _____ how to analyze that information to make good supply chain decisions.

4. Managers must understand how information is _____ and _____ because information is critical to a supply chain's success.

5. An advanced order _____ system is capable of providing a wealth of information to various departments within the organization.

6. The basic functions of warehousing are movement, storage, and information _____.

7. In the future, warehousing will move toward more and more computer _____.

8. The ability to set inventory levels _____ is crucial in the PC business.

9. _____ data interchange applications in logistics are growing among all firms especially among Fortune 500 manufacturers and merchandisers.

10. In the supermarket sector, computers, in _____ with information systems, have been used with great effect.

Ⅳ. Translate the following sentences into Chinese.

1. Information flow was brought into full play in each links of the logistics activities.

2. IT provides the underlying links as well as the data collection and analysis platform for these companies to deliver goods purchased online.

3. Information is of vital importance for supply chain managers as it supplies useful facts to them.

4. The design of a logistics management information system should begin with a survey of customer needs and a determination of standards of performance for meeting these needs.

5. An advanced order processing system is capable of providing a wealth of information to various departments within the organization.

Ⅴ. Translate the following sentences into English.
1. 大数据通过信息系统收集。
2. 物流信息系统是由人员、设备、程序和网络构成的。
3. 物流信息系统不是独立存在的,而是企业信息系统的一部分。
4. 物流信息系统是整个物流系统的指挥和控制系统。
5. 物流系统是企业经营管理系统的一部分。

Ⅵ. Read the following passages and answer the questions.

The characters of modern logistics are huge quantity, quick response and globalization. In order to meet the needs, information technology has become the brain to control them.

Bar code, POS, EDI, GPS and internet are the main choices for the operation of logistics. Bar code system can get the goods information fast and exactly. By the data processing unit, POS system can check the inventory of warehouse at any time. When the super center adopts POS system, it can check the sales record, inventory even cash flow easily. EDI is a magic tool that can translate your documents into electronic data, sent it to your partner in any location by cable. In this way, we don't need to make deal face-to-face. Revise the documents, declare to customs before the shipments arrived, and more. Now, EDI is the most essential information tool for international trade and logistics. All of information tools are based on internet. In today's society, the organs of commercial and government, schools, even individual can make E-commerce with internet. So, Internet is the greatest revolution to influence the mankind.

1. Information technology can help the operation of the logistics, but can't change its future.

Is it correct or not? (   )

  A. Correct.   B. Wrong.

  C. In limited way.   D. The role is not decided.

2. EDI is the core of information technology used in international trade and transportation.

Is it a fact? (   )

  A. Correct.   B. Wrong.   C. Not mentioned.   D. Not clear.

3. What is the meaning of "magic tool" in the paragraph? (   )

  A. Visible.   B. Invisible.

C. Net. D. You can't imagine it.

4. What is most important information technology in the logistics? (　　)

   A. Bar Code.　　B. DOS.　　C. EDI.　　D. GPS.

5. The Internet is a great revolution because it is (　　).

   A. the newest scientific and technology invention

   B. the most advanced technology

   C. the valuable tool

   D. helping the mankind greatly

Dialogue 2　Introduction to Supply Chain Management Information System

(*Wilston was talking with John, they were discussing how to make decisions regarding supply chain management information system.*)

Wilston: Since management information systems play a significant role in every stage of the supply chain by enabling companies to gather and analyze information, at present, our biggest problem is how to make a decision on supply chain management information system.

John: I think there are several general ideas we should take into account.

Wilston: Oh, what are they?

John: Firstly, a management information system that addresses the company's key success factors should be selected.

Wilston: How important about this, John?

John: Every industry and even companies within an industry can have very different key success factors. By key success factors, the two or three elements that really determine whether a company is going to be successful.

Wilston: I am sorry. I don't quite understand what you said. Could you explain it by giving me some examples?

John: Of course. For instance, the ability to set inventory levels optimally is crucial in the PC business, in which product life cycles are short and inventory becomes obsolete very quickly. In contrast, inventory levels are not nearly as crucial for an oil company, in which demand is fairly stable and the product has a very long life cycle. For the oil company, the key to success would depend more on utilization of the refinery. Given these success factors, a PC company might pick a package that is strong in setting inventory levels even if it is weak in maximizing utilization of production capacity, and the oil company should choose a different product, one that excels at maximizing utilization even if its inventory components are not especially strong.

Wilston: Now I understand. I think, Secondly, we should align the level of sophistication with the need for sophistication.

John: I agree with you. Management must consider the depth to which a management information system deals with the firm's key success factors. There can be a trade-off between the ease of implementing a system and that system's level of complexity.

Wilston: That's right!

John: Then, we should make clear that use management information systems to support decision making instead of making decisions. Management must keep its focus on the supply chain because as the competitive and customer landscape changes, there needs to be a corresponding change in the supply chain.

Wilston: That's really a big question we should keep in mind.

John: In addition, as we think about these, we should think about the future at the same time. The key here is to ensure that the software not only fits a company's current needs but also, and even more importantly, it will meet the company's future needs.

Wilston: That's good! By the way, we'll have a meeting next Wednesday to make the decision, please inform all the people concerned.

John: OK.

New Words and Phrases

significant [sig'nifikənt] adj. 有意义的，重要的
element ['elimənt] n. 要素，元素
optimal ['ɔptiməl] adj. 最佳的，最理想的
crucial ['kru:ʃəl] adj. 至关紧要的
obsolete ['ɔbsəli:t] adj. 荒废的，陈旧的
stable ['steibl] adj. 稳定的
utilization [ˌju:tilai'zeiʃən] n. 利用
refinery [ri'fainəri] n. 精炼厂

excel [ik'sel] v. 优秀，胜过他人
align [ə'lain] v. 排列，使结盟
sophistication [səˌfisti'keiʃən] n. 复杂，尖端
implement ['impliment] v. 贯彻，实现，执行
focus ['fəukəs] v. 定焦点，集中
corresponding [ˌkɔris'pɔndiŋ] adj. 相应的
life cycle   生命周期
make clear   弄清楚

Notes

1. Since management information systems play a significant role in every stage of the supply chain by enabling companies to gather and analyze information. 管理信息系统通过使公司能够收集和分析信息的方式，在供应链的各个环节起到了重要作用。

2. A management information system that addresses the company's key success factors should be selected. 应该选择那些能够促进公司成功的关键的管理信息系统因素。

3. Management must consider the depth to which a management information system deals with the firm's key success factors. There can be a trade-off between the ease of implementing a system and that system's level of complexity. 经营必须考虑到针对公司成功因素的管理信息系统的深度，在系统执行的简单性和系统水平的复杂性之间

要有一个平衡。

 Exercises

Ⅰ. Oral practice: Practice the above dialogue with your partner until you can learn the lines by heart.

Ⅱ. Team work: Make up a dialogue according to the following situation and practice it with your partner.

Situation:

Jane is a secretary of a logistical software after-sale service center. Now she is receiving the guest, who is willing to inquiry something about after-sale service.

Tips:

1. If … may I return it?
2. If it doesn't work properly, you may bring it back within a month.
3. The warranty is good for 2 years.
4. We have some questions about after-sale services.
5. Repairs take a maximum of 10 days.
6. How long is the warranty?
7. When will the guarantee expire?
8. All repairs are billed at cost.

Ⅲ. Write an E-mail to your customer, telling them about the following information.

Contents:

1. 询问客户购买的物流信息软件运行的情况。
2. 向客户介绍本公司新开发的系统升级软件。
3. 征询客户对本公司的系统软件的意见或建议。

Ⅳ. Fill in the blanks with the words in the following box. Change the forms if necessary.

cut	accept	confirmed	adjusted	investigated
increased	original	agreement	profit	cancel

(*Mr. James is negotiating the price for the software on logistical information system they developed with Mr. Brown whose corporation intends to buy it …*)

James: According to your requirements, we have _____ our information system and calculated the quotation again. As a result, we should have _____ our price by 5%. But in order to come to _____, our original quote remains unchanged. Hope you can make more efforts.

Brown: Thanks. We've _____ current market price, too. We're surprised that your price is 30% higher compared with other companies. Even if you do not increase it, we can't _____ it.

James: 30%? You can't be serious!

Brown: That has been _____ by our survey. I'm afraid I'll have to _____ the deal if you don't reduce your price.

James: How much do you want to take off?

Brown: 30% according to the listed price.

James: But that's impossible. We won't make any _____ at that price, 10% off the _____ price. How's that?

Brown: No way. 10% is still too high.

James: (thinking about his proposal for a while) All right then. I'll _____ another 3%, and that's my rock bottom price.

Brown: All right, that's a deal.

Supplementary Reading

Information Technology

Just a few years ago, the Internet was something new that not many people knew much about. Now, it is changing the way we communicate and conduct business. The Internet provides users the opportunity to search for information at any time of the day or night and to communicate instantly with the use of E-mail and electronic forms. Exciting technology-based approaches emerge almost daily. Many of these innovations are well suited to the enhancement of logistics management, including Just-in-time, Quick Response, Efficient Consumer Response, and Continuous Replenishment Program. Some kinds of information technology are described briefly as below:

E-Commerce

Electronic commerce is the term used to describe the wide range of tools and technology utilized to conduct business in paperless environment. The main vehicle of E-commerce remains the Internet and the World Wide Web, but uses of E-mail, fax and telephone are also prevalent. The benefits of E-commerce include facilitation of information-based business processes for reaching and interacting with customers, online order taking, online customer service, etc. E-commerce also reduces costs in managing orders and interacting with a wide range of suppliers and trading partners, areas that typically add significant overheads to the cost of products and services.

E-commerce is a way of marketing and selling your products through the Internet. The Internet enables transactions to take place between your company and customers, and between businesses. Business-to-customer is where an actual financial transaction takes place for customers to purchase products. Business-to-business E-commerce is when companies deal with suppliers online. It would be here that your suppliers would take orders, do their billing and get paid online.

E-commerce can be defined as modern business methodology that addresses the needs of the organization, merchants and consumers to cut costs while improving the quality of goods and services and speed of service delivery. E-commerce can allow existing merchants the opportunity to expand their client base. It can also be a cost-effective method of marketing products or services and displaying an inventory of products. Traditionally, merchants had to set up physical show rooms or produce costly catalogues to preview their products. Now, the Internet can provide an electronic vehicle to enhance this marketing strategy.

E-commerce includes the following activities:
- Commercial transactions conducted by Internet, telephone and fax
- Electronic banking and payment systems
- Trade in digitized goods and services
- Electronic purchasing and restocking systems (supply chain management)
- Business-to-business exchange of data
- Delivery of goods and/or services purchased (order fulfillment), and customer service

Electronic Data Interchange

EDI refers to a computer-to-computer exchange of business documents in a standard format. EDI is being utilized to link supply chain members together in terms of order processing, production, inventory, accounting, and transportation. It allows members of the supply chain to reduce paperwork and share information on invoices, orders, payments and inquiries. EDI improves productivity through faster information transmission as well as reduced information entry redundancy.

The benefits of EDI are numerous, including:
- Quick access to information
- Better customer service
- Reduced paperwork
- Increased productivity
- Cost efficiency
- Competitive advantage

Bar Coding and Scanning

Bar coding refers to the placement of computer readable codes on items, cartons, containers, and even railcars. This particular technology application drastically influenced the flows of product and information within the supply chain. In the past, this exchange was conducted manually, with error prone and time-consuming paper-based procedures. Bar coding and electronic scanning are identification technologies that facilitate information collection and exchange, allowing supply chain members to track and communicate movement details quickly with a greatly reduced probability of error. The critical point-of-sale data that organizations such as Wal-Mart provide to their supply chain partners is made possible through the use of bar coding and scanning technology. This technology is critical to transportation companies, such as FedEx, by enabling them to provide their customers with detailed tracking information in a mater of seconds.

Answer the following questions.
1. What kinds of information are applied in the logistics activities?
2. How do you think of E-Commerce?
3. How is EDI used to the logistics industry?
4. How do you understand Bar coding?

参 考 文 献

[1] 庄佩君.物流专业英语[M].北京：电子工业出版社,2005.
[2] 程世平.物流专业英语[M].北京：机械工业出版社,2006.
[3] 白世贞.物流专业英语[M].北京：中国物资出版社,2006.
[4] 景平.物流英语[M].上海：上海财经大学出版社,2004.
[5] 杨瑛.物流英语口语教程[M].天津：南开大学出版社,2005.
[6] 刘醒吾.经贸英语口语[M].北京：外语教学与研究出版社,2003.
[7] 周宁.物流英语[M].北京：电子工业出版社,2007.
[8] 闫静雅.物流专业英语[M].北京：机械工业出版社,2007.
[9] 贾虹.物流英语听力教程[M].天津：南开大学出版社,2005.
[10] 刘冉昕.物流专业英语[M].北京：中国劳动社会保障出版社,2006.
[11] 毛浚纯.物流英语[M].北京：高等教育出版社,2005.
[12] 赵娟.物流英语[M].北京：中国劳动社会保障出版社,2006.
[13] 段云礼.物流英语阅读教程[M].天津：南开大学出版社 2005.
[14] 王洪章,杨昌蓉.物流英语[M].北京：科学出版社,2006.
[15] 王朝晖.实用外贸英语谈判与函电[M].北京：对外经济贸易大学出版社,2006.
[16] 佟勇臣.现代物流专业英语[M].北京：中国水利水电出版社,2006.
[17] 王传见.国际货代物流实务英语手册[M].上海：华东理工大学出版社,2011.
[18] 陈丹,李硕.物流英语脱口秀[M].北京：北京师范大学出版社,2013.
[19] 王睿.物流实务英语[M].北京：清华大学出版社,2013.
[20] 齐利梅,牛国崎.物流专业英语[M].北京：北京理工大学出版社,2013.
[21] Robert Monczka, Roobert Trent, Robert Handfield.采购与供应链管理[M].4 版.北京：清华大学出版社,2010.

Appendix Ⅰ Logistics Terms

A

ABC classification　ABC 分类法
airfreight forwarding agent　航空货运代理
application identifier (AI)　应用标识符
assembly　组配货
attachments of fork lift trucks　叉车属具
automatic guided vehicle (AGV)　自动导引车
automatic identification and data capture (AIDC)　自动识别与数据采集
automatic replenishment　自动补货
automatic storage and retrieval system (AS/RS)　自动化立体仓库

B

bar code　条码
bar code automatic identification technology　条码自动识别技术
bar code system　条码系统
base port　基本港口
bonded area　保税区
bonded factory　保税工厂
bonded goods　保税货物
boned warehouse　保税仓库
box car　箱式车

C

cargo damages rate　货损率
cargo under custom's supervision　海关监管货物
carriage of goods under charter　租船运输
carrier　承运人
carton　周转箱
certificate of origin　原产地证明
chill space　冷藏区
claim for damages　索赔
class rate　等级费率
clearance　清关,结关
cold chain　冷链
collaborative planning, forecasting and replenishment (CPFR)　协同计划、预测与补货
consigner　托运人
consistency of the pallet transit　托盘作业一贯化

container　集装箱
container freight station（CFS）　集装箱货运站
container terminal　集装箱码头
containerization　集装化
containerized transport　集装运输
continuous replenishment program（CRP）　连续补货计划
conveyors　输送机
cost and freight（CFR）　成本加运费
cost，insurance and freight（CIF）　成本加保险费加运费
cross docking　直接换装
customer relationships management（CRM）　客户关系管理
customized logistics　定制物流
customs declaration　报关
customs ratable price　海关估价

D

delivered price　到货价格
distribution　配送
distribution center　配送中心
distribution logistics　销售物流
distribution processing　流通加工
distribution requirements planning（DRP）　配送需求计划
distribution resource planning（DRPⅡ）　配送资源计划
distribution-mode support　配送式保障
dock levelers　站台登车桥
door to door service　门到门运输服务
drawback　出口退税
drive-in rack　驶入式货架
drop and pull transport　甩挂运输

E

e-commerce（EC）　电子商务
economic order quantity（EOQ）　经济订货批量
efficient customer response（ECR）　有效客户反应
electronic authentication　电子认证
electronic clearance　电子通关
electronic data interchange（EDI）　电子数据交换
electronic order system（EOS）　电子订货系统
electronic product code（EPC）　产品电子代码
emergency logistics　应急物流
empty-loaded rate　车辆空驶率
enterprise logistics　企业物流
enterprise resource planning（ERP）　企业资源计划
EPC system　产品电子代码系统

e-procurement 电子采购
e-report 电子报表
export processing zone 出口加工区
export supervised warehouse 出口监管仓库

F

fee for delayed declaration 滞报金
fixed-interval system (FIS) 定期订货制
fixed-quantity system (FQS) 定量订货制
flexible freight bags 集装袋,柔性集装箱
fork lift truck 叉车
free on board (FOB) 装运港船上交货
freeze space 冷冻区
freight unit price 基本运价
fulfillment rate 订单满足率
full container ship 全集装箱船

G

geographical information system (GIS) 地理信息系统
global individual asset identifier (GIAI) 单个资产标识代码
global location number (GLN) 全球位置码
global positioning system (GPS) 全球定位系统
global returnable asset identifier (GRAI) 可回收资产标识代码
global trade item number (GTIN) 全球贸易项目标识代码
goods 物品,货物
goods coding 货物编码
goods consolidation 集货
goods reserves 物品储备
goods stack 货垛
goods-tracked system 货物跟踪系统
grade labeling 等级标签

H

handling/carrying 搬运
hoisting machinery 起重机械
humidity controlled space 控温储存区

I

identification code for commodity 商品标识代码
import and export commodity inspection 进出口商品检验
in bulk 散装化
integrated logistics service 一体化物流服务
integration of military logistics and civil logistics 军地物流一体化
intelligent transportation system (ITS) 智能交通系统

international airline transport　国际航空货物运输
international forwarder　国际货运代理
international logistics　国际物流
international multimodal transport　国际多式联运
international through railway transport　国际铁路联运
inventory control　存货控制
inventory cost　存货成本
inventory cycle time　存货周期
inventory financing　存货质押融资

J

joint distribution　共同配送
joint managed inventory (JMI)　联合库存管理
joint transport　联合运输
just-in-time logistics　准时制物流

L

land bridge transport　大陆桥运输
lean logistics　精益物流
less-than-truck-load transportation　零担运输
lift table (LT)　升降机
liner transport　班轮运输
live pallet rack　重力式货架
load weighing devices　称量装置
loading and unloading　装卸
logistics　物流
logistics activity　物流活动
logistics activity-based costing　物流作业成本法
logistics alliance　物流联盟
logistics center　物流中心
logistics contract　物流合同
logistics cost　物流成本
logistics cost control　物流成本管理
logistics customer service　物流客户服务
logistics enterprise　物流企业
logistics enterprise's liability insurance　物流企业责任保险
logistics facilities　物流设施
logistics information　物流信息
logistics information coding　物流信息编码
logistics information platforms　物流公共信息平台
logistics information technology　物流信息技术
logistics label　物流标签
logistics management　物流管理
logistics management information system　物流管理信息系统

logistics modulus　物流模数
logistics network　物流网络
logistics outsourcing　物流外包
logistics park　物流园区
logistics process reengineering　物流流程重组
logistics resource planning（LRP）　物流资源计划
logistics service　物流服务
logistics service quality　物流服务质量
logistics strategy management　物流战略管理
logistics system simulation　物流系统仿真
logistics technology　物流技术
logistics unit　物流单元

M

manufacturing resource planning（MRPⅡ）　制造资源计划
material requirements planning（MRP）　物料需求计划
military logistics　军事物流
mobile rack　移动式货架
multimodal transport　多式联运

N

national product code（NPC）　全国产品与服务统一代码
non-vessel operating common carrier(NVOCC)　无船承运人

O

order cycle time　订货周期
order picking　拣选

P

packaging/package　包装
pallet　托盘
pallet pool system　托盘共用系统
palletized unit　集装单元
palletized unit implements　集装单元器具
palletizing　码盘作业
point of sale（POS）　销售时点系统
postponement strategy　延迟策略
private warehouse　自营仓库
processing with imported materials　进料加工
processing with supplied materials　来料加工
production logistics　生产物流
public warehouse　公共仓库

Q

quick response（QR）　快速反应

R

rack　货架
radio frequency identification（RFID）　射频识别
radio frequency identification system　射频识别系统
rate of the goods in good condition　商品完好率
receiving space　收货区
regional logistics center　区域物流中心
reverse logistics　逆向物流,反向物流
robot palletizer　垛码机器人

S

safety stock　安全库存,保险库存
sales package　销售包装
scissor lift table　手动液压升降平台车
serial shipping container code（SSCC）　系列货运包装箱代码
settlement of claim　理赔
shipper's own container　自备箱
shipping agency　船务代理
sorting　物品分类
sorting & picking system　分拣输送系统
special railway line　铁路专用线
stacking　堆码
stock　库存
stock-out rate　缺货率
storage　保管
storing　储存
supplier relationships management（SRM）　供应商关系管理
supply chain　供应链
supply chain management　供应链管理
supply logistics　供应物流

T

tally　理货
tallying space　理货区
third party logistics（TPL,3PL）　第三方物流
through goods　通运货物
through transportation　直达运输
total asset visibility　全资产可见性
total cost analysis　物流总成本分析
total social logistics costs　社会物流总费用
total value of social logistics goods　社会物流总额
tow tractor　牵引车
trade item　贸易项目

trade off　效益背反
traffic hub　交通枢纽
trans-customs transportation　转关运输
transaction warehouse　交割仓库
transfer transportation　中转运输
transit cargo　转运货物
transit goods　过境货物
transport package　运输包装
transportation　运输
truck-load transportation　整车运输
twenty-feet equivalent unit (TEU)　标准箱
two-dimensional bar code　二维码

U

unit loading & unloading　单元装卸

V

value-added logistics service　增值物流服务
vendor managed inventory (VMI)　供应商管理库存

W

warehouse goods turnover rate　仓库货物周转率
warehouse ground area utilization rate　仓库面积利用率
warehouse ground load utilization rate　仓库地面载荷利用率
warehouse layout　仓库布局
warehouse management system (WMS)　仓库管理系统
warehouse receipt　仓单
warehouse receipt financing　仓单质押融资
warehouse space utilization rate　仓库空间利用率
warehousing　仓储
warehousing fee　仓储费用
warehousing management　仓储管理
waste material logistics　废弃物物流

Z

zero-inventory technology　零库存技术

Appendix Ⅱ Reference Keys

Unit 1

Text 1

Ⅱ 1. inventory 2. Logistics 3. route 4. flow 5. movement 6. purchase 7. originated 8. storage 9. importance 10. location

Ⅲ 1. 现代物流是全球最富挑战性和激动人心的工作之一。
2. 每个销售商品的公司都需要物流服务。
3. 许多专家都认为物流成本是一座冰山,能看见的仅是小部分,下面看不见的是绝大部分。
4. 随着物流经理的地位和价值日益提高,社会大量需求拥有各种技能、接收过良好教育的专业人才。
5. 物流是一个独特的全球"管道",每天 24 小时运营,计划和协调产品的运输来为全球客户提供服务。

Ⅳ 1. The overall goal of logistics is to achieve an expected level of customer service at the lowest possible total cost.
2. With the help of logistics expert, the company has made a significant rise in profits.
3. The international logistics company plans, coordinates and controls the transport and delivery of products all over the world.
4. In recent years, our country has made very significant developments in the structure, organization and operation of logistics.
5. Ocean transport has been the most important mode of transport in international trade.

Ⅴ 1. B 2. D 3. B 4. D 5. C

Dialogue 1

Ⅳ representative Corporation honestly establish deal with manager luggage a good idea

Text 2

Ⅱ 1. land 2. manager 3. costs 4. success 5. business 6. source 7. alike 8. activities 9. Procurement 10. analysis

Ⅲ 1. 在过去的几十年中,采购在现代物流系统中的角色发生了重要的变化。
2. 包装有消费包装和物流包装两种类型。
3. 为了有效地利用仓库空间,你应该决定下多少订单。
4. 我们应该知道没有一个物流系统适合所有的公司,物流系统的具体活动随着公司不同而随之变化。
5. 将仓库战略性地布置在公司主要的市场附近,就可提高公司的客户服务水平。

Ⅳ 1. Our company has a very perfect customer service system.
2. JD has built a world-class logistics system in 10 years.
3. Excessive inventory will ultimately result in higher than necessary total logistic cost.
4. Freight rates are based on three factors, namely, distances, shipment, and competition.
5. Packaging is a means of ensuring the safe delivery of a product to the consumer at minimum cost.

Appendix Ⅱ Reference Keys

Dialogue 2

Ⅳ keeping   appointment   enlarge   satisfied   reliable   quality   workable
concession   expect   treat

Ⅴ A   G   D   L   J   C   F   I   B   H

Supplementary Reading

Ⅰ 1. Historically, the concept of logistics stems from specific facets of military and industrial management.
2. In the industrial or commercial sector, logistics has been defined to include such activities as material flow, product distribution, transportation, warehousing, and the like.
3. In recent years, systems and products have become more complex as technology advances.
4. The costs associated with system/product acquisition and the costs of logistics support have also been increasing at an alarming rate.
5. Because the current economic dilemma of decreasing budgets combined with upward inflationary trends cause the situation.

Ⅱ 1. F   2. F   3. T   4. F   5. F

Unit 2

Text 1

Ⅱ 1. place utility   2. personal   3. external customers   4. demand   5. analysis
6. convenient   7. output   8. available   9. response   10. retail

Ⅲ 1. 在客户服务绩效方面,可用性就是在预测的基础上提供产品或原料。
2. 基本的客户服务是从可得性、绩效和可靠性三个方面来衡量的。
3. 如果客户的期望值没有完全实现,其他任何东西就都不重要了。
4. 物流绩效随时调整,以适应不断变化的市场需求。
5. 在确定物流策略时,完整理解客户服务的要求是很重要的。

Ⅳ 1. In the logistics system customer service is one of the key activities.
2. The perfect customer service can add value for all members of the supply chain.
3. Customer service is a measure of the effectiveness of the logistics system.
4. As far as we know, the ultimate purpose of any logistics system is to satisfy customers.
5. There is no value in the product or service until it is in the hands of customers.

Ⅴ 1. B   2. D   3. A   4. A   5. B

Dialogue 1

Ⅳ sales assistant   order   gold   in store   convenient   Delivery Department
charge any money   charge   in cash

Text 2

Ⅱ 1. basic service   2. determine   3. role   4. handle   5. coordinate   6. competitive
7. response   8. profits   9. proximity   10. offset

Ⅲ 1. 互联网时代,公司都通过大数据分析客户需求。
2. 因为市场的不断开拓,公司今年年底的效益一定非常可观。
3. 许多公司都在努力创造自己的特色品牌以引导消费者偏好。
4. 实现顾客的期望值是成功物流的一个核心战略。
5. 我们必须把产品尽可能多地分配到尽可能多的地方,这样我们的客户就能方便地得到它们。

Ⅳ 1. In the long run, it is economic to buy good quality goods, even though they cost more.
2. The company should take relevant measures to improve customer service level.
3. You find it difficult to explain what customer service is and does.

4. Many firms have established the customer-focused marketing strategy.

5. In addition to basic service, the company will provide special service for key customers.

Dialogue 2

Ⅳ complained   bothering   satisfied   arrived   beyond   considerate   comment   pleased   feedback   hesitate

Supplementary Reading

1. A   2. B   3. D   4. A   5. D

Unit 3

Text 1

Ⅱ 1. moderate   2. temporary   3. order   4. desired   5. proximity   6. automated
   7. bridge   8. achieve   9. sufficient   10. verified

Ⅲ 1. 仓库的位置由客户、生产地点和产品需求决定。

2. 仓库、庭院、车间、运输设备和零售商店货架上都会存有货物。

3. 仓库管理人员必须减少对需求的响应时间和分派中的错误。

4. 他晋升为仓库经理的要求被拒绝了。

5. 数据仓库应该是为数据分析而设计的。

Ⅳ 1. Warehousing is an important link between the producer and the consumer.

2. Warehouses store all products, and distribution centers hold minimum inventories to satisfy maximum demand.

3. The larger the quantities of goods, the larger the size of warehouse.

4. Warehousing facilities and equipment technologies have improved greatly in recent years.

5. Products must be stored for later use and consumption.

Dialogue 1

Ⅳ forwarding   allocate   shelves   acquainted   chassis   discharging   exported   end

Text 2

Ⅱ 1. strategic   2. expanding   3. inventory   4. warehouse   5. stocks   6. reordered
   7. cause   8. balance   9. declining   10. specialize

Ⅲ 1. 库存广泛存在于供应链的每一个环节中,从供应商的原材料、制造商的加工过程到分销商和零售商持有的产成品。

2. 库存存在的原因是供给和需求的失配。

3. 企业必须持有额外的库存以满足需求的变化,以防万一。

4. 如果产品需求相对稳定,但原材料是季节性的,那么当无法获得原材料时就必须保证成品库存满足需求。

5. 不论你将货物存放在公共仓库,租用的私人仓库还是你自己的仓库,你都必须承担储存费用。

Ⅳ 1. Replenishing inventory will only be a temporary stimulus without an increase in consumer demand.

2. Some stores inventory their stock once a week.

3. The product will first look for the local inventory system.

4. The aim of inventory management is to minimize the amount of material in stock.

5. The classification of products is necessary for the application of choosing inventory.

Ⅴ 1. B   2. D   3. B   4. C   5. B

Dialogue 2

Ⅳ　1. warehousing　　2. shipping, handling　　3. Purchasing　　4. running firms　　5. minimum

Ⅴ　1. materials, goods, warehouse　　2. customer service　　3. Purchasing, needs

　　4. Inventories, period

Ⅵ　1. D　　2. C　　3. A　　4. A　　5. D

Supplementary Reading

1. The important warehouse activities in the warehouse include handling, receiving, in-storage handling, shipping, and storage.
2. Order selection is one of the major activities within warehouses. The selection process requires that materials, parts, and products be grouped to facilitate order assembly. After it is incorporated into a machine.
3. The active storage concept includes flow-through distribution, which uses warehouses for consolidation and assortment while maintaining minimal or no inventory in storage.
4. Extended storage, a somewhat misleading term, refers to inventory in excess of that required for normal replenishment of customer stocks.

Unit 4

Text 1

Ⅱ　1. cheapest　　2. important　　3. maritime　　4. movement　　5. features　　6. low

　　7. door-to-door　　8. unique　　9. proportion　　10. advantage

Ⅲ　1. 管道可以一周七天、一天二十四小时运作,只需要更换运输的产品和进行必要的维修保养。

　　2. 水运特别适合于大量的、散装的、单位价值低的货物。

　　3. 水路运输的主要缺点是运输范围和速度受到限制。

　　4. 两方就运输方式问题最终达成一致。

　　5. 运费主要取决于运输距离、装运条件和竞争条件三种因素。

Ⅳ　1. If the cost of railway transportation is high, we prefer sea transportation.

　　2. Air transport is the safest mode of transportation.

　　3. Recently the company have laid an underground pipeline.

　　4. The company has the highest transportation cost in the total logistics cost.

　　5. The development potential of air transport is huge.

Dialogue 1

Ⅴ　1. D　　2. A　　3. A　　4. B　　5. B

Text 2

Ⅱ　1. focus on　　2. load volume　　3. facilitate　　4. relationship　　5. fulfill　　6. transport lane

　　7. value-added　　8. advantage　　9. contact　　10. automated

Ⅲ　1. 运输费用占到商品总成本的20%并不稀奇。

　　2. 铁路运输只能提供车站之间的服务,而不能提供门到门的运输。

　　3. 你们必须在6月前交货,否则我们就赶不上销售季节了。

　　4. 我们通知供货单位及时安排公路或铁路运输以便及时装船。

　　5. 空运业务不断增长,某些商品如新鲜食品、鲜花以及贵重物品是最佳选择。

Ⅳ　1. Distribution is the most recent logistics link to consumers.

　　2. Zara air expresses goods from its single distribution center in Spain, usually in small quantities.

　　3. Milk will be sent from the distribution center to the supermarkets in Beijing.

4. The goods are not allowed partial shipment.

5. I'm sorry to tell you that we are unable to give you a definite date of shipment for the time being.

Dialogue 2

Ⅴ　1. A　　2. D　　3. B　　4. C　　5. D

Supplementary Reading

Ⅰ　1. Maersk Logistics China opened in mid June a large National Distribution Center(NDC) in Jiu ting Town in Shanghai.

2. The new Maersk Logistics facility is about 14000 sqm large and is located in the jiuting economic development zone of Songjiang District, an ideal location for an integrated logistics center in the greater Shanghai area, The NDC is conveniently linked to Shanghai's outer expressway, providing easy access to and from key ports, roads and other distribution channels for importers, local manufacturers and exporters.

3. The new NDC will offer customers specialized Supply Chain Management services including cross docking, storage, sorting facilities, import, export, and distribution in China.

4. Maersk Logistics provides customized solutions for integrated supply chain management, warehousing and distribution, and sea and airfreight transport in the international logistics market.

Ⅱ　1. F　　2. T　　3. F　　4. F

Unit 5

Text 1

Ⅱ　1. confuse　　2. fulfill　　3. containers　　4. exterior　　5. discard　　6. appealing
　　7. significance　　8. withstand　　9. widespread　　10. insufficient

Ⅲ　1. 包装对仓储和物资搬运作业至关重要,它在全球日益受到关注。

2. 不论遇上什么样的环境,包装是用来保护产品,在它最终到达消费者手中的这段过程中,保护产品状态完好。

3. 新型材料和智能保护性包装系统有助于减少环境负担。

4. 良好的包装能够有效利用存储空间、运输空间以及重量的约束条件。

5. 这种包装材料在产品上架之前就被丢弃,所以消费者将不会看到这种包装。

Ⅳ　1. Industrial packaging has an important impact on the cost and efficiency of logistics.

2. Confirm they have received your package.

3. Packaging is an important part of logistics.

4. Different products require different sales packages.

5. In recent years, logistics packaging technology has made rapid progress.

Dialogue 1

Ⅳ　consignment　　take place　　record　　damp-proof　　rest　　safety　　a lot of　　worry about

Ⅴ　1. C　　2. B　　3. D　　4. C　　5. A

Text 2

Ⅱ　1. dictate　　2. reinforce　　3. instill　　4. entice　　5. oddly　　6. shun　　7. marketplace
　　8. residual　　9. standpoint　　10. forbid

Ⅲ　1. 在过去的两年里,这家公司为了满足消费者的需要,增加了它的包装业的投资。

2. 良好的包装能对仓库的陈列、设计和仓库的总体生产效率产生积极的影响。

3. 我们一个纸箱装两打,每箱毛重25公斤。

4. 我们已经特意加固包装,以便使货物可能遭到的损坏减小到最低限度。

5. 包装的真正艺术在于把被包装物包装成好看、紧凑的形状,并使其在粗率的运送过程中保持这种形状。

Ⅳ 1. Our packages are recyclable.
2. Packaging materials need to meet the needs of green logistics.
3. Environmental packaging is the development trend of future logistics.
4. The transport packaging of cold chain logistics is in urgent need of improvement.
5. In the development of smart logistics, packaging technology needs to be improved constantly.

Ⅴ 1. A   2. C   3. D   4. C   5. D

Dialogue 2

Ⅳ suggestion   Go ahead   improvement   attractive   function   fall into love
    lost   eye-catching   handle   reinforce

Supplementary Reading

Ⅰ 1. Prior to World War Ⅱ, packaging was used primarily to surround and protect products during storage, transportation, and distribution.
2. After World War Ⅱ, manufacturers began to view packaging as an integral element of overall business marketing strategies to lure buyers.
3. The importance of consumer packaging was elevated in the United States during the late 1970s and 1980s.
4. During the late 1970s and 1980s, rapid post-war economic expansion and market growth waned.
5. Today, good package design is regarded as an essential part of successful business practice.

Ⅱ 1. F   2. F   3. T   4. T   5. F

Unit 6

Text 1

Ⅱ 1. A   2. C   3. D   4. B   5. C   6. A   7. C   8. C   9. D   10. B

Ⅲ 1. 多式联运也可以被视作一种解决方法,在某些情况下也会起作用。
2. 控温集装箱可以向有特殊要求的货物提供相应的服务。
3. 随着国际贸易的发展,集装箱服务受到越来越广泛的欢迎。
4. 在集装箱运输出现前,散装货运很难达到规模经济效益。
5. 马士基海运公司是全世界最大的航运公司之一,在全球范围内从事海运服务。

Ⅳ 1. Economic globalization has created more challenges for the infrastructure of inter-modal transport.
2. I propose inter-modal transport. The goods can be carried first by rail to Ningbo and then by sea to London.
3. The use of container has greatly improved the logistics efficiency.
4. The freight rate of the FCL is lower than the LCL.
5. The international freight forwarding company can provide the LCL service.

Ⅴ 1. C   2. D   3. B   4. A   5. A

Text 2

Ⅱ 1. document   2. cargo   3. transport   4. destination   5. receipt   6. negotiable
   7. functions   8. exporters   9. insurance   10. amount

Ⅲ 1. 海上贸易最重要的单证之一就是提单。
2. 货物清单提供装上船的货物信息。

3. 托运单是托运人托运货物的承诺，也是填制提单的依据。

4. 提单的主要当事人包括托运人、收货人、通知方和承运人。

5. 大幅收据是承运人承认收到货物并装船的依据。

Ⅳ 1. The B/L shows that when the shipping company received the goods, they were in apparent good condition.

2. The second B/L was marked as original.

3. The copy B/L is not negotiable.

4. B/L is divided into many categories from different angles.

5. A large number of documents are used in international logistics.

Ⅴ 1. B 2. C 3. A 4. A

Supplementary Reading

1. (1) In terms of whether or not the goods are on board: On Board B/L and Received for Shipment B/L

(2) On the basis of the apparent condition of goods noted: Clean B/L and Unclean (or Foul) B/L

(3) In the light of different characteristics of consignees: Straight B/L, Order B/L and Open (or Bearer) B/L

(4) In terms of modes of transport: Direct B/L, Transshipment B/L, Through B/L and Combined Transport (or Container) B/L

(5) In conformity with the form and clauses: Long Form B/L and Short Form B/L

2. (1) On Board B/L is issued by the carrier or its agent when all the goods are loaded on board of the ship, and must bear the name of the ship and the date of shipment. Received for Shipment B/L is issued by the carrier or its agent when the goods are under his control before loaded on boarded the shipment.

(2) When the shipping company writes on the B/L "The goods loaded are in apparent good order", this B/L is a clean one. When the shipping line gives such an indication as "The goods loaded are not in apparent good order" or "The packing is broken or … is polluted, etc.", this B/L is a foul one and non-negotiable at the bank.

(3) Straight B/L has a specified name in the column of consignee, which means that the goods can only be received by the specified person. Order B/L does not have a specified name but the phraseology of "To order", or "To the order of …" in the column of consignee.

(4) Under Direct B/L, the goods will be directly carried to the port of destination without transshipment, while with transshipment under Transshipment B/L. Through B/L is a development of these two B/L. Under Through B/L, the goods will at least be carried by two different modes of transport before arriving at the port of destination. A multi-modal operator responsible for the whole voyage issues combined Transport B/L, involving two or more different kinds of transport. This kind of B/L is usually used in container transport and may be a Received for Shipment B/L, but a Through B/L must be a Clean Shipped B/L.

(5) A Long Form B/L has detailed clauses printed on its back concerning the transport of goods so as to solve any possible disputes. While a Short Form B/L does not have such clauses on its back.

3. Straight B/L has a specified name in the column of consignee, which means that the goods can only be received by the specified person and the B/L cannot be transferred to a third person. So it is not negotiable.

Unit 7

Text 1

Ⅱ 1. F 2. T 3. N 4. T 5. T 6. F 7. F 8. N 9. F 10. T

Ⅲ 1. B 2. D 3. D 4. D 5. A

Ⅳ 1. 采购的最重要职责之一是正确地选择供应商。
2. 大多数公司把采购作为主要的供应链活动。
3. 采购部门进行许多活动来保证为公司创造价值。
4. 供应商有助于区别生产商的最终产品和服务。
5. 运作良好的供应商有助于企业更有效率地运作、生产更高质量的产品和服务、降低成本和增加利润。

Ⅴ 1. Purchasing contributes to the firm's efficiency and effectiveness in many ways.
2. Purchasing goods and services are one of the largest elements of costs for many firms.
3. The company purchased new hardware for the construction of the database.
4. Procurement has become an important part of supply chain management.
5. Purchasing is not just buying raw materials.

Dialogue 1

Ⅳ 1. purchasing 2. identify 3. major 4. negotiate 5. strategy 6. profitable
7. unfortunately 8. management 9. reasonable 10. competitive

Ⅴ 1. B 2. A 3. A 4. D 5. B

Text 2

Ⅰ 1. F 2. T 3. F 4. F 5. N 6. N 7. T 8. F

Ⅱ 1. Minimizing 2. identifying 3. accomplish 4. performance 5. bidding
6. maintenance 7. Effective 8. efficient 9. goal 10. Negotiating

Ⅲ 1. 采购逐渐接受来自高层领导更大的关注。
2. 采购流程包括了几个阶段的周期。
3. 需求产品不同,买方选择供应商的流程也随之变化。
4. 当评估潜在供应商时,买方使用不同的衡量标准。
5. 在线订货系统包括从买方系统到卖方系统的直接电子联络。

Ⅳ 1. Each company has its own purchasing methods and procedures.
2. The supermarket group has to purchase 400 TEU of cargos from China every year.
3. The use of the Internet for procurement has become a common means of enterprise procurement.
4. The procurement department is usually responsible for contract and supplier management.
5. China's official purchasing managers' index — a key measure of the manufacturing sector-dropped to 50.9 in June.

Ⅴ 1. A 2. C 3. A 4. D 5. A

Dialogue 2

Ⅳ 1. accessory 2. financial 3. invoice 4. bid 5. receipt 6. reference
7. discount 8. installation

Supplementary Reading

1. Yes 2. No 3. No 4. Yes 5. Yes 6. No 7. Yes 8. Yes 9. Yes
10. No

Unit 8

Text 1

Ⅱ 1. F 2. N 3. T 4. T 5. F 6. T 7. N 8. F

Ⅲ 1. facilitate 2. outsource 3. expertise 4. economies of scale 5. multiple
6. in-house 7. integrated 8. define 9. resulted from 10. pursue

Ⅳ 1. 第三方物流业已经进入快速扩张和转型时期。
2. 我们可以利用在物流管理方面的专业知识来增加你的利润。
3. 我们可以让你及时跟上国内和国际的船运需求。
4. 第三方物流提供者一般分为资产型和非资产型公司。
5. 有时最低的成本并不是最佳的选择。

Ⅴ 1. In recent years, the logistics industry has created a large number of employment opportunities.
2. Compared with other e-commerce enterprises, JD's advantage is its powerful logistics system.
3. The government should adopt various effective policy measures to promote the fine development of the logistics industry.
4. The rapid development of e-commerce develops a greater challenge to the logistics industry.
5. Some third-party logistics companies focus on providing supply chain management services to customers.

Dialogue 1

Ⅳ 1. comprehensive 2. in brief 3. leading 4. guarantee 5. track 6. confirmation
7. compliance 8. count on

Ⅴ 1. A 2. A 3. B 4. D

Text 2

Ⅱ 1. T 2. F 3. F 4. F 5. T 6. T 7. T 8. F 9. T 10. T

Ⅲ 1. rely on 2. conducted 3. promising 4. network 5. focus 6. good at
7. revenue 8. benefit 9. simplify 10. survey

Ⅳ 1. 在与第三方物流企业建立合作关系之前，你需要清楚希望达到的目标。
2. 物流外包可以使企业集中在自己的核心业务上，成本的节约也是可观的。
3. 如果你还没有认识到第三方物流的优点，你可能会失去这次机会。
4. 与适当规模的物流公司合作是非常重要的，公司大到能够提供你所需要的服务，但又小到能够专注于客户的需求。
5. 一份合同界定了双方的合作关系。

Ⅴ 1. The 3PL is called contract logistics or outsourcing logistics.
2. Third party logistics should provide personalized service according to customers' different needs.
3. JD will also share its logistics resources with merchants within Jiangsu province to provide online stores and professional markets, etc.
4. The 3PL should provide customers with more value-added services.
5. Cainiao logistics integrates the resources of many express delivery companies for customer service.

Dialogue 2

Ⅴ 1. criteria 2. dozens of 3. impact 4. take into account 5. participate
6. correction 7. quantitative 8. measure

Ⅶ 1. B 2. B 3. D 4. B 5. C

Supplementary Reading

Ⅰ 1. Numbered in their millions and located in almost every corner of the world.
   2. It plays the key role.
   3. The chairman, chief executive officer and key people. To consult with brokers and clients.
   4. To create a unified processing structure for the London market thereby providing superior service to clients.

Ⅱ specialist   behalf   asbestos   pollution   health   concentration   legacy   benefit   insurers

Unit 9

Text 1

Ⅱ 1. downstream   2. linkage   3. procurement   4. Competitiveness   5. shareholder
   6. utilization   7. optimization   8. modeling   9. margin   10. throughput

Ⅲ 1. 传统意义上供应链中的营销、配送、计划、生产和采购部门各自独立经营。
   2. 供应链管理是一种一体化哲学,管理着分销渠道中货物从供应商到最终用户的整个流动过程。
   3. 供应链管理把一家公司及其分销、供应网络和其最终用户联系起来。
   4. 除了采用准时制生产及精益制造之外,很多著名的大公司还采取了其他的经营策略。
   5. 自从第二次世界大战以来,随着运筹学和管理科学的发展,人们对供应链计划及管理的兴趣与日俱增。

Ⅳ 1. We always balance the two in supply chain management.
   2. A supply chain is a system that includes multiple principals, including suppliers, manufacturers, transporters, retailers, and customers.
   3. There is usually a core business in a supply chain.
   4. The supply chain is the strategic management of the whole process.
   5. Successful supply chain management can coordinate and integrate all activities in the supply chain.

Dialogue 1

Ⅳ catalogues   suppliers   according to   indication   favorably   subject to   discount   negotiate

Ⅴ 1. B   2. D   3. A   4. B   5. A

Text 2

Ⅱ 1. turbulence   2. advent   3. configuration   4. ultimately   5. impeccable   6. deflation
   7. prominent   8. collaborate   9. accommodate   10. entail

Ⅲ 1. 动态市场的特点就是,从客户需求、降低成本和利润合理化等多方面进行战略规划,以使市场维持长久竞争力。
   2. 要取得供应链的成功,需要在管理和合作上付出很大的努力。
   3. 供应链管理相对来说是一个比较新的概念,但其事实上就是物流管理的一个延伸。
   4. 整合供应链带来的众多优势,使其管理成为一个巨大的挑战。
   5. 对大多数制造商来说,与其说供应链像个管道或链条还不如说更像棵连根拔起的大树,它的枝干和根是客户和供应商建立起来的广泛延伸的网络。

Ⅳ 1. The goal of supply chain management is to maximize customer satisfaction and reduce the cost of the company.
   2. In supply chain management, everything revolves around the concept of "customer-centric".
   3. The supply chain focuses more on the network chain of core enterprises.

4. Through supply chain management, the company build the core competitiveness of the enterprise.
   5. The supply chain management considers all joint enterprises as a whole.
Ⅴ 1. C   2. A   3. D   4. D

Dialogue 2

Ⅳ   stack   molded   fork-lifts   piled up   individually   transportation
     unless   communication   in order to   so that

Supplementary Reading

Ⅰ 1. In the 1980s the term Supply Chain Management (SCM) was developed.
   2. The basic idea behind the SCM is that companies and corporations involved in a supply chain by exchanging information regarding market fluctuations, production capabilities etc. can rationalize the processes involved in the supply chain resulting in mutual gains.
   3. On the global market where competition is no longer of the company versus company form but rather takes on a supply chain versus supply chain form.
   4. The primary objective of supply chain management is to fulfill customer demands through the most efficient use of resources, including distribution capacity, inventory and labor.
   5. 3PL, third-party logistics provider, is a firm that specializes in providing logistics services and which is independent from the manufacturer's division.
Ⅱ 1. T   2. F   3. T   4. T   5. F

Unit 10

Text 1

Ⅱ 1. A   2. C   3. B   4. C   5. D
Ⅲ 1. 通过一些例子发现,现在及时、准确的信息比美国商务历史上任何时候都要重要。
   2. 为了实现降低供应链总资产的目标,经理们意识到使用信息可以降低库存和对人力资源的需求。
   3. 这样,信息可用性能够降低操作和规划的不确定性。
   4. 订单处理的自动化和一体化可节约时间和减少信息耽搁的可能性。
   5. 在物流信息系统的发展和维持中,硬件和软件均应受到重视。
Ⅳ 1. Our company has a perfect customer service information system.
   2. An information system generally consists of hardware and software.
   3. We can now perform real time tracking of products with bar codes
   4. In recent years, the status of information flow has been increasing.
   5. I work in the information technology department of this logistics company.
Ⅴ 1. B   2. B   3. D   4. C   5. C

Dialogue 1

Ⅳ   through   Hold   module   Room   Building   Road   District   than

Text 2

Ⅱ 1. key   2. enables   3. broad   4. strategy   5. individual   6. craft   7. affect
   8. entire   9. maximizes   10. higher
Ⅲ 1. serves   2. installing   3. capturing,understanding   4. gathered,analyzed   5. processing
   6. transfer   7. utilization   8. optimally   9. Electronic   10. combination
Ⅳ 1. 信息流在物流活动中的各个环节上发挥了应有的作用。
   2. 信息技术提供了潜在的联系,还为这些递送在线出售商品的公司提供了数据收集和分析的

3. 信息对供应链经理们很重要,因为它向他们提供实用的事实。
4. 对物流管理信息系统的设计要从对顾客需求的调查和为满足顾客需求执行标准的决定开始。
5. 先进的订单处理系统能够向组织内不同部门提供许多信息。

Ⅴ 1. Big data is collected through the information system.
2. Logistics information system is composed of personnel, equipment, program and network.
3. Logistics information system is not independent, but is part of enterprise information system.
4. The logistics information system is the command and control system of the whole logistics system.
5. The logistics system is part of the enterprise management system.

Ⅵ 1. B   2. A   3. B   4. C   5. D

Dialogue 2

Ⅳ adjusted   increased   agreement   investigated   accept   confirmed   cancel
Profit   original   cut

Supplementary Reading

1. E-commerce, electronic data interchange, bar coding and scanning are applied in the logistics activities.
2. Electronic commerce is the term used to describe the wide range of tools and technology utilized to conduct business in paperless environment.
3. EDI is being utilized to link supply chain members together in terms of order processing, production, inventory, accounting, and transportation.
4. Bar coding refers to the placement of computer readable codes on items, cartons, containers, and even railcars.

Appendix Ⅲ International Logistics Vocabulary

A

@ at
20' container 20英尺柜
3PL 第三方物流
40' container 40英尺柜
40' HQ 40高柜
A/ agent
A/C account
A/F air freight
A/P airport
Abbreviation 简称,缩写
ABD aboard
aboard 上船
above-mentioned fees 以上所提的费用
ABT about
ABV above
acceptable 可接受的
acceptance 接受
acceptance for carriage 承运
accessorial charges 附件费
accident handling 装卸事故
accordingly 一致地
account 账目,客户
account No. 账号
accountant 会计员
accounting 会计
accredited 被认可的
accumulated 积累的
ACK acknowledge 承认
ACPT accept
acquaintance 熟人
acquire a new customer 赢得新客户
ACTL actual
actual weight 实际重量
ad val 从价
ADD addition

additional 额外的
address 地址;称呼;向……提出
ADMIN administration 管理
administration 管理
ADV advise
advise 通知
AFTN afternoon
agency agreement 代理协议
agency network 代理网络
agent 代理
AGN again
agreement 协议
AGRMT agreement
AGT agent
air freight 空运
air waybill 空运单
airborne 上飞机的
Airline fuel surcharge 航空燃油附加费
airlines 航空器
all in rate (AL) 全价
all water 全水
allocate 分配
allowable 可允许的
AMNDMT amendment 修改
AMT amount
annual reports 年报
annually 每年地
APL 总统轮船
applicable 适用的
apply 申请,适用
appointments 约会,约定
appreciate 感激
APPROX approximate 大约
appt. appointment
APRV approval 通过
APRVD approved
arbitration 仲裁

Appendix III International Logistics Vocabulary

arranging cargo pickup 安排提货
arrival 到达
arrogant 自负的
ARV arrive
as per 根据
ASA as soon as
ASAP as soon as possible
asf as the following
assembling 组装
assigned sailings 指定航班
at rear of 后面
at your earlist convenience 尽早地
ATCH attach
ATL Atlanta
attached 随附的
ATTN attention
audit 审计
automatically 自动
AVAL available 可得到的
AW all water
AWTG awaiting

B

B be
B/E bill of exchange 汇票
B/G bond goods 保税货物
B/L bill of lading
B/L issuing 提单签单
B/N booking note 订舱单
B/R best regards
B4 before
back up 后备
bad debts 坏账
BAF 燃油附加费
BAL balance
balance 余额
balance due 欠款
balance sheet 负债表
bank transfer 银行转账
barcoded 贴条形码的
barge 驳船
base port 基本港
BCOZ/BCZ because
beneficiary 收益人

beneficiary's certificate/statement 寄单证明
berthing 停泊
betray 背叛
BIBI bye bye
bill of exchanger/draft 汇票
bill of lading 海运提单
bill to 向……收款
BIZ business
BK book
BKG booking
BN been
bonded warehousing 报税仓储
booking advice 订舱通知
booking agency 订舱代理
booking instruction 订舱委托书
booking module 订舱模块
bookkeeper 出纳
breakbulk 分拨
breakdown 分类, 分项
broker 报关行
BTWN between
budget 预算
bundles 捆、批
business intelligence 业务信息
buying rate 买价

C

C. A. D cash against document
C. O (county of origin) 原产地
C. O. D collect on delivery 货到付款
C/ consignee
C/D (customs declaration) 报关
C/I commercial invoice
C/N credit note
CAAC 民航总局
CAF currency adjustment factor 货币调整因素
cancellation 取消
canvassing 揽货
CAPA capacity
CARBON COPY 抄送
cargo 货物
cargo agent 货运代理人
cargo canvassing 揽货
cargo handling facility 货物搬运设施

cargo receipt, C/R 承运货物收据
carriage 运输
carrier 承运人
cartage service 运输服务
carton 纸箱
case by case 个案处理
cash 现金
CAT a client name
CBM 立方米
CC charges collect 到付（freightage）
CC copy
CCA cargo correction advice
CERT certificate 证书
certificate of origin 产地证明
certificate of sample 寄样证明
CFM confirm
CFMTN confirmation
CFR（cost and freight） 成本加运费价
CFS 货运站
CGO 计费重量
chargeable weight 计费重量
charges 费用
charter vessel 租船
chartering 租（船、飞机）
chassis cost 底盘使用费
CHB customs house broker
Check 检查，支票
CHGBL chargeable
CHGS charges
CHRG charging
CIF cost, insurance & freight
circular 通知文件
city-pair trucking 城市间运输
CK check
CKG checking
claim 索赔
clarification 澄清
Class A forwarder 一级货代
Class B forwarder 二级货代
class rate 等级运价
clean bill 光票
clearance of goods 货物清关
clients 客户
close-out reservation 截止订舱

CLP container load plan
CLT Charlotte,城市名
cm 厘米
CM (CONTAINER MANIFEST) 舱单
CMA NAME OF carrier
CMBNG combining
CNCL cancel
CNEE consignee
CATG contacting
CNTR container
CO company
coastal ports 沿海港口
codes 代号,代码
cold storage 冷藏
CO-LDR co-loader 货运操作伙伴
collection of documents 收集单证
collection report 收款报告
collection freight 收运费
Co-loader 运输合作方
column 栏目
Combined transport, B/L 联运提单
COMM commodity
commercial invoice 商业发票
commission agent 佣金代理
CMDTY commodity 货物
commodity inspection 货物检验
communicating 通信
company stamp 公司图章
comparable 可比的
compensation 赔偿
competitors 竞争者
competitive 有竞争力的
compliance 服从
comply with 遵守
comprehensive 综合的
concentration 注意力
conciliation 安抚
concurrence 一致
conference freight 协定运费
confidence 机密,信心
confidential 机密的
confidential exchange 秘密交换
confirm 确认
consecutive days 连续工作日

consign 托运
consignee 收货人
consignment 货物
consistent 不断的
consolidate 合并
consolidation 集运
consolidators 集运人
consular invoice 领事发票
consulting 咨询
container 集装箱
container booking/release 订箱/放箱
container control 箱管
container freight station 货运站
container freight station (CFS) 货运站
container load plan (CLP) 集装箱装箱单
container manifest 舱单
container yards (CY) 堆场
contract 合同
contract for carriage 运送契约
conveyor belts 传输带
coordination 协调
core business 主营业务
COSCO 中远
cost 成本
courier 快件
cranes 起重机
credit 信用
credit note 贷记证明
credit status 信用状况
crucial 重要
crushed 压碎的
CTC contact
c'tion competition
CTN carton 纸箱
cubic meter 立方米
CUD could
currency 货币
currency exchange rate 汇率
customary 一贯
customer demands 客户需求
customer service 客服
customized solution 个性化解决方案
customs 海关
customs broker 报关行
customs declaration 报关
Customs declaration entrustment note 报关委托书
Customs declaration form 报关单
customs duties 关税
customs invoice 海关发票
customs registration 海关登记
cutoff date 截止日
CW chargeable weight
CY container yard

D

D/A (document against acceptance) 承兑交单
D/D door to door
D/G dangerous goods
D/N debit note
D/O delivery order
D/P (document against payment) 付款交单
daily bookings 每日订舱
daily cargo receiving report 每日入库报告
damage ratio 损坏率
data input 数据录入
DBL double
DD dated
DDC destination
DDC、IAC 直航附加费
DDS code of client
dead freight 空舱费
deadweight cargo or heavy goods 重货
debit note 借记证明
deduct 削减
deem 认为
delivery 运送
delivery against letter of guarantee 凭保证书提货
demurrage 滞期费
DEN city code
DEP departure
departure 出发
DESC description
despatch money 速遣费
destination 目的地
destined to 以……为目的地
DESTN destination

detention　延误
DG surcharge　危险品附加费
DHL　敦豪, name of courier
DIFF　difference
dimensions　尺寸
DIMS　dimensions
dip　下降
diplomatic goods　外交货物
discharging　卸货
disclosure　公布
discrepancy　错误
dispatch　派送
disposal　处理
distribution centers　配送中心
distributor　分销商
DLR　deliver
DLVRY　delivery
DLY　delay
DMG　damage
DOC　documents
dock receipt　集装箱场站收据
DOCS　documents
document cover sheet　寄单表
document retrieval　文件回收
documentation　制单
documents　单证
domestic　国内的
door to port　门到港
door-to-door　门到门
DOZ/DZ (dozen)　一打
draft　草稿
drumming　装桶
DT　dated
DTLS　details
due　到期的
due amount　应付账
due to　因为
duly informed　及时告知
duplicate　副本
duration　期限
Duty　关税

E

EA (each)　每个, 各

EB　east bound
EDC　express delivery charge
EDI　electronics data interchange
effective immediately　立刻生效
efficient　有效的
elaborate　详细说明
electronics data interchange　电子数据交换
elevators　升降机
emergency　加急
emergency bunker fuel adjustment　紧急燃油附加费
EMS (express mail special)　特快专递
ENCL　enclosed
enclosed　内附
encounter space problem　遇到舱位问题
endorsement　背书
end-user　最终用户
enlighten　取悦
enquiries　询价
ensure　保证
entail　包括
enter into an agreement　达成协议
EQL　equal
ERR　error
ESP　especially
EST　estimate
ETA　estimate time of arrival
ETD　estimated time of delivery
EUR/EU　europe
EX　export
exceed　超过
excel　表现优异
exchange rate　汇率
EXCL　exclude
exclude　不包含
exclusive handling agent　独家操作代理
execute this agreement　执行协议
exhibition logistics　展览品物流
expansion　扩张
expedite　加速
expenditures　成本, 花费
expense　成本
EXPLN　explain
explore market　开发市场

export license   出口许可证
export tax rebate form   出口退税单
exposure   接触
express   速递
EXRATE   exchange rate
ex-Shanghai   从上海出口

F

F. I.   free in
F. O.   free out
facilitate   促进
facility   设施
FAF   燃油价调整附加费
FAK   设施
familiarization   熟悉
Far East   远东
favorable   有利的
fax   传真 facsimile
FCL   full container load
FCR   forwarder's cargo receipt
FCTY   factory
FDD   a name of client
FDR   feeder
fee   费
feedback   反馈
feeders   支线船
FEU   forty equivalent unit
FF   freight forwarder
FGV   code of client
FIATA   货运联合会
FIATA   国际货代协会
fig.   Figure
file   文件夹
filter   过滤
finance   财务
financial condition   财务状况
financial report   财务报告
flight   航班
flow of goods   货物流动
FLT   flight
FLWG   following
FM   from
FOB   free on board
follow up   跟踪

followed to the letter   应由……汇款
for the time being   目前
foreign currency   外汇
forklifts   叉车
formalities   手续
formula   公式
forwarders' certificate of receipt (FCR)   货代收货收据
foul bill   不清洁提单
FPA   free of particular average
FR   for
free out/in   船方不负担装卸货费用
freight collect-CC   运费待付
freight forwarder/FF   货代
freight prepaid   运费已预付
Freight Unit Price   运费率
frequency   频率
frozen goods service   冷冻货服务
FRT   freight
FT   feet
fumigation   熏蒸
further to   附加
FW   forward
FWDR   forwarder
FYG   for your guidance
FYI   for your information
FYR   for your reference

G

G. S. P (generalized system of preferences)   普惠制
G. T.   gross ton
G. W. (gross weight)   毛重
G/CGO   general cargo
gallon   加仑
garments   服装
GDS   goods
GDSM   百货商品
GEN   general
general cargo   普货
globalization   全球化
GOH   挂衣 garment on hanger
GOVT   government
gp/hc   一般用途集装箱

GRI　general rate increase　一般性涨价
gross　总的
groupage　合并运输
GSA　general sales agent
guarantee　保证
guidelines　指令

H

H. O.　head office
H/C handling charge　处理费
HAFFA　香港空运协会
Hamper　阻止
handling agent　操作代理
hazard surcharge　危险品附加费
HAWB　house airway bill
HDL　handle
heating　加热
HEC　health (inspection) charge
heel　紧追
hence　因此
hereafter known as　以下简称
hereby　特此
HKG　Hong Kong
HL　name of carrier
HLD　hold
HMF　harbor maintenance fee　港口维修费
hold up　阻止
hot　（货物）紧俏的
household goods mover　家用品运输行
HQ　母公司
HR　hour
HV　have
HVY　heavy
HWVR　however

I

I/O　instead of
IATA　国际航协
identify　辨认
IFA　临时燃油附加费
IFM　inform
illustrate　证明
IMM　immediate
IMP/IM　import

impact　影响
imperative　必要的
impractical　不实际
IMPT　important
IN　inch
in accordance with　根据
in case of　一旦
in collaboration with　联合
in connection with　关于
in effect　有效
in force　有效
in lieu of　代替
in line with the market　与市场一致
in place　适当的
in reference to　关于
in terms of　关于
in the meantime　同时
in this regard　就此而言
in witness of　作为……的证据
inbound/outbound　进口/出口
INCL　include
inclusive　包含在内的
income　收入
incorporate　包含
INFO　information
inform　通知
inland drayage　内陆托运
inspection certificate　检验证明
INSTD　instead
instructions　指令
INSUR　insurance
insurance policy　保险单
intergrated logistics　综合物流
interim footwear invoice　临时鞋业发票
international chamber of commerce　国际商会
INT'L　international
INV/I/V　invoice
inventory　存货
invoice　发票
invoicing　开发票
IOT　in order to
IOU　I owe you
irregularities　不规则
ISO　国际标准组织

issue documents　签发单证
IT scan-in/out　电子扫描进货/出货

J

JFK　airport
jointly　共同
just-in-time　及时

K

KDLY　kindly
keep you advised　告知你
KG　kilograms
KL　KLINE
KLINE　carrier code
KM　kilometer
KP　keep

L

L　length
L/C　letter of credit
L/C provisions　信用证条款
labeling　贴标签……
land haulage　陆路托运
land-bridge　陆桥
lax　松懈
lay days　允许装卸时间
layout　布局,安排
lbs　磅
LCL　less than container load　拼箱
LDD　loaded
LDN　London
lead time　前置期
leaks　漏洞
lease　租赁
ledger　账目
LET　letter
letter of credit　信用证
letter of indemnity/trust receipt　赔偿保证书(信托收据)
levy　征收
LGB　Long Beach(美国城市)
LH　name of airline
licensed freight forwarders　注册货代
LIM　code of a client

line mumber mixed up　线号混淆
liner services　班轮服务
linkage　联系
liquidity　资产流动性
litre　升
LMT　limit
loading/unloading　装/卸
loan　贷款
local supplier　当地供应商
location　地点
logistics　物流
Long Beach　长滩
LT　意邮
LTR　litre

M

M　meter
M/F　manifest
M/R　mate receipt
M/T　metric ton
M/V (merchant vessel)　商船
maintaining container　集装箱维护
management　管理
manufacturer　生产商
marine　海运
maritime　海运的
mark　标记
market trends　市场趋势
mate's receipt　收货单/大副收据
MAWB　master airway bill　航空主单
MAX　maximum
maximum　最大
MBL　主单
measure　衡量
measurement cargo or light goods　轻货
MED　地中海
Memphis　name of city
merchandise　商品
MFR　manufacturer
MGR　manager
MIN　minimum
Ministry of Communication　交通部
MISC　miscellaneous
MISG　missing

Mission statement   目标宣言
MKT   market
MLB   mini land bridge   小路桥
mode of transport   运输方式
MoFTEC   外经贸委
momentum   高潮
MON   month/Monday
money order   汇款单
monitor the movement   监控运输
mooring   停泊
most likely   很可能
MPF   merchandise processing fee
MSC   Mediterranean Shipping Company
MSG   message
MSP   code of a city
MTG   meeting
MTH   code of city
MTIME   meantime
MTY   empty
MU   东航
multimode transport/intermodal transport   多式联运
multinational   跨国的
mutual consent   一致同意
mutually   共同,一致
MVMT   movement

N

N   and
N. W.（net weight）   净重
N. Y.   new york
ND   need
needless to mention   不用说
negative   消极的
NEGO   negotiate
negotiable   可转让的
net rate   净价
NIL   nothing
NITE   night
NLT   no later than
No.   number
No. of jobs   票数/作业数
nominated carrier   指定的承运人
Non-Base Port   非基本港口
non-hazardous cargo   非危险品
non-negotiable   不可转让
notification   通知
notwithstanding   不论
NTD   noted
NU   new
NVOCC   无船承运人
NW   net weight
NXT   next
NYC   New York City
NYK   日本邮船
NYK PAX   NYK Pacific Atlantic Express

O

O/B   on board
O/F   ocean freight
O/N   over night
OBC   on board courier
ocean quotes   海运报价
OCP   overland common bridge   大陆桥
offending   冒犯
offer   报价
offloaded   （货）卸下
offset   抵扣
on a daily basis   每日的
on board date   装船期
on part A'behalf   代表甲方
one-stop-shop   一站式服务
opening invoices   开发票
operation revenue   营业收入
operation staff   操作人员
operations   操作
option   选择
ORC   本地出口附加费
order tracing   订单跟踪
ORIG   original
origin   原产地/起运港
other than   除……之外,不是
outcome   结果
outstanding   欠款
overcharge   超额受费
overdue account   过期账
overheads   管理费用
overnight delivery   连夜运送

overseas agents　海外代理
oversized　超尺寸的
overweight　超重的
OZWS　otherwise

P

p. o. details　购货单明细
P/L　packing list
package　包装
packing list　装箱单
palletizing　装托盘
PARA　paragraph
parcels　包裹
partial goods　分批货物
partial shipment　部分运输
participation　进入
partnership　联合
passenger　旅客
payable　应支付的
payee　收款人
payer　付款人
payload　商务载重
payment collection　收款
payment negotiation　议付款
payment terms　支付条款
PC　personal computer
PCE/PCS（piece/pieces）　只、个、支等
PCS　港口拥挤费
peak season　旺季
penalty fee　罚金
pending　未定的
penetrate　深入
per diem　每日,按日
per shipment　每票货
personal goods　私人物品
pertaining to　关于
physical inspection　物品检查
pier charges　码头费
pilotage　引航费
PKG（package）　一包、一捆、一扎、一件等
PLND　planned
PLS　please
PLSD　pleased
PLT　pallet

PO　purchase order
POD　port of discharge
POD　proof of delivery
POL　port of loading
port of call　停泊港
port of discharging　卸货港
port of entry　进口港
port of exit　出口港
port of loading　装货港
positive　积极有效的
potential　潜在的
pouch　（文件）袋
PP　prepaid　预付
pre-advice/alert/pre-alert　预报
pre-clearance　预清关
preliminary　预先
premises　地点
presentation of invoice　出示发票
prior notice　提前通知
prior to　在……之前
prioritize　以重要性区分
proactive　积极的
procedure　流程
process improvement　改进程序
professional staff　专业人员
profit margin　利润率
profit share　利润分成
project cargo　项目货物
promote　提高
promotional campaigns　促销活动
proof copy　证明复印件
proportion　比例
proposal　提议
prospects　潜在客户
providers　供应商
PSBL　possible
PSS　peak season surcharge　旺季附加费
PTF　巴拿马运河处理费
purchase order processing　订单处理
push　催促
PYMY　payment

Q

Q. A. center　质保中心

QIN/DAL/XIN/SHA/XIA code of city
QK   quick
QLTY   quality
QNTY   quantity
QR   quarter
QSTN   question
QTE   quote
QTN   quotation
quality inspection   质检
quarantine inspection   检疫
quotation sheet   报价单

R

R   are
rail freight   铁路运输
railway bill   铁路运单（一式五联）
range of services   服务范围
rapport   关系
rate   运价
rate request   运价请求
RCFM   reconfirm
RCPT   receipt
RCV   receive
RCVD   received
RDY   ready
RE   regarding
real-time visibility   实时可见性
rebates   回扣
receipts   收据
receivable amount   应收账
receivables   应收账
recommend   推荐
reconciliation of statement of account   对账单
reefer   冷藏车
REF (reference)   参考,查价
reference   关于/参考
refrigerated storage service   冷藏服务
refund   退还
regarding   关于
regardless of   不论
register   注册
release of goods   放货
reminder   提醒
remit   汇款

render   提供
rental   租赁
REP   representative
repackaging   再包装
representation   代表
REPT   report
request   请求
rescinded   取消
residule   积淀
resolve the problem   解决问题
respectively   各自地
respond   回应
retention   滞留
retrieval   收回
revenue   收入
revert to   转向
RGDG   regarding
RGDS   regards
RLSG   releasing
RM   room
RMKS   remarks
road feeder   公路集配车
road restriction   公路载重限制
rollovers   滚装车
routed shipment   指定货
routing   路线
routing instructions   运输路径指令
RSPNSBL   responsible
RTM/LEH/BHW/ANR   city code
RTN   return
RYF   re your fax

S

S. S.（steamship）   船运
S/   shipper
S/Ls   steamship lines
S/O   shipping order
sales leads   销售线索
sales proposal   销售提议
sanitary inspection   卫检
SBJ   subject
scan   扫描
SCHDL   schedule
schedule   日程,船期

Appendix III International Logistics Vocabulary

SEA   south east asia
sea freight   海运
sea portion   海运部分
sea-air combined   海空联运
seal #   封箱号
seamen recruitment   海员招聘
seaway bill   海运单
SEC   service charge
secured   获得
security surcharge   安全附加费
segregation   分割
selling rate   销售价
SEN   德国胜利,code of carrier
sensitive shipment   敏感货物
sequence   次序
service contract   服务合同
SES   name of a forwarder
settle account   结账
settle payment   结账
SHA   Shanghai
shipment status   货物动态
shipper   发货人
shipper's letter of instruction   出口货物代运委托书
shipping advice   装船通知
shipping agency   船代
shipping order S/O   装货单
shipping schedule   船期
shipping window   运输窗口
shortshipped   少装
SHP   ship
SHPD   shipped
SHPMT/SHPT   shipment
SHPR   shipper
shrinking   捆扎
SHUD   should
signature   签名
signing bill of lading   签提单
Sino-foreign joint ventures   中外合资
sinotrans   中外运
SKED   schedule
SKU   stock unit
SLD   sailed
SLG   sailing
slots   箱位
SMPL   sample
SNST   soonest
SOP   storage charge
sophistication   复杂
sorting   分拣
sourcing   采购
space booking   订舱
space booking note   订舱单
SPCL   special
split   分割
SPS   上海港口附加费
square meters   立方米
SRY   sorry
SS   steamship lines
standard procedure   标准流程
state of the art   先进的
statement of all transactions   所有交易账目报表
status   状况
stipulate   标明,规定
stipulated time   规定的时间
STL   still
STN   station
storage   仓储
strategic partner   战略伙伴
stuffing & drayage   装箱托运
subject to   取决于,以……为准
submit shipping documents   交寄运输文件
suffix   后缀
SUG   suggest
supervisor   主管
supply chain   供应链
surcharge   附加费
surplus   多余
SVC   service
swap and drop basis   以交换/卸载方式
swissair cargo   瑞航货运处
switch booking   变更订舱
SZ   size

T

T   ton
T/T   transit time
T/T (telegraphic transfer)   电汇

T4　therefore
table of contents　目录
TACT　the air cargo tariff
tailor-made　量身定做的
tally　理货
tank container　集装罐
tariffs　运费率
TDY　today
TEL　telephone
telex-released fee　电放费
terminal　装卸区,码头,终点站
termination　停止,取消
terms and conditions　条款,条件
TEU　twenty-feet equivalent unit　20尺换算单位
THC　terminal handling charge
thereafter　之后
through rate　直达费率
THRU　through
Thru　通过
time charter　期租船
title　物权
TK　thank
TKS　thanks
TKU　thank you
TMNL　terminal
TMW　tomorrow
TN　a state in USA
TNTE　tonight
TOD　time of departure
toll fee　桥境费
top urgent　加急
total logistics services　综合物流服务
tracking　跟踪
trade fair cargo　展览物品
trade shows　展览会
transaction　交易
transferal　交换
transit time T/T　运输时间
transmitting　发送,运输
transportation　运输
transshipment　转运
TRBL　trouble
tremendous initiative　重要主张
trial period　试用期

trucking　卡车托运
trucking fleet　卡车车队
TT　that
TTL　total
TWN　台湾
TXT　text

U

U　you
U/STNDG　understanding
UA/FX/NW　name of airline
UGT　urgent
ultimate consignee　最终收货人
under no account　在任何情况下都不能
unimodal　单式
unsettled　未解决的,未付款的
update　提供最新消息
upon request　收到请求马上……
UR　your
urgent　重要的
U'STOOD　understood
utilize　利用
utmost　最……的

V

V　voyage/volume
validity　有效期
value-added services　增值服务
vanning/devanning containers　装/卸集装箱货物
vehicle detention　拖车延误
vendor　售货方
via HKG　通过香港
vice versa　反之亦然
violation of this clause　违犯此条款
VIP clients　大客户
visa　签证
VLDY　validity
VNDR　vendor
VOL　voyage
volume　货量
volume cargo　轻抛货
VOY　voyage
voyage charter　程租船
VS　name of airline

VSL　vessel　船
VW　volume weight

W

W　weight
W Med/E Med　West Med./East Med.（地中海）
W. P. A　with particular average
W. R.　war risk
W/　with
w/c　west coast
W/H　warehouse
W/I　within
W/O　without
waive　取消
war risk　战争险
warehousing　仓储
weigh　称重
weight breaks　重量分级
westbound　向西的
WFOE　外商独资
whereby　由此
wholesalers　批发商
WHSE　warehouse
WHZ　whether
wire　打电报
WK　week
WL　will
WLB　will be
WME　code of a city
write off　取消
WRTG　writing
WRU　who are you
WT　weight
WTO　commitments
WUD　would

X

X　stop
XCPT　accept
XMAS　christmas
XPLN　explain
XPR　expire

Y

Y　yard
YAS　日元升值附加费
YDY　yesterday
YL　your letter
YR　your

Z

ZIM　name of a carrier

Appendix Ⅳ Logistics Documents

海 运 提 单

Shipper		B/L NO.
Consignee		**COSCO** 中国远洋运输（集团）总公司 CHINA OCEAN SHIPPING(GROUP)CO.
Notify Party		

Pre-carriage by	Place of Receipt	
Ocean Vessel Voy. No.	Port of Loading	**Combined Transport BILL OF LADING**
Port of Discharge	Place of Delivery	

Marks & Nos. Container/Seal No.	No. of Containers or Packages	Kind of Packages. Description of Goods	Gross WeightKgs	Measurement

TOTAL NO. OF CONTAINERS OR PACKAGES (IN WORDS)

FREIGHT & CHARGES	Revenue Tons	Rate	Per	Prepaid	Collect

Ex. Rate:	Prepaid at	Payable at	Place and date of issue
	Total Prepaid	No. of Original B(s)/L	Signed for the Carrier

商 业 发 票

Exporter (Name, Address)		发 票 INVOICE	
To:			
Issued by (Bank and Branch)		Invoice No.	Date
		Your Order No.	Our S/C No.
		Documentary Credit No.	
Vessel/Aircraft etc.	From	Country of Origin of Goods	
To		Terms of Delivery and Payment	
Marks and Numbers:	Description of Goods	Quantity Unit Price	Amount

海 运 提 单

Shipper		B/L NO. COSCO10567
CNTIC-SHANGHAI IMPORT AND EXPORT COMPANY 4TH/FL., ZHONGCHENG BIUILDING, 8 RUIJING YI ROAD, SHANGHAI 200020, CHINA		**COSCO** 中国远洋运输（集团）总公司 CHINA OCEAN SHIPPING (GROUP) CO. CABLE: COSCO DELING TLX: 210746 CPC CN
Consignee TO ORDER		
Notify Party ABC STATIONERY CO., LTD. RM. 219, GARDEN HOTEL, 28 STREET 6, HAMBURG, GERMANY		ORIGINAL Combined Transport BILL OF LADING

Pre-carriage by	Place of Receipt	RECEIVED in external apparent good order and condition except as otherwise noted...
Ocean Vessel Voy. No. FENGHE V. 082W	Port of Loading NINGBO CHINA	
Port of Discharge HAMBURG GERMANY	Place of Delivery	

Marks & Nos. Container / Seal No. ABC S/C 02ABC-123 HAMBURG GERMANY NO. 1—140	No. of Containers or Packages 140CNTS	Kind of Packages. Description of Goods HAND PENCIL SHARPENER 空白背书： CNTIC-SHANGHAI IMPORT AND EXPORT COMPANY 佟东海(手签章) LCL CFS/CFS	Gross Weight Kgs 3070KGS	Measurement 12.881CBM
TOTAL NO. OF CONTAINERS OR PACKAGES (IN WORDS)	SAY ONE HUNDRED AND FORTY CARTONS ONLY			

FREIGHT & CHARGES FREIGHT PREPAID	Revenue Tons WARRANT GROPU PLC, NO. 16 KEENLY STREET, HAMBURG 0215, GERMANY TEL: 6077 0272 FAX: 6077 3458	Rate	Per	Prepaid	Collect
Ex. Rate:	Prepaid at	Payable at		Place and date of issue NINGBO JULY 28, 2002	
	Total Prepaid	No. of Original B(s)/L THREE		Signed for the Carrier NINGBO DONGFANG SHIPPING AGENCY	

LANDEN ON BOARD THE VESSEL
DATE JULY 28, 2002 BY 刘知平(手签章)
　　　　　　　　　　　　　　　AS AGENT FOR THE CARRIER ——COSCO

NINGBO DONGFANG SHIPPING AGENCY
刘知平(手签章)
AS AGENT FOR THE CARRIER ——COSCO

Appendix IV Logistics Documents

航空主运单

MASTER AIR WAYBILL 航空主运单

Master Air Waybill	航空主运单		
999			999

Shipper's Name and Address	Shipper's Account Number	NOT NEGOTIABLE 中国民航 CCAC
		AIR WAYBILL(AIR CONSIGNMENT NOTE ISSUED BY:THE CIVIL AVIATION ADMINISTRATION OF CHINA BEIJING CHINA)
		Copies 1,2 and 3 of this Air Waybill are originals and have the same validity
Consignee's Name and Address	Consignee's Account Number	It is agreed that the goods described herein are accepted in apparent good order and condition(except as noted)for carriage SUBJECT TO THE CONDITIONS OF CONTRACT ON THE REVERSE HERE OF THE SHIPPER'S ATTENTION IS DRAWN TO THE NOTICE CONCERNING CARRIER'S LIMITATION OF LIABILITY.Shipper may increase such limitation of liability be declaring a highter value for carriage and paying a supplemental charge if required. ISSUING CARRIER MAINTAINS CARGO ACCIDENT LIABILITY INSURANCE
Issuing Carrier's Agent Name and City		Accounting Information
Agent's IATA Code	Account No.	

port of Departure(Addr, of First Carrier)and Requested Routing

to	By First Carrier	Routing and Destination	to	by	to	by	Cutency	Code	CHGS WINAL	Other	Declared Value for Carriage	Declared Value for Carriage
									PPD COLL	PPD COLL		

Airport Destination	Flight/Date	For Carrier Use only	Flight/Date	Amount of Insurance	INSURANCE if carrier offers insurance,and such insurance is requested in accordance with conditions on reverse here of,indicate amount to be insured infigure in box marked amount of insurance.

Handling Information
(for USA only)Those commodities licensed by U.S. for ultimate destination...Diversion contrary to U.S.law is prohibited

No. of Pieces RCP	Gross Weight	kg/lb	Rate Class Commodity Item No.	Chargeable Weight	Rate Charge	Total	Nature and Quantity of Goods (incl Dimensions or Volume)

Prepaid Weight Charge Collect	Other Charge
Valuation Charge	
Tax	
Total Other Charges Due Agent	Shipper certifies that the particulars on the face hereof are correct and that insofar as any part of the consignment contains dangerous goods,such part is properly described by name and is in proper condition for carriage by air according to the applicable Dangerous Goods Regulations.
Total Other Charges Due Carrier	
	Signature of Shipper or his Agent
Total Prepaid Total Collect	
Currency Conversion Rates CC Charges in Dest.Currency	Executed on(date) at(place) Signature of Issuing Carrier or its Agent
For Carriers Use only at Destination Charges at Destination Total Collect Charges	999—

航空分运单

HOUSE AIR WAYBILL   航空分运单

House Air Waybill   航空分运单

AIRPORT OF DEPARTURE			AIRPORT OF DESTINATION			MASTER AIR WAYBILL NUMBER	AIR WAYBILL NUMBER No. 322297
ROUTING AND DESTINATION						NOT NECOTIABLE AIR WAYBILL (AIR CONSICNMENT NOTE) ISSUED BY	
TO	BY FIRST CARRIER	TO	BY	TO	BY		
CONSIGNEE'S ACCOUNT NUMBER		CONSIGNEE'S NAME AND ADDRESS				中国对外贸易运输总公司 China National Foreign Trade Transportation Corporation Beijing, China Member of FIATA Copies 1, 2and 3 of this Air Waybill are originals and have the same validity	
		ALSO NOTIFY				It is agreed that the goods deseribed here are accepted in apparent good order and condition(except as noted)for carriage SUBJECT TO THE CONDITIONS OF CONTRACT ON THE REVERSE HEREOF.THE SHIPPER'S ATTENTION IS DRAWN TO THE NOTICE CONCERNINC CARRIERS, LIMITATION OF LIABILITY.Shipper may increase such limitation of liability by declaring a higher value for curriage and paying a supplemental charge if required. EXECUTED ON _____ AT _____ (Date) (Place) SIGNATURE OF ISSUING CARRIER OR ITS AGENT	
SHIPPER'S ACCOUNT NUMBER		SHIPPER'S NAME AND ADDRESS					

CURRENCY	WTNAL		OTHER		DECLARED VALUE FOR CARRIAGE	DECLARED VALUE FOR CUSTOMS	AMOUNT OF INSURANCE	INSVRANCE. IF Carrier offers insurance,and such insurance is requesied in accordance with conditions on reverse hereof,indicate amount to be insured in figures in box marked amount of insurance
	PPD	COLL	PPD	COLL				
NO. OF PACKAGES RCP	ACTUAL GROSS WEIGHT		kg / lb	RATE CLASS		CHARGEABLE WEIGHT	RATE	WEIGHT CHARGE	NATURE AND QUANTITY OF GOODS (INCL DIMENSIONS OR VOLUME)
				COMMODITY ITEM NO.					
SPECIAL HANDLING INFORMATION (INCLUDING MARKS. NUMBERS AND METHOD OF PACKING)									

P R E P A I D	WEIGHT CHARGE	OTHER CHARGES	TOTAL OTHER CHARGES
	VALUATION CHARGE		TOTAL PREPAID
C O L L E C T	WEIGHT CHARGE	OTHER CHARGES	TOTAL OTHER CHARGES
	VALUATION CHARGE		TOTAL COLLECT

The shipper Certifies that the particulars on the face here of are correct and agrees to the Conditions of Carriage of the carrier

No. 322297

ORIGINAL 3 (FOR SHIPPER)

保 险 单

PICC 中国人民保险公司 宁波市分公司
The People's Insurance Company of China Ningbo Branch

总公司设于北京　一九四九年创立
Head Office Beijing　Established in 1949

货物运输保险单
CARGO TRANSPORTATION INSURANCE POLICY

发票号(INVOICE NO.)　　　　　　　　　　保单号次
合同号(CONTRACT NO.)　　　　　　　　　POLICY NO.
信用证号(L/C NO.)
被保险人：
Insured：

中国人民保险公司(以下简称本公司)根据被保险人的要求,由被保险人向本公司缴付约定的保险费,按照本保险单承保险别和背面所载条款与下列特款承保下述货物运输保险,特立本保险单。
THIS POLICY OF INSURANCE WITNESSES THAT THE PEOPLE'S INSURANCE COMPANY OF CHINA (HEREINAFTER CALLED "THE COMPANY") AT THE REQUEST OF THE INSURED AND IN CONSIDERATION OF THE AGREED PREMIUM PAID TO THE COMPANY BY THE INSURED. UNDER TAKES TO INSURE THE UNDERMENTIONED GOODS IN TRANSPORTATION SUBJECT TO THE CONDMONS OF THIS POLICY AS PER THE CLAUSES PRINTED OVERLEAF AND OTHER SPECIAL CLAUSES ATTACHED HEREON.

标　记 MARKS & NOS.	包装及数量 QUANTITY	保险货物项目 DESCRIPTION OF GOODS	保险金额 AMOUNT INSURED

保险金额：
TOTAL AMOUNT INSURED：_____
保费：　　　　　　起运日期：　　　　　　装载运输工具：
PREMIUM　AS ARRANGED　DATE OF COMMENCEMENT_____ PER CONVEYANCE：_____
自　　　　　　　　经　　　　　　　　至
FROM_____ VIA_____ TO_____
承保险别：
CONDITIONS：

所保货物,如发生保险单项下可能引起索赔的损失或损坏,应立即通知本公司下述代理人查勘。如有索赔,应向本公司提交保单正本(本保险共有　1　份正本)及有关文件。
IN THE EVENT OF LOSS OR DAMAGE WHICH MAY RESULT IN A CLAIM UNDER THIS POLICY. IMMEDIATE NOTICE MUST BE GIVEN TO THE COMPANY'S AGENT AS MENTIONED HEREUNDER CLAIMS. IF ANY. ONE OF THE ORIGINAL POLICY WHICH HAS BEEN ISSUED IN ONE ORIGINAL(S) TOGETHER WITH THE RELEVANT DOCUMENTS SHALL BE SURRENDERED TO THE COMPANY.

中国人民保险公司宁波市分公司
The People's Insurance Company of China Ningbo Branch

赔款偿付地点
CLAIM PAYABLE AT _____
出单日期
ISSUING DATE _____

Authorized Signature

地址：中国宁波药行街151号　　　　　电话(TEL)：0574-87196111-80220、80219
ADD：151# YAOHANG STREET NINGBO CHINA　　传真(FAX)：0574-87199058
邮编(POST CODE)：315000

报单顺序号：PICC0301010589

中华人民共和国原产地证

ORIGINAL

1. Exporter (full name and address)	CERTIFICATE NO. CERTIFICATE OF ORIGIN OF THE PEOPLE'S REPUBLIC OF CHINA
2. Consignee (full name, address, country)	
3. Means of transport and route	5. For certifying authority use only
4. Country/region of Destination	

6. Marks and numbers of packages	7. Description of goods; number and kind of packages	8. H.S Code	9. Quantity or weight	10. Number and date of invoices

11. Declaration by the exporter
 	
    The undersigned hereby declares that the above details and statements are correct; that all the goods were produced in China an that they comply with the Rules of Origin of the People's Republic of China.
	12. Certification
	
	    It is hereby certified that the declaration by the exporter is correct.

Place and date, signature and stamp of authorized signatory	Place and date, signature and stamp of certifying authority

装 运 通 知

SHIPPING ADVICE

Inv. No. <u>ABC020630</u>
L/C No. <u>00/089/CBG/600</u>
Date: <u>JULY 28, 2002</u>

To:
    ABC STATIONERY CO., LTD.,
    RM. 219, GARDEN HOTEL, 28 STREET 6, HAMBURG, GERMANY

We are glad to inform you that the captioned shipment has been effected. The details of the shipment are as follows:

Shipping Marks	Description of Goods	Quantity	Invoice value
ABC S/C 02ABC-123 HAMBURG GERMANY NO. 1—140	HAND PENCIL SHARPENER	140CTNS	USD15348.96 CIFC5 HAMBURG

B/L No and Date: COSCO10567 JULY 28, 2002
Vessel: FENGHE V. 082W
Port of Loading: NINGBO CHINA
Port of Destination: HAMBURG GERMANY
ETA: ABOUT AUG 28, 2002

CNTIC-SHANGHAI IMPORT AND EXPORT COMPANY

佟东海(手签章)

托 运 单

Shipper

D/R No.

Consignee

Notify Party

集装箱货物托运单

货代留底

第一联

泛洋

Pre-carriage by　　Place of Receipt

Ocean vessel　Voy. No.　Port of Loading

Port of Discharge	Place of Delivery		Final Destination for the Merchant's Reference	
Container No. Seal No. Marks & Nos.	No. of containers or P'kgs.	Kind of Packages, Description of Goods	Gross Weight	Measurement
TOTAL NUMBER OF CONTAINERS OR PACKAGES (IN WORDS)				
FREGHT & CHARGES	Revenue Tone	Rate	Per	Prepaid	Collect
Ex. Rate	Prepaid at	Payable at		Place of issue
	Total Prepaid	No. of Original B(s)/L		

Service Type on Receiving □—CY, □—CFS, □—DOOR	Service Type on Delivery □—CY, □—CFS, □—DOOR	Reefer Temperature Required	°F	℃
TYPE OF GOODS	□ Ordinary, □ Reefer, □ Dangerous, □ Auto □ Liquid, □ Live Animal, □ Bulk, □_____	危险品	Class: Property: IVDG Code Page: UN No.:	

可否转船：　　　可否分批：　　　联系人：　　　电话：

装　　期：　　　效　　期：

金　　额：

制单日期：　　　　　　　　　　　　　　　　　　　业务章：

Appendix Ⅳ　Logistics Documents

装　箱　单

Exporter (Name, Address)	
	装　箱　单 **PACKING LIST**
To:	Invoice No.:
	Date:
	L/C NO.

Shipping Marks	Descriptions of Goods	Quantity	G.W. / N.W.	Measurement
	TOTAL:			